# The Liturgical Sense of The Readings at Mass – Year A

# The Liturgical Sense of The Readings at Mass - Year A

*David L. Gray*

Saint Dominic's Media
Warren, Ohio

The Liturgical Sense of the Readings at Mass (Year A)
© 2025 David L. Gray

All rights reserved. No part of this book may be reproduced, stored in a retrieval system, or transmitted in any form or by any means—electronic, mechanical, photocopying, recording, or otherwise—without the prior written permission of the publisher, except for brief quotations in critical articles or reviews.

Published by:
Saint Dominic's Media
www.saintdominicsmedia.com

Printed in the United States of America
1 2 3 4 5 6 7

BISAC Categories:
RELIGION / Christianity / Catholic
RELIGION / Christian Rituals & Practice / Worship & Liturgy
RELIGION / Biblical Commentary / New Testament

ISBN-13 (Hardcover): 979-8-9857040-5-1

# Dedication

This book is lovingly dedicated to the memory of Dorothy O'Niell Weimar, a lay Dominican whose faith and devotion continue to inspire all who knew her and continue to learn about her.

# Contents

**Dedication** .................................................................... 5

**Foreword** ...................................................................... 14

**Preface** ........................................................................ 17

   *The Liturgical Sense of the Sacred Scriptures Defined* ............. 18

   *How to Utilize This Book* ............................................... 18

   *In Gratitude* ............................................................... 19

**The Season of Advent** ................................................... 21

**The First Sunday in Advent** ........................................... 22

   *The Liturgy of the Catholic Mass Teaches Us Four Holy Desires* 23

**The Second Sunday in Advent** ........................................ 26

   *The Liturgy of the Catholic Mass is for People Who Know Their Lives Are Messy* ................................................................... 27

**Third Sunday in Advent** ................................................. 31

   *The Liturgy of the Catholic Mass Comes to Make Us New in Christ* ................................................................................ 32

**Fourth Sunday in Advent** ............................................... 36

   *The Theology of the Incarnation Through the Liturgy of the Catholic Mass* ........................................................................... 37

**The Nativity of the Lord** ................................................ 40

   *The Liturgical Paradox of the Nativity of the Lord* .................. 41

**The Octave of Christmas** ............................................... 45

   *The Liturgical Life of Saint Joseph,* ................................... 46

*Father of the Holy Family* .......................................................... 46

*Through the Liturgy, we are Born Again through the Womb of Mary, Mother of God and Mother of the Church* ................................ 50

## The Epiphany & The Baptism of the Lord ............................. 53

*The Liturgy of the Holy Mass is the Epiphany Event* ................. 54

*The Baptism of the Lord* ........................................................ 58

## 2nd Sunday in Ordinary Time .................................................. 62

*You Have Been Called to the Liturgy of the Holy Mass* ............. 63

## 3rd Sunday in Ordinary Time ................................................... 66

*The Liturgy of the Catholic Mass: A Journey from Darkness to Light and Back Again* ........................................................................ 67

## 4th Sunday in Ordinary Time ................................................... 70

*The Liturgy Forms the Spirit of Humility in the Hearts of God's Remnant People* ...................................................................... 71

## 5th Sunday in Ordinary Time ................................................... 74

*In the Liturgy, we consume the Light of the World, thereby becoming the Light of the World* ............................................................. 75

## 6th Sunday in Ordinary Time ................................................... 79

*The Liturgy and the Law Share the Same Source and Purpose* 80

## 7th Sunday in Ordinary Time ................................................... 84

*The Liturgical Teaching on the Imago Dei* ................................ 85

## 8th Sunday in Ordinary Time ................................................... 90

*The Liturgy of the Catholic Mass Draws Us into the Divine Reliance* ................................................................................................ 91

## 9th Sunday in Ordinary Time ................................................... 94

## Table of Contents

*The Phylactery is Fulfilled in Liturgy and the Sacraments of the Church* ................................................................... 95

**10th Sunday in Ordinary Time** .................................................. 98

*Liturgy and the Ite, Missa Est is the Activity of Knowing and Loving God* ................................................................................ 99

**11th Sunday in Ordinary Time** .................................................103

*How the Liturgy Communicates God's Mercy of Remembrance and Mission* ............................................................................ 104

**12th Sunday in Ordinary Time** .................................................108

*In the Liturgy of the Catholic Mass, Divine Justice and Peace Kiss* ................................................................................ 109

**13th Sunday in Ordinary Time** .................................................113

*The Fulfillment of the Liturgies of Shunem and Zarephath*.... 114

**14th Sunday in Ordinary Time** .................................................117

*How the Liturgy Participates in the Call of Christ Jesus for the Conversion of Jews* ............................................................ 118

**15th Sunday in Ordinary Time** .................................................122

*The Liturgy of the Catholic Mass is the Rich Soil, and We are the Seeds* ................................................................................ 123

**16th Sunday in Ordinary Time** .................................................126

*The Liturgy of the Mass is the Best Evidence of God's Loving Patience* ............................................................................ 127

**17th Sunday in Ordinary Time** .................................................131

*The Liturgy of the Mass Creates in Us a Servant's Heart* ....... 132

**18th Sunday in Ordinary Time** .................................................135

*The Liturgical Teaching on How to Avoid Separation from God* 136

**19th Sunday in Ordinary Time** .................................................139

  The Liturgy of the Catholic Mass is Forming Us to Have No Fear of the World .................................................................................... 140

## 20th Sunday in Ordinary Time ................................................ 143

  The Liturgical Teaching on the Catholicity of God ................. 144

## 21st Sunday in Ordinary Time ................................................ 148

  The Liturgical Teaching on the Two Types of People ............. 149

## 22nd Sunday in Ordinary Time ............................................... 153

  How the Liturgy Trains Us to Make Ourselves a Living Sacrifice 154

## 23rd Sunday in Ordinary Time ................................................ 158

  The Liturgy is Building a Culture and a Community of Mercy, Love, and Healing ............................................................................ 159

## 24th Sunday in Ordinary Time ............................................... 163

  The Liturgical Teaching on the Relationship Between Sin and Forgiveness ............................................................................ 164

## 25th Sunday in Ordinary Time ............................................... 167

  The Liturgy is Forming Us to Have a Holy Indifference ........... 168

## 26th Sunday in Ordinary Time ............................................... 172

  The Liturgy is Us, Taking Personal Responsibility for Our Lives 173

## 27th Sunday in Ordinary Time ............................................... 176

  The Liturgy is the Fertile Ground, and We are the Harvest .... 177

## 28th Sunday in Ordinary Time ............................................... 180

  The Liturgy Wants You to Invite People to Come Feast with Jesus .................................................................................................. 181

## 29th Sunday in Ordinary Time ............................................... 184

  The Liturgy Teaches Us Who Created Us and Why He Created 185

## 30th Sunday in Ordinary Time ............................................... 189

## Table of Contents

*The Liturgy Equips Us to Love the Least Among Us* .............. 190

**31st Sunday in Ordinary Time** ................................................. 193

*The Liturgy of the Catholic Mass is Our Way Home* ............... 194

**32nd Sunday in Ordinary Time** ................................................ 198

*The Call to Pursue Wisdom Outside of Liturgical Worship* ..... 199

**33rd Sunday in Ordinary Time** ................................................ 202

*The Liturgy is a Type of Mother Who Instructs Us* ................. 203

**34th Sunday in Ordinary Time (The Solemnity of Our Lord Jesus Christ, King of the Universe)** ............................................ 206

*The Liturgy is Christ Jesus Taking Responsibility for Us* .......... 207

**The Season of Lent** ................................................................. 210

**First Sunday of Lent** ............................................................... 211

*The Liturgy Teaches Us How to Resist Every Evil Temptation* 212

**Second Sunday of Lent** .......................................................... 216

*The Liturgy Wants to Make Us Uncomfortably Comfortable* 217

**Third Sunday of Lent** ............................................................. 221

*The Teachings of the Liturgy Versus the Quarrelsome Spirit* . 222

**Fourth Sunday of Lent** ........................................................... 227

*The Liturgy of the Catholic Mass Leads Us into a Spiritual Awakening* ................................................................................ 228

**Fifth Sunday of Lent** .............................................................. 232

*The Liturgy Empowers and Equips Us to Bring the Dead to Life* 233

**Easter Season** ........................................................................ 237

**Palm Sunday** ......................................................................... 238

*The Liturgy teaches us that what Belongs to God, Stays with God* ............................................................................................ 239

**Resurrection Sunday ............................................................. 243**

    *The Great Sunday, Our Day of Remembrance, Our Day of Life 244*

**Second Sunday of Easter (Divine Mercy) ............................... 247**

    *The Liturgy of the Church and Her Sacraments are God Being Merciful with Us ................................................................. 248*

**Third Sunday of Easter ........................................................ 251**

    *The Liturgy of the Catholic Mass is Unique, Exceptional, and Extraordinarily Transformative ............................................. 252*

**Fourth Sunday of Easter ...................................................... 256**

    *Through the Liturgy, Our Lord Shepherds Us ......................... 257*

**Fifth Sunday of Easter ......................................................... 260**

    *The Liturgy is not an Appeal to Diversity, but a Call to Oneness In Christ ................................................................................ 261*

**Sixth Sunday of Easter ........................................................ 265**

    *The Liturgy of the Catholic Church Prepares us for the Coming Persecution ......................................................................... 266*

**Seventh Sunday of Easter .................................................... 270**

    *The Lord is Risen, Now What? ............................................. 271*

**Other Holy Days of Obligation ............................................... 274**

**Solemnity of Mary, the Holy Mother of God .......................... 275**

    *Through the Catholic Mass, we are Born Again through the Womb of Mary, Mother of God, Mother of the Church, and Mother of the Liturgy ............................................................................... 276*

**The Feast of the Presentation of the Lord ............................. 280**

    *The Feast of the Presentation of the Lord ............................. 281*

**The Solemnity of the Ascension of the Lord ......................... 285**

*The Relationship Between Ascension and Descension, Anabainō and Katabainō* .............................................................. 286

**Pentecost Sunday** ................................................................. **291**

*The Liturgy of the Catholic Mass Fulfills the Human Desire for Unity* ............................................................................................... 292

**Solemnity of the Most Holy Trinity** ....................................... **296**

*The Solemnity of the Most Holy Trinity* ................................ 297

**Solemnity of the Body and Blood of Christ** .......................... **302**

*The Most Holy Body and Blood of the Lord* ......................... 303

**Saint Joseph, Spouse of the Blessed Virgin Mary** .................. **307**

*The Liturgical Symphony of Saint Joseph's Obedient Faith* ... 308

**The Annunciation of the Lord** .............................................. **312**

*A Feast of Incarnation, Obedience, and Liturgical Conversion* 313

**Nativity of Saint John the Baptist** ........................................ **317**

*The Turning of the Liturgical Year, the Herald of the Dawn* ... 318

**Feast of Saints Peter and Paul** June 29 ................................. **322**

*Liturgical Unity in Martyria, the Broken Rock, and the Outpoured Word*........................................................................... 323

**Feast of the Transfiguration of the Lord** .............................. **327**

*Divine Majesty, Prophetic Fulfillment, and the Call to Transformation* ............................................................................................... 328

**The Assumption of the Blessed Mother of Mary** .................. **332**

*The Solemnity of the Assumption of the Blessed Mother of Mary* 333

**Feast of the Exaltation of the Cross** ..................................... **338**

*The Exaltation of the Cross: Liturgical Paradox and Promise at the Heart of the Catholic Christian Faith* ....................................... 339

## Dedication of the Lateran Basilica ...........342
*The House Not Made by Hands............... 343*

## The Solemnity of All Saints ....................346
*The Solemnity of All Saints ...................... 347*

## The Commemoration of all the Faithfully Departed (All Souls' Day) ...................351
*The Liturgy of Remembrance, Intercession, and the Hope Beyond Death................ 352*

## The Solemnity of the Immaculate Conception of the Blessed Virgin Mary ...............356
*Far Above All Angles and Saints ............ 357*

## Feast of the Holy Family ......................361
*The Liturgy of the Domestic Church: Holiness in the Ordinary 362*

# Foreword

On May 28, 2022, I was ordained to the Diaconate by Archbishop Salvatore Cordileone of San Francisco. My path to this moment was shaped by a rich educational foundation—beginning at Saint Bede Catholic Elementary and Moreau Catholic High School in Hayward, continuing at Saint Mary's College of California, and culminating at the University of San Francisco. Throughout this journey, I have been a proud member of the Black Catholic community.

While academic study has undeniable value, it is clear to me that not all theological perspectives impact one's knowledge, understanding, or personal growth in the same way. True transformation often arises from life experience and the perseverance required to navigate its challenges. These experiences shape our character and influence the decisions we make for ourselves and for those we love.

During the tumultuous events of 2020—including the COVID-19 pandemic, civil unrest, and partisan social movements—I found myself deeply reflecting on my vocation to the Diaconate. This period of widespread uncertainty and division, especially along religious, racial, and political lines, prompted me to seek perspective and understanding. At the time, Archbishop Cordileone appointed me to lead the Racial Reconciliation team in the Archdiocese of San Francisco. This responsibility, amid turmoil and distress, led to a period of personal isolation—not only from liberal Black Catholics but also from conservative voices within my diocese. It was a lonely season, and I longed for a traditional voice of reason, someone who understood the path I was walking.

In my search, I encountered the theological work of David L. Gray—a Catholic theologian, author, speaker, and media host known for his humility and compassionate approach. Through my membership at Saint Dominic Media and his books, such as "The Divine Symphony: An

Exordium to the Theology of the Catholic Mass" and "Catholic, Traditional & Black: In Anthology and Discourse," I found both guidance and inspiration. David's personal witness and theological insights profoundly transformed my understanding of faith.

Those who inspire me most are individuals who, through Christ's redemption, have triumphed over despair. Their witness is marked by humility and the boldness that comes from redemption. Such people are not mere copies of others; they live authentically, shaped by their struggles and victories. These "great warriors" and "hounds of heaven" have overcome significant challenges, inspiring all who encounter them.

It is in the sacred study of Scripture and the silence of our hearts that we truly hear God speaking. In moments of turmoil, disillusionment, pain, or misery, God's voice brings peace to our hearts. Personal experiences grant us spiritual wisdom that penetrates deeply. David L. Gray, in particular, rose in the spirit of God's redemption during his times of desperation, finding solace in the sacred silence of his heart.

The angels spoke to David when he most needed God's mercy and love, and—most importantly—he listened. He thirsts passionately to fulfill God's plan, not just for his own life, but for all the faithful who engage with his work. His writings ignite in us a desire for greater understanding, revealing how the message of salvation is actively at work in each of us.

The Gospel of Matthew, written for a first-century Jewish-Christian audience, is deeply rooted in the history of Israel. "The Liturgical Sense of The Readings at Mass—Year A" explains how the political and religious tensions of the time—especially between Jewish followers of Jesus and the Pharisees—influenced the text. Without this context, Jesus' stern rebukes of the Pharisees can be misunderstood. Commentaries, such as those by David L. Gray, help bridge these gaps, guiding us away from misunderstandings and toward a richer and more intentional sacramental Catholic faith.

David's personal journey echoes the central theme of Matthew: that those who endure trials and serve others in sacrifice will be saved. He helps us see that the Old and New Testaments are one seamless narrative of God's love, meant for all who seek Him and live according to His Word.

For anyone seeking to move beyond surface-level engagement with the lectionary, David's commentaries offer scholarly expertise presented in accessible language. By exploring historical context, cultural background, linguistic meanings, and Old Testament echoes, he transforms the New Testament into a living word for our daily lives. His work provides a "telescope" through which we can better understand and apply Scripture with confidence and abundance.

Ultimately, greater fulfillment comes from a deeper study of God's Word, paired with the voices of those who have truly experienced grace. As Jesus promises, "Come to me, all you who are weary and are carrying heavy burdens, and I will give you rest" (Matthew 11:28). David L. Gray has experienced that rest and transformation, and his voice speaks to the daily courage required of ordinary believers. He reminds us that only in the sacred silence of the heart do we encounter the mystery of God and the more profound meaning found in the Gospel of Matthew.

May the Lord continue to guide your heart in peace as you explore this mystery with David L. Gray.

Rev. Mr. Christopher Major, Deacon
Archdiocese of San Francisco

# Preface

This collection of commentaries and reflections on the Sunday Mass Readings and Holy Days of Obligation seeks to invite every reader—clergy and laity alike—into a deeper communion between the Liturgy of the Word and every other movement of the Mass: the Opening Rite, the Liturgy of the Eucharist, and the Concluding Rite. The hope is to illuminate how the sacred liturgy overflows into our daily lives, transforming the moments between our gatherings for worship into opportunities for grace and growth.

When a homily fails to connect with the present realities of our lives, the faithful may feel distanced from the liturgy, as though standing at the edge of a bridge that leads nowhere. They may glimpse the destination but cannot set foot upon it. Alternatively, some may cross but remain unsure how they arrived, never fully present in heart or mind. Our shared journey as believers calls us to experience the liturgy as a living encounter—a unity of mind, body, and spirit—with the living Body of Christ.

To truly respond to God's invitation in the liturgy—to be made fully alive in Him—we must embrace the Mass in its fullness. Every prayer, confession, and gesture of worship finds meaning in our union with Christ and His Church. Just as a seed needs water, sunlight, and good soil to flourish, so every Christian needs repentance, attentive hearing and proclamation of God's Word, nourishment at the Lord's Table, and the commission to carry Christ's message into the world.

The Holy Spirit, who stirs our hearts to repentance and animates our worship, breathes life into the sacred Scriptures and into us, uniting us with Christ's mission in every dimension of the liturgy. This same Spirit draws us ever deeper into the mysteries we celebrate at Mass and sends us forth, renewed and strengthened, to embody those mysteries in our lives.

# The Liturgical Sense of the Sacred Scriptures Defined

Traditionally, we have entered the Scriptures through their literal meaning and spiritual senses—moral, allegorical, and anagogical. Yet, these approaches alone do not always reveal the vibrant connection between the life of the Holy Trinity and the living reality of the Mass. The Word of God is not a lifeless text to be consumed and discarded, but sustenance for body and soul, entirely nourishing and life-giving. The liturgy, too, is not a collection of rituals, but the living presence of Christ drawing His people into communion.

The Liturgical Sense of the Scriptures is the lens through which we perceive the Scriptures alive within the liturgy, and the liturgy radiant within the Scriptures. It is the Catholic Mass casting its light upon the Word, and the Word coming alive within the celebration of the Mass. Through this perspective, the events and teachings of the Bible—along with their deeper meanings—become tools to recognize how salvation history is fulfilled and continually made present through the liturgy, in the sacraments, sacred symbols, appointed times and places, and above all, in the persons of the Holy Trinity. In this way, the Liturgical Sense unites Scripture and liturgy, drawing together the literal and spiritual senses, and inviting us to encounter the living God.

# How to Utilize This Book

The principal purpose of the liturgy of the Catholic Mass is not to serve as a mere subject for debate, contention, or personal grievance. Instead, its purpose is to promote spiritual transformation by guiding practitioners to embody its teachings. Fundamentally, the liturgy focuses not on a 'what' but on a 'who': Christ Jesus, who invites the faithful into the liturgical life to participate fully in His and the Holy Spirit's mission. The utmost good of the Mass liturgy is not that we stay with her, but that we might leave – act her dismissal, and act in the world who she has pedagogically formed us to become. By accepting her dismissal, we can shape the world into a liturgical space oriented towards Christ Jesus. This shaping is how the world becomes one, as the Father and the Son are one. We live the liturgical life so that we may influence the world to partake in the liturgical life.

Therefore, how might you utilize this book? To study diligently, thereby enabling you to contemplate profoundly, to pray sincerely, and to become the individual whom the liturgy has cultivated you to be, ultimately inspiring, in a divinely infectious way, those around you.

## In Gratitude

This work intentionally began in 2019 as a follow-up to my book, The Divine Symphony: An Exordium to the Theology of the Catholic Mass, and continued my desire to help others understand the real meaning of the Mass—not only through analogies, but by discovering a liturgical sense of the Scriptures themselves.

Throughout, my wife, Felicia, and our daughter, Olivia, have graciously endured my long hours spent writing, recording, and reflecting every Saturday morning, sometimes even during family vacations. Thank you both for all your patience and understanding.

In the final years of my studies at the Catholic University of America, I encountered inspiring faculty and peers who helped me refine my understanding of the Mass's true meaning. I am deeply grateful for God's timing and the blessings received along this path.

I am genuinely grateful to everyone who took the time to read this work in its early stages on 'A Commentary on the Spiritual Life with Yoseph Daviyd (blogspot),' at davidlgray.info, and who listened to the podcast version available at saintdomincsmedia.com. Your comments and sharing have kept me inspired. I believe it is easier to know your calling, but very hard to act on it when you feel like it may not matter to anyone if I do it or don't. During those dark moments, many of you, in small ways, helped me stay motivated. Thank you!

May these commentaries and reflections lead you ever deeper into the Sacred Heart of the liturgy, and may you discover anew how the living Word and the living Church draw us into the very life of God.

Pax per veritatem,
*David L. Gray*
November 11, 2025, the Feast of Saint Martin of Tours

Saint Martin of Tours, Pray for Us!

# The Season of Advent

# The First Sunday in Advent

|  |  |
|--:|:--|
| First Reading | Isaiah 2:1-5 |
| Responsorial Psalm | Psalm 122 |
| Second Reading | Romans 13:11-14 |
| Gospel Acclamation | Psalm 85:8 |
| Gospel Reading | Matthew 24:37-44 |

# The Liturgy of the Catholic Mass Teaches Us Four Holy Desires

The magisterium and theologians of our Catholic Church have spent nearly two thousand years discussing ontological arguments concerning how original sin affects our nature. Common terms used to describe the effect of the sin against God committed by Adam and Eve, which continues to influence those affected by this sin, include 'weakened human nature,' 'nature subject to ignorance,' and 'nature suffering from the domination of death.' Words like "wounded" and "fallen" are also frequently used.

Here, I offer a different perspective on the effects of original sin: human nature has a strong tendency to desire less than what God intended for us. We often settle for less than God's plan, strive for less, long for less, wake up for less, sleep for less, hope for less, and pray for less than what God has ordained. As a result, there is an ongoing struggle between the Creator and the creature, causing us to continually wrestle with God, resist His will, and turn away from Him. The comforting message is that, despite our tendencies toward what may hurt us or fall short of our true potential, God's desires for us stay the same. No matter how little we aim for ourselves, God is always ready to generously share His greatest blessings with us, and there is no action on our part that can reduce God's desire for us more than what He knows we genuinely need.

In today's first reading from Isaiah 2:1-5, what the prophet "saw concerning Judah and Jerusalem, in days to come" was precisely that—an era when it is not man who establishes himself as king; a king capable only of dividing God's people. Rather, it will be a day when the "LORD's house shall be established as the highest mountain and raised above the hills. All nations shall stream toward it; many peoples shall come and say: "Come, let us climb the LORD's mountain, to the house of the God of Jacob, that he may instruct us in his ways, and we may walk in his paths.'" Although the human nature is naturally inclined toward division, hatred, and war, the prophet Isaiah envisioned a day of true peace when men "shall beat their swords into plowshares and their spears into pruning hooks; one nation shall not raise the sword against another, nor shall they train for war again." On this day, the liturgical kiss of peace and the sign of peace will be fulfilled.

Furthermore, it is greatly beneficial for us to accept that the number of days we have left in this life is very limited, and our personal judgment day could even occur after the next breath we take. For if we accept that death and judgment are near, as the Apostle Paul states in today's second reading from Romans 13:11-14, we would "throw off the works of darkness and put on the armor of light" and "conduct ourselves properly as in the day, not in orgies and drunkenness, not in promiscuity and lust, not in rivalry and jealousy. But put on the Lord Jesus Christ and make no provision for the desires of the flesh."

Similarly, in the Gospel reading from Matthew 24:37-44, our Lord Jesus recapitulated the events surrounding Noah's time, when people thought they had plenty of time and ignored the warnings. "So will it be also at the coming of the Son of Man. Two men will be out in the field; one will be taken, and one will be left. Two women will be grinding at the mill; one will be taken, and one will be left. Therefore, stay awake! For you do not know on which day your Lord will come... So too, you also must be prepared, for at an hour you do not expect, the Son of Man will come."

I appreciate that the Year A readings for the First Sunday in Advent are clear, bold, and challenging in their instructions. Yes, the Christ Mass is coming. Baby Jesus is near to be born of the Virgin. Yes, prepare your gifts around the table. Enjoy your time eating with your family. But how would your life be different right now if the approaching Christmas were one of judgment? What our Lord and the Apostle are teaching here is not harsh, radical, or impossible at all once we digest the habits that the liturgy is forming in us and how we are cooperating with God's grace through the liturgy to elevate our human nature to a supernature in Him who was raised on the Cross of Sacrifice and is lifted before us today on the altar of sacrifice.

Indeed, the Holy Eucharist itself exemplifies the transformation of a lifeless element into a living entity. Consequently, it follows that God can accomplish even greater works within us, which He has elected to transubstantiate from simple bread and wine. Through this, the liturgy fosters proper desires within our hearts. Although we continually grapple with the struggle to desire God's goodness, and at times wish for less for ourselves than what God desires for us, attentive participation in the liturgy—through its four stages: the Rite of Penance, the Liturgy of the Word, the Liturgy of the Holy Eucharist, and the Rite of Sending (*Ite, Missa est* – the Concluding Rite)—teaches us the four sacred desires that God wishes us to cultivate: 1) Contrition, Repentance, and Confession; 2) Hearing and Responding to His Word; 3) Worthy Reception of Our Daily Bread; and 4) Becoming Missionaries of Christ within the World.

This commentary is not the place to provide an exhaustive discussion regarding these four sacred desires or the liberty to arrange various subcategories beneath them; however, it suffices to pose the question: if these four sacred desires bestowed upon us through the liturgy serve as the foundation of our existence, what could be held against us by God? Accordingly, let us concentrate on cultivating, during this Advent season, the desires that the Church's liturgy has formed in us throughout our Catholic lives.

# The Second Sunday in Advent

| | |
|---:|:---|
| First Reading | Isaiah 11:1-10 |
| Responsorial Psalm | Psalm 72:1-2, 7-8, 12-13, 17 |
| Second Reading | Romans 15:4-9 |
| Gospel Acclamation | Luke 3:4, 6 |
| Gospel Reading | Matthew 3:1-12 |

# The Liturgy of the Catholic Mass is for People Who Know Their Lives Are Messy

As we continue our approach to the Christ Mass this Advent, this selection of readings today gives us an opportunity to marvel at the intentionality of the religion that God has gifted us with.

I am not quite sure when religion became such a taboo word in our society, but the idea that one can have a Christian spirituality outside of a Catholic Christian religion is the height of Protestant hubris and the folly of Eve, who wanted to be like God and have us worship at the altar of self-determination. The presumption that I can have Christ without His Church and that I can set my own path is antithetical to the entirety of sacred Scripture.

Nowhere does God say, go ahead, do your own thing, set your own path, and try to find me that way. God never says I will not provide you with precepts, commandments, grace, or anything to help you know and follow what is good and true. Nor does God ever say that I will not bring you into my community for you to live in communion with all my children; rather, I'll just let you figure it out on your own. Not only do the sacred Scriptures of our Catholic faith flatly reject the idea of God being such an apathetic clown, but a narcissist would dare say they believe in a God who does not believe in you.

When one practices a religion, it involves an invitation, a pathway, and a route to their deity. However, within Catholicism, religion extends beyond a unilateral approach. This is because the Holy Spirit, the Third Person of the Holy Trinity, resides within us through Baptism, and Christ Jesus, the Second Person of the Holy Trinity, enters into communion with us during the Holy Mass as the Holy Eucharist. Thus, religion becomes more than merely an invitation, a pathway, or a route to access God; it also transforms into a divine invitation, path, and route for God to reach us through His magnanimity.

## Second Sunday of Advent

When discussing religion, we are elucidating a method for interpreting the interaction between the created and their Creator, as well as the intricate and intimate process of continual transformation that arises from this encounter. Indeed, religion can be disorderly; however, this disorderliness should not serve as a motive for its rejection. Rather, it is precisely because of its messiness that we ought to embrace it. Even the liturgy embodies disorder—not due to its structure or form, but owing to the individuals being shaped by it. In this regard, liturgy can be compared to the process of making sausage. What do we observe during the Holy Mass? Disordered individuals advancing to meet the God who engages with them amidst their disorder, so that they may collaborate with Him to foster peace amid conflict, establish order within chaos, and create harmony from cacophony.

It was not the coming of ice cream and cherries that the prophet Isaiah foretold in today's First Reading from Isaiah 11:1-10, saying, "On that day, a shoot shall sprout from the stump of Jesse." That image itself is messy and unorderly—hardly an ideal picture of what one would like to see. Usually, you would expect to see a new tree grow from rich soil, not a stump. A stump is something cut down or sawed off; it's broken, stepped on, discarded, overlooked. Yet, out of the crack of a stump of Jesse, Isaiah prophesied that a new tree would sprout and begin to grow, even if things are messy at times. "He shall strike the ruthless with the rod of his mouth; with the breath of his lips he shall slay the wicked." But out of that messiness, "shall come abundant joy and peace; "the wolf shall be a guest of the lamb, and the leopard shall lie down with the kid; the calf and the young lion shall browse together, with a little child to guide them. The cow and the bear shall be neighbors, and their young shall rest together; the lion shall eat hay like the ox. The baby shall play by the cobra's den, and the child shall lay his hand on the adder's lair. There shall be no harm or ruin on all my holy mountain; for the earth shall be filled with the knowledge of the LORD, as water covers the sea. On that day, the root of Jesse, set up as a signal for the nations, the Gentiles shall seek out, for his dwelling shall be glorious."

What Isaiah is talking about here is religion—that is, the ongoing transformation through encounter that results in true peace.

Reflect on Saint Paul's letter to the Church in Rome in today's Second Reading from Romans 15:4-9. It would be one thing for us gathered now to hear the words, "May the God of endurance and encouragement grant you to think in harmony with one another, in keeping with Christ Jesus, that with one accord you may with one voice glorify the God and Father of our Lord Jesus Christ." Speaking with unity should be simple for us today, given our sacred Scriptures, Creeds, dogmatic teachings, and even a Catechism. But imagine the original call: Jews and Gentiles, circumcised and uncircumcised, asked to abandon their old perspectives and adopt a new way of thinking—one in harmony through our Lord Jesus Christ. "Welcome one another, then, as Christ welcomed you, for the glory of God." What a messy religion this is, many must have thought.

The letters and epistles of the New Testament show that this was a tumultuous time in the history of the Catholic Church. Yet, many in the Church Triumphant today—those who intercede for us—began their ongoing transformation through encounters with Christ Jesus in those difficult moments. Their testimony affirms that our faith is from God; it is effective not because of us or our messy lives, but despite us. Out of our cacophony, does our Lord not conduct us toward His divine symphony?

We encounter fewer people in the sacred Scriptures whose lives seem messier than John the Waymaker. We are reading about a man in Matthew 3:1-12 who was completely unconcerned about his appearance or diet; utterly indifferent about what people thought of him; and entirely unconcerned about being accepted by the religious establishment. This prophet of the Old Covenant, whom Christ Himself said no prophet was greater than, devoted his life to religion. He said, himself, "I am the 'voice of one crying out in the desert, 'Make straight the way of the Lord.'" This is why I prefer to call him John the Waymaker rather than John the Baptist: he did not come to baptize, but to make a way. What is this way, one might ask – or where does this way lead? John came baptizing repentant sinners, meaning people who knew their lives were messy. Baptizing these messy people in the Jordan provided them with the way to encounter Christ Jesus, who was born of the Virgin, so that He might meet them.

Those who approach worship through the Divine Symphony of the Holy Mass enter a realm of disorder. They arrive noisy, disorganized, broken, and troubled, and there we encounter what? Broken Bread. A fractured image of God, our creator, who knows us intimately because He dwelt among us. Despite this, He comes to meet us in our brokenness, so that we might unite with Him and the Father through the Holy Spirit.

The Holy Mass is the privileged and pedagogical method by which Christ and His Church share His glory with us. This divine pedagogy is the pathway of ongoing transformation through continuous encounter with the Holy Eucharist, for which Christ Jesus sacrificed His life so that we may participate in it. The sacraments are not intended for the righteous, but for the imperfect.

Remember this journey of this religion of encounter and transformation as you commence your movement towards the communion line today.

# Third Sunday in Advent

        First Reading   Isaiah 35:1-6a, 10
Responsorial Psalm   Psalm 146:6-7, 8-9, 9-10.
    Second Reading   James 5:7-10
Gospel Acclamation   Isaiah 61:1 (cited in Lk 4:18)
     Gospel Reading   Matthew 11:2-11

# The Liturgy of the Catholic Mass Comes to Make Us New in Christ

As we continue our journey to experience the joy and newness that many felt at the birth of our Lord Jesus Christ, the readings for the Third Sunday in Advent draw us into the joy and newness we should feel for having been reborn in Him. This Third Sunday in Advent is also called Gaudete Sunday (*Gaudete*, meaning 'joy' in Latin); so, this is Joy Sunday. The liturgical color is rose, and we light what is called the Shepherd's candle because it emphasizes the joy of finding the Christ Child and sharing or evangelizing this joy with others.

To participate in this season of joy, the liturgists have chosen Isaiah 35:1-6 for the First Reading at Mass today. These verses belong to a section that begins in 34:1 and ends in 35:10, which includes an oracle of judgment against Edom—once a symbol of evil—and a prophecy of salvation, describing how Edom, now fallen and deserted, will show signs of rebirth and new life after the exodus, with "abundant flowers" blooming and the sounds of rejoicing "with joyful song." Who has saved these people? Who has granted them new life?

In verse four, the oracle becomes especially meaningful for Christians because it states that God will come in person to save His people. "Here is God," the text says, "He comes with vindication; with divine recompense, he comes to save you." This prophecy by Isaiah, centuries before the Virgin's birth, points to the coming of Immanuel, and even describes the miracles by which we will recognize Him: "Then the eyes of the blind will be opened, the ears of the deaf will be cleared; then the lame will leap like a stag, and the tongue of the mute will sing. Those whom the LORD has ransomed will return and enter Zion singing, crowned with everlasting joy."

The nature of prophecy is analogous to that of any promise; the expression 'I promise you I will' is articulated by countless individuals—

potentially millions—throughout the day worldwide. The typical response frequently is, '... but when?'—When will you honor that promise?"

Indeed, since the beginning, numerous members of the Jewish community have inquired, 'When will that prophecy be fulfilled?' regarding the anticipated Messiah, just as many recent converts to Christianity—who have heard about these oracles and prophecies—have posed similar questions. The response given to them was, well... Christ has come to us in person; He continues to come to us through the Holy Eucharist; and He will come again... but when? In this context, Saint James responds, writing, "Be patient, brothers and sisters, until the coming of the Lord. See how the farmer waits for the precious fruit of the earth, being patient with it until it receives the early and late rains. You, too, must be patient. Make your hearts firm because the coming of the Lord is near. Do not complain, brothers and sisters, about one another, so that you may not be judged. Behold, the Judge is standing at the gates. Take as an example of hardship and patience, brothers and sisters, the prophets who spoke in the name of the Lord."

All writings of Saint James emphasize the significance of the liturgy of the Mass. There exists a reason why the Holy Mass does not commence with the Liturgy of the Holy Eucharist. Patience is required in receiving Him, because first, we must be properly prepared to accept Him. Therefore, the liturgy serves as a pedagogical reflection of salvation history. Salvation was not instant after the expulsion of Adam and Eve from the Garden of Eden, nor immediately after the Children of Israel crossed the Red Sea. It did not arrive within a short span, but Christ Jesus came when humanity was prepared to receive Him. The Scriptures record the names of individuals who were blessed for patiently awaiting His arrival, such as the Magi who journeyed from afar to visit the newborn King of the Universe, and Simeon and the prophetess Anna, whose moment of prophecy coincided with the circumcision of the young King.

Saint James again emphasizes the importance of the liturgy in verse nine, writing, "Do not complain, brothers, about one another, that you may not be judged." Do we not ask the Lord to forgive us our sins as we forgive those who have sinned against us before we are able to receive the Holy Eucharist? Have many liturgical rites throughout Church history asked us to exchange a kiss of peace or sign of peace with our brothers and sisters before receiving the Holy Eucharist? For before joy comes, according to Saint James, we must endure the same hardship and patience as the prophets and saints who came before us.

Another prophet who demonstrated resilience through hardship and patience was John the Waymaker. He likely rejoiced in prison when Jesus responded to his question, "Are you the one to come, or should we expect another," by echoing the words of his ancestor, the prophet Isaiah. In today's Gospel from *Matthew* 11:2-11, we learn that Jesus sent John's disciples back to him with the message: "Go and tell John what you hear and see: the blind regain their sight, the lame walk, lepers are cleansed, the deaf hear, the dead are raised, and the poor have the good news proclaimed to them. And blessed is the one who takes no offense at me."

Since the creation of the universe, God has continuously created new life within and around us. New life and renewal invariably evoke joy, whether it is the birth of a child, the sight of gifts beneath the Christmas tree, or the experience of new love. These are just foretastes of the divine gift brought forth by the nativity of Christ Jesus: renewed sight for the blind, restored mobility for the lame, new skin for the leper, improved hearing for the deaf, and renewed life for the deceased and the impoverished.

Moreover, the most beautiful thing about the liturgy of the Mass is that Christ Jesus not only presents us with new offerings, but He Himself embodies that newness. He is the new wine and the new bread, which becomes the foundation of our renewed life through His body and blood. What manner of God is this who comes with the gift of a new thing every day, who renews our lives continuously, who arrives repeatedly? Not only does our Lord assure us that those who are not offended by His offering of this new life are blessed, but He also bestows blessings upon those who find delight in His existence.

    Persevere through your hardships and patience, for the moment you are about to receive — when you reach the end of the communion line — is a divine gift. It will introduce something new into your life and ignite a fresh work within you. Embrace this transformation, for the old you must die so that a new, transformed life in Him can emerge. Are you willing to accept this challenge and step into the renewal that awaits?

# Fourth Sunday in Advent

First Reading    Isaiah 7:10-14
Responsorial Psalm    Psalm 24:1-2, 3-4, 5-6
Second Reading    Romans 1:1-7
Gospel Acclamation    Matthew 1:23
Gospel Reading    Matthew 1:18-24

## The Theology of the Incarnation Through the Liturgy of the Catholic Mass

On the Fourth Sunday in Advent, we celebrate the fulfillment of God's promise through the Incarnation of our Lord and Savior, Jesus Christ. Our First Reading comes from Isaiah 7:10-14, where the Lord speaks to Ahaz, the twelfth King of Judah and son of Jotham, offering him a sign: "the virgin shall conceive, and bear a son, and shall name him Emmanuel,' which means 'God with you.' In the Second Reading, the Apostle Saint Paul expands on this ancient promise, writing to the Church in Rome in 1:1-7, "Paul, a servant of Christ Jesus, called to be an apostle and set apart for the gospel of God, which he promised previously through his prophets in the holy Scriptures, the gospel about his Son, descended from David according to the flesh."

In the Gospel Reading, Matthew relies on the Septuagint, the Greek translation of the Old Testament from the 3rd to 1st centuries B.C., for his citation of Isaiah 7:14. In this translation, the Hebrew term *almah*, meaning 'maiden' or 'young woman of marriageable age,' is translated as the Greek *parthenos*, which means 'virgin.' Matthew 1:18-24 presents an account of the birth of Jesus Christ, including references to the roles of Mary and Joseph, their betrothal, the naming of Jesus (*Yeshua*, meaning 'God saves'), and the Incarnation through the Holy Spirit. The passage states: "All this took place to fulfill what the Lord had said through the prophet: Behold, the virgin shall conceive and bear a son, and they shall name him Emmanuel, which means 'God is with us.'"

It is imperative to recognize that the Incarnation event in the Gospel of Matthew is narrated from Saint Joseph's perspective, including the dream he received. This revelation elucidates why the genealogy in Matthew commences with Abraham and terminates with Joseph, the husband of Mary. Conversely, the Incarnation in the Gospel of Luke is described from Mary's perspective and her visitation by the Angel Gabriel. Therefore, Luke's genealogy begins with Adam and culminates with Joseph, son of Heli. Specifically, in Matthew, Jesus is acknowledged as genuinely belonging to the Tribe of Judah, a descendant of Abraham and the house of David, as Joseph is informed in a dream that he "will save his people from their sins."

In contrast, Luke depicts Jesus as a descendant of Adam and the house of David, emphasizing His divine origin and eternal reign, as indicated by the belief that "there will be no end." Furthermore, Matthew underscores the Incarnation of Jesus primarily for the salvation of the Jewish community. Simultaneously, Luke situates the event at the beginning of salvation history, emphasizing its significance for the entire human race, including those affected by Adam and Eve's original sin.

This discussion does not intend to revisit the long-standing debates or differing views between Jewish and Christian communities regarding the translation of the Hebrew term almah as the Greek *parthenos* in Matthew 1:23. It is sufficient at this juncture to note that the incarnation itself is cited by some as evidence supporting the translators' choice, implying both prudence and possible divine guidance in their work, which was accomplished two to three centuries before the advent of Christ. Moreover, there is no necessity here to reconsider Protestant concerns that almah does not necessarily mean 'perpetual virgin,' because that objection is one merely born out of the necessity of their hatred of Christ and His Church and our love for the Blessed Virgin Mary.

Notably, Isaiah's prophecy about the Incarnation in verse 7:14 is just one of five promises made to King Ahaz—none of which he sought out for himself. According to the text, the Lord offered Ahaz the chance to ask for a sign, saying it could be as deep as Sheol or as high as the sky. In this encounter, God showed a willingness to reveal any part of His divine plan that Ahaz might want to see. However, Ahaz refused, saying, "I will not ask! I will not tempt the LORD!" In this way, Ahaz is similar to Mary, as both received promises they did not explicitly ask for.

Furthermore, through the first promise, Ahaz also parallels Adam and Eve; like them, he was told about the coming birth of the New Eve:

"the young woman, pregnant and about to give birth to a son, shall call him Emmanuel." So, Ahaz—the twelfth king of Judah mentioned in Matthew's genealogy—also connects to Luke's account. The other four signs, in verses 18 through 23, provide vivid imagery of the destruction that would come upon Israel after Emmanuel's birth.

Chapter seven of Isaiah is crucial in Catholic theology, laying the groundwork for Christian beliefs about Jesus Christ as Lord, Savior, and Redeemer. This early mention of the Incarnation is significant in the context of liturgical practices. Both King Ahaz and the Blessed Virgin Mary received messages highlighting God's imminent presence: Ahaz was told that a child born of a virgin would be called Emmanuel, meaning 'God is with us.' At the same time, Mary learned he would be named Yeshua, which means 'God saves.' These titles reflect core aspects of the Holy Mass, which seeks to convey the reality of eternal life in Christ through God's presence and saving action. The ideas of 'being with' and 'saving' emphasize a personal and communal dimension, showing that true communion requires both closeness and redemptive purpose.

It is frequently observed that individuals tend to retain items they deem valuable or meaningful, typically objects with which they can engage. Conversely, individuals are less inclined to preserve unfamiliar or otherwise insignificant items; instead, they tend to retain those of personal importance. In this manner, the Catholic tradition asserts that divine interaction occurs through the Holy Mass, with particular emphasis on the importance of the Holy Eucharist. Catholic doctrine regards the Holy Eucharist as both a symbol and a practice essential to the faith, subject to various interpretations and responses among followers.

During liturgical observances, such as the Fourth Sunday in Advent, we are encouraged to contemplate these concepts and their implications within the broader framework of our creed. Let us not merely contemplate but also act on the more profound truths they reveal.

# The Nativity of the Lord
*December 25*

# The Liturgical Paradox of the Nativity of the Lord

The Theophany of the Nativity of the Lord and the celebration of the Christ Mass have inspired centuries of contemplation, offering abundant richness for thoughtful reflection and spiritual growth. At the heart of this mystery lies a wondrous paradox: the birth of Christ is at once forever ancient and always new. This truth is experienced most vividly in the living memorial of the Holy Mass, where the coming of Christ is not only remembered but made present with every celebration.

How can we grasp this miracle, something that, though rooted in history, renews itself in every age, every heart, every prayer? This miracle is the marvel at the center of our faith: the Nativity of the Lord is not simply an event to remember, but a living reality that shines forth in the liturgy of the Church and in the life of every believer.

As we continue to contemplate this sacred mystery, we are drawn into a sense of wonder that refreshes the soul and awakens the spirit with hope. The story of Christ's birth does not fade with the passing of years; instead, it continually invites us to experience its promise again. In the sacred celebration of the Mass, God's timeless presence is poured into our moment, bringing illumination, peace, and the joy of renewal to all who open their hearts.

For this reason, we enter this season with gratitude, allowing the beauty of the Nativity to fill us with hope and inspire us to share the message of "God is with us" with kindness, generosity, and faith. In this way, the story of Christ's birth becomes the bright dawn of every day, drawing us ever deeper into the love that changes our lives and the world.

The novelty of the Nativity of the Lord is clearly manifested in the Scripture readings observed throughout this day, from the Vigil Mass to the Mass during the Night, the Dawn, and Christmas Day. The passages from the prophet *Isaiah* and *Deutero-Isaiah* consistently affirm this truth. Isaiah 9:5 states, "For a child is born to us, a son is given us; upon his shoulder dominion rests. They name him Wonder-Counselor, God-Hero, Father-Forever, Prince of Peace." Isaiah 52:8 proclaims, "Hark! Your sentinels raise a cry, together they shout for joy, for they see directly, before their eyes, the LORD restoring Zion." Isaiah 62:2 declares, "Nations shall behold your vindication, and all kings your glory; You shall be called by a new name bestowed by the mouth of the LORD." Isaiah 62:11 announces, "See, the LORD proclaims to the ends of the earth: say to daughter Zion, your savior comes! Here is his reward with him, his recompense before him."

The Second Reading from Titus, Acts, and Hebrews also sings of the joy and renewal experienced when God fulfills His promise through His Son, our Lord, Christ Jesus. The motif of newness is conveyed through the language of purification within these scriptures. Titus 3:5-6 states, "He saved us through the bath of rebirth and renewal by the Holy Spirit, whom he richly poured out on us through Jesus Christ, our savior." Titus 3:13-14 affirms, "Jesus Christ, who gave himself for us to deliver us from all lawlessness and to purify for himself a people as his own, eager to do what is good." Acts 13:24 notes, "John heralded his coming by proclaiming a baptism of repentance to all the people of Israel." Hebrews 1:3 elucidates, "When he had accomplished purification from sins, he took his seat at the right hand of the Majesty on high."

Mark is the sole Synoptic Gospel that omits the account of the Nativity of the Lord; therefore, on this day, we focus on the birth of Christ Jesus as presented in Matthew and Luke. Subsequently, the Gospel of John describes our Lord as the preexistent Word of God, who "became flesh and made his dwelling among us."

While people born in the flesh often celebrate their birthdays as annual milestones, what is truly being marked is another year of life. Usually, we don't revisit images from our birth or gather around our first crib with symbolic representations of those present at the event, such as doctors, nurses, or distant relatives. Such practices are generally avoided because it might seem presumptuous to assume that our birth was universally welcomed. The existence of sin suggests that our arrival may have had adverse effects on others; it is possible that someone, somewhere, views our birth unfavorably.

Moreover, we typically do not celebrate our own birthdays with the same reverence as important historical or religious events because we realize that our birth didn't fundamentally change the world for the better. There's a common belief that our greatest achievements and contributions are still ahead of us, making future years more significant than the day we were born. As a result, milestones later in life, like major anniversaries or accomplishments, often hold more meaning than simply being born.

In this manner, the divine is fundamentally distinguished from humanity, and it is noteworthy that theological traditions frequently emphasize this distinction. Regarding liturgy, particularly within the context of the Ordinary Form, it has become customary on certain occasions for the priest celebrant or master of ceremonies to inquire whether any individuals are celebrating a birthday at the conclusion of the service. However, such a practice may undermine the primary purpose of the liturgy, which is centered not on personal milestones but rather on spiritual renewal and rebirth in Christ. Even if the Concluding Rite permitted such acknowledgments, the more pertinent focus would be on the individuals' spiritual renewal through the Sacrament of Baptism, or as effected through the sacraments of Penance and Reconciliation or the Holy Eucharist. Consequently, the introduction of personal celebrations into the liturgical setting can be regarded as inconsistent with the intended spiritual emphasis of the rite.

In every celebration of the Christ Mass—the very heart of the liturgy—we experience the wonder and promise of the Nativity, ever ancient and ever new. Day after day, year after year, for nearly two millennia, the faithful have gathered to rejoice in the birth of our Lord, whose presence graces the world anew with each Mass. The Nativity of the Lord, then, is not relegated to history, but breathes with life in every moment we approach the altar.

This ongoing renewal is most profoundly experienced through the sacraments. In the living waters of Baptism, individuals are initiated into hope; through Confession and Anointing of the Sick, their spirits are purified, and hearts are mended. Marriage and Holy Orders introduce new avenues of self-sacrifice and service, while the Holy Eucharist sustains us with the love and strength of Christ Himself. Each sacrament, administered within the liturgical context, unites us with the mystery of Christ's coming—an existence that is both eternal and perpetually developing.

Therefore, today, as we contemplate the Holy Infant, we rejoice in this gift of newness, given without measure. Through the Church's sacred celebrations and sacraments, we are continually invited into the grace of that first Holy Night—a miracle that transforms not only the passing of years, but the very depths of our souls. Let our hearts be lifted by gratitude and hope, for the Nativity's radiant promise is ours to receive, cherish, and share with the world.

# The Octave of Christmas

# The Liturgical Life of Saint Joseph, Father of the Holy Family

The veneration of the Holy Family of Jesus, Mary, and Joseph possesses a longstanding and distinguished history within the Catholic Church. Its origins can be traced to 14th century art representing the trio. Nevertheless, it gained heightened prominence in the 17th century when Saint François de Laval, the inaugural bishop of New France, established the Confraternity of the Holy Family, thereby facilitating the dissemination and promotion of devotion to the Holy Family worldwide.

The liturgical celebration of the Feast of the Holy Family was instituted by Pope Leo XIII in 1893, initially scheduled on the Sunday following Epiphany. However, in 1969, it was relocated to the first Sunday after Christmas to coincide with the Octave of Christmas. This veneration and celebration serve to inspire reverence for the Holy Family of Nazareth as an exemplary model of Christian familial life and obedience to God. Concurrent with this development, Catholics also began to utilize the initials "JMJ" to refer to Jesus, Mary, and Joseph, following the example set by venerable individuals such as Saint Thérèse of Lisieux and Venerable Fulton J. Sheen, who employed this abbreviation in their correspondence.

I am amazed at how this tradition has developed in our faith, evolving from a local veneration of art to a worldwide celebration of the Church and inspiring many parish names. This tradition is more woven into the fabric of the Church's life than it is present in the actual accounts of the Holy Family in the sacred Scriptures. In fact, aside from the stories of Jesus' birth and childhood, we do not see Jesus, Mary, and Joseph together anywhere else in the Bible. Because there are few testimonies and stories about the daily life of the Holy Family in the scriptures, we must use our imagination to contemplate this mystery. One question is why we consider Joseph to have been holy during his life on earth, given that the sacred Scripture does not suggest he was born immaculately or incarnate. How is it that we call the Holy Family to include Jesus, Mary, and Joseph, in light of Joseph's not being identified by the Angel Gabriel as full of grace nor being conceived by the Holy Spirit? How is Joseph of Bethlehem considered holy?

We answer the question by affirming that God is the one who makes persons, places, and objects sacred or holy by giving them a special name. The process by which God makes something holy is by setting it apart for a specific purpose that demonstrates His divine and perfect goodness.

In the case of Joseph, we see that God chose and set him apart to be the father of Jesus and the husband of Mary. Since the roles of a husband and father are to protect, provide, and guide, Joseph surpasses other men because he was assigned and set apart by God for the most sacred work of all. He is rightly called Joseph, Head of the Holy Family, Husband of the Mother of God, and the Father of the Son of God on Earth. Therefore, Joseph is called holy through the work he was set apart to do as the husband of a holy wife and the father of a holy son. Additionally, because the principle of work of husband and father is to sacrifice for those he is set apart to protect, provide, and guide—and only holy sacrifices are acceptable to God—we believe that by sacrificing himself for his holy wife and son, Joseph of Bethlehem is also rightly called Joseph the Holy Sacrifice.

Few men would sacrifice the life they believed they would have, the type of wife they thought they would marry, and the children they expected to have with her, to instead be with a woman pregnant with a child who was not theirs. A man who was simply righteous before God would have quietly divorced her to avoid exposing her to shame[1] or accusations of adultery that could have led to her receiving the death penalty. However, when the angel of the Lord appeared to Joseph in a dream and said, "Yoseph, son of Daviyd, do not be afraid to take Mary

---

[1] Cf. Mt. 1:19.

your wife into your home. For it is through the holy Spirit that this child has been conceived in her. She will bear a son and you are to name him Yeshua because he will save his people from their sins," Joseph responded by showing obedience to God, demonstrating that he loves and fears Him. As *1* John 5:3 states, "For this is the love of God, that we keep his commandments. And his commandments are not burdensome," but it is not solely love that makes us obedient to God, but also faith for His name's sake.[2] Therefore, Joseph is rightly called holy because of his faith and love for God, which compelled him to prioritize obedience to God above all else, even when faced with a command no other man had been asked to follow.

In the liturgy's processes of birthing, nurturing, contemplative reflection, pedagogical instruction, anagogical interpretation, prayerfulness, attentiveness, and rhythmic expression, it is exceedingly apparent what commonalities she shares with the Holy Mother and the reasons why Mary is rightly revered as the Mother of the Church and should be called Mother of the Liturgy. Nevertheless, it is within the liturgy's invocation of interior silence and obedient action through the dismissal – *Ite, Missa est* – that we appropriately regard Joseph as the Father of the Church.

Indeed, silence and obedience represent the most profound summons of the liturgy, and it is there that the husband of the Mother of the Liturgy emerges as our exemplar of excellence. Joseph the Silent and Contemplative, who uttered no words in sacred Scripture but bore witness loudly to his obedient faith through his deeds, demonstrates how we ought to be in the world, forming us through liturgical practice. We do not observe Joseph praying, nor do we hear him speaking verbally about his wife or son. Conversely, we only learn of a dream he was given. Nevertheless, no individual can be called to undertake what Joseph of Bethlehem did, nor perform what he was called to do, without

---

[2] Cf. Romans 1:5

possessing a deeply prayerful and contemplative life that is closely connected to God; such a life enables a person to sacrifice his dreams solely to fulfill his role of providing for, protecting, and guiding the desires of God's heart.

# Through the Liturgy, we are Born Again through the Womb of Mary, Mother of God and Mother of the Church

The Catholic Church's dogmatic teaching that the Blessed Virgin Mary is truly the Mother of God—the Theotokos—requires faithful assent to a profound mystery: That Mary is mother in every natural sense to Christ Jesus, the Second Person of the Holy Trinity. The Word became flesh—flesh through her flesh. Through her womb and her DNA, the Blessed Mother contributed to the formation of His human nature.

He who is eternally begotten of the Father, consubstantial with Him in divinity, is also truly the Son of Mary in humanity. The Second Person of the Trinity is, by blood and lineage, intimately related to the Blessed Virgin. Christ Jesus is, in every way, the Son of Mary—and in every way, the Son of the Eternal Father Almighty. This truth stands without confusion, contradiction, or conflict: one Person, fully divine and fully human, born of the Virgin, begotten of the Father.

This reality is affirmed in the sacred Tradition of the Church. In the Apostles' Creed, which affirms that the Son of God was "born of the Virgin Mary," the declaration made against Nestorius, the former Archbishop of Constantinople, at the Council of Ephesus in 431 A.D., states, "If anyone does not confess that the Emmanuel (Christ) in truth is God and that, on this account, the Holy Virgin is the Mother of God – since she brought forth the Word of God made flesh according to the flesh – let him be anathema." That is, anyone who teaches that Mary is not truly the Mother of God because she only gave birth to Jesus' human nature, not His divine nature, is guilty of the heresy of Nestorius. For who Mary gave birth to was fully God and fully Man; therefore, she is the Mother of God, the Theotokos. In other words, it is a lie to claim that the Virgin gave birth to a human boy who later became God.

This truth is confirmed in sacred Scripture; in Isaiah 7:14, which is repeated in Luke 1:31, "Behold a virgin shall conceive and bear a Son and His name shall be called Emmanuel;" in Luke 1:43 where Elizabeth calls Mary, "the Mother of my Lord;" throughout the Gospel of Matthew, where she is referred to as "His Mother;" at the Incarnation event in Luke 1:35, where the Angel Gabriel announced, "The Holy Spirit will come upon you, and the power of the Most High will overshadow you. Therefore, the child to be born will be called Holy, the Son of God;" in John 2:1, where it is said, ". . . the mother of Jesus was there," and in the Second Reading at Mass today from Galatians 4:4-7, which states, "When the fullness of time had come, God sent his Son, born of a woman, born under the law."

Therefore, as the Mother of God, the Blessed Mother remains in a dignity far exceeding that of any other human being, angel, or created entity. Consequently, all generations will deem her blessed. No human has ever been closer to God than Mary, who carried the Second Person of the Holy Trinity within her womb, gave birth to Him, clothed Him, nurtured Him, and raised Him in the world. Accordingly, she is recognized as the mother of adoration of the Blessed Sacrament and the esteemed icon of a worthy reception of the Body, Blood, Soul, and Divinity of Jesus Christ.

Considering that Mary is recognized as the Mother of the physical body of Christ, it logically follows that she is also regarded as the Mother of all individuals who have been adopted into the spiritual Body of Christ and the Mother of the Liturgy through which the sacraments give God's children new life. Consequently, a part of the honor of the Blessed Mother is that she is the sole woman born of flesh whose life is inextricably linked by necessity to the life of the Church; that is, the ecclesiology of our Catholic Church. For this reason, Saint Augustine articulated that, given her status as the Virgin Mary being truly the Mother of God and the Redeemer, she is "clearly the mother of the members of Christ... since she has, through her charity, participated in the spiritual rebirth of believers in the Church, who are members of its head."

In recognition of this, Pope Saint Paul VI bestowed upon our Mother the title, "Mary, Mother of Christ, Mother of the Church."

Let us now proceed to embed this divine reality into the very fabric of the liturgy. If Mary is acknowledged as the Mother of the Church, our discourse concerning the liturgy remains incomplete unless we consider the extent to which it venerates her motherhood and her participation in shaping us through the liturgical rites, just as she contributed to the formation of Christ Jesus within her womb. Permit me to extend this analogy further. As Christ Jesus was formed within the womb of Mary, adopting her lineage, genetic traits, and natural features, so too does the liturgy mold us to be tangible representatives of the Blessed Mother in the world, enabling others to recognize our Mother and our Father through us when they observe our lives.

I have shared before how the liturgy helps shape us, much like the comforting rhythm of standing, sitting, kneeling, praying, and confessing. Think of this formation as a gentle process, similar to how a baby is born in the warmth of Mary's womb—a sacred space where, in every rhythm of our worship, we are being gently brought into new life. The bread we receive is her Son, a nourishing gift prepared with love, and the procession to receive Him is like an umbilical cord, reconnecting us to divine life—only sin can sever it. When we hear '*Ite, Missa est*,' it's like being gently pushed out into the world, ready to live out the purpose God has lovingly shaped us for. The beautiful part is that we can always return to this sacred womb through the liturgy, guided by Mary, our Mother. There, we are renewed as spiritual babies, nurtured again with divine nourishment, so that we can be born anew in Christ—becoming more holy and ready to serve Him with joy.

# The Epiphany
*January 6 (or nearest Sunday)*

# & The Baptism of the Lord
*First Sunday after the Epiphany*

# The Liturgy of the Holy Mass is the Epiphany Event

Epiphany (or Theophany, as it is known in the Eastern Rite Catholic Church), also recognized as Three Kings' Day, is a Christian liturgical celebration that honors the revelation of God, the Second Person of the Holy Trinity, as entirely divine and dwelling among us as Jesus of Nazareth. The term 'epiphany' originates from the Greek word meaning "manifestation." This feast also commemorates the visit of the Magi to the Christ child, thereby symbolizing Jesus' physical manifestation to the Gentiles.

In consideration of the Gospel of Matthew's account of the Epiphany event found in 2:1-12, I have always been intrigued by the fact that several magi (also known as wise persons) from the East observed a star ascending and subsequently followed it in order to pay homage to the newborn King of the Jews. Such an act represents a remarkably bold response to a rare celestial event.

Questions emerge regarding the duration of their planning for this journey, the size of their retinue, the stops they made along the way, and the information they conveyed to those who inquired about their destination. It is highly probable that individuals asked them, 'Where are you going?' or 'Who are you going to see?' What responses did they provide? Were they the first evangelists, declaring, 'We are going to meet the Savior King?' Furthermore, it remains uncertain whether others were influenced by their testimony to believe in the coming of Jesus. Ambiguity persists concerning whether these Magi were of Jewish origin, their number, or whether all of them were male. Numerous questions regarding the Magi continue to lack definitive answers; however, it is certain that these individuals recognized the significance of the moment and acted in accordance with the insights gained through their discernment.

On a crisp, starlit night, the Magi journeyed across the desert, the cool air swirling with the earthy scents of leather and frankincense. Above, the brilliant star shimmered as a beacon, guiding them toward Bethlehem, the House of Bread. Dawn painted the quiet town in soft gold, mingling aromas of baking loaves and olive oil with the distant hum of merchants and sheep. Within a humble home, Mary cradled the Child, her eyes reflecting wonder and exhaustion. The Wise Men entered, reverently kneeling on the cool earthen floor, their treasures—gold gleaming, frankincense swirling, myrrh's bittersweet tang—filling the sacred space as candlelight danced and the soft sounds of life embraced the moment.

While joy and awe filled the modest room, elsewhere, Herod's palace echoed with the metallic scent of suspicion and fear. The proximity to light did not determine one's response; some sought the divine and offered themselves, while others recoiled, consumed by darkness. The world, for a brief moment, was divided along the line between adoration and anxiety, as bread and incense mingled in the air and the gentle glow of the Epiphany called all hearts to choose how they would receive the light.

The unconventional message about the difference between the Magi's and Herod's responses is this: The proximity to light has no bearing upon the reception of light. In other words, God is always the same – He never changes, but what does change is how our hearts respond to Him. What varies is the most inconsistent aspect of humanity: although God reveals and manifests Himself to us, our reactions to His light, revelation, and manifestation are often erratic, conflicting, and lacking. In that lack of genuine interest to respond rightly to God in love, man opens the door to respond to his own base and fleshly desires to sin. This is the dichotomy we face: we either pursue God or pursue sin. There is no third option.

Once again, the proximity to light does not influence its reception. A child born to devout parents and even a saintly priest as a close sibling may grow into someone capable of committing great, unrepentant evil;

conversely, a child whose parents are the firstborn of Satan may attain sainthood. Similarly, if an egg and a stick of butter are placed in a pot of boiling water, each will respond differently to the environment. The egg will become firm, and the butter will melt, not because the water discriminates between them, but because each reacts uniquely to the surrounding conditions.

I understand many parents face this challenge—loving one child completely while feeling uncertain about another's behavior. Imagine if Herod had lived to witness Jesus beginning His ministry; maybe he might have believed. Perhaps he could have been the first Saint Paul. Who can say? Each of us is simply who we are in that moment, responding to our surrounding conditions with the best of our ability at that time.

Jesus is the light of the world; He is the eastern star; He is the truth; He is the bread of life, and people will always respond differently to these truths. Some will love Him, hate Him, or be indifferent, but there are also those who seek Him even if they don't know His name, like the magi—they search for the light and truth. Humanity has always been in search of these treasures, and as children of the Light, we are called to let our light shine brightly, so others can see the light in us (Christ Jesus) and be drawn to the source, just as many followed the Magi.

Indeed, the liturgy of the Holy Mass, itself a form of epiphany, is a manifestation of Jesus Christ in the Holy Eucharist. We resemble the Magi in our journey to the altar, meet our King, and in presenting Him with our gifts, offerings, and the labor of our human hands—an extraordinary facet of the Divine Symphony. We embody the Magi; we journey to behold our King; and we offer Him the gifts He has bestowed upon us. Yet, we are even more blessed than the Magi; while the Blessed Mother Mary permitted them to hold the Infant Lord briefly, we have the privilege of consuming Him into our bodies—His body and blood entering into us.

For this profound act, we prostrate ourselves as the Magi did. While the Magi departed Bethlehem and returned home with only a memory of their encounter with the newborn King of the Universe, we depart the Mass with Him and the indwelling of God Himself—the Holy Spirit. Moreover, we have the opportunity to experience this liturgical epiphany daily throughout the year, except on Good Friday.

Furthermore, what did the Magi hear from Jesus on the day of their visit? A silent infant—neither speaking nor crying, swaddled in cloth. Here, we are even more blessed, for we hear the words of Jesus through the Scriptures and in His words of consecration, through which He comes to meet us, the adopted sons and daughters of His Eternal Father. It is moments like this that make the liturgy of the Holy Mass the greatest, the most timeless, and most renewing event in the universe. Thanks be to God.

# The Baptism of the Lord

**I**nitially, it may seem unusual to celebrate an event that occurred thirty years after the Nativity within the Christmas season. However, early Catholic traditions commemorated Christmas and Epiphany together and encapsulated four of the five great theophanies of Jesus' divine revelation to the world: the Nativity,[3] the visit of the Magi,[4] the Baptism of Jesus,[5] and the Wedding at Cana.[6] The fifth great theophany, the Transfiguration,[7] is celebrated later on August 6th. By the 4th century, the Western liturgical rites distinguished between Christmas on December 25th and Epiphany on January 6th. The Council of Tours in 567 further established these as distinct feast days, with the twelve days between them marking the joyous Christmas season.

In 1955, the reformed liturgical calendar under Pope Pius XII designated the Feast of the Baptism of the Lord with a specific observance, held on the Sunday following Epiphany. If Epiphany occurs on January 7th or 8th, the feast is observed on the subsequent Monday. This procedural distinction occasionally results in the celebration of the Baptism of the Lord outside the Christmas Season and into Ordinary Time.

Derived from the Greek terms *theos* (meaning "god") and *phaino* (meaning "to show"), a theophany constitutes a visible and tangible manifestation of a deity to a human individual, frequently accompanied by events that evoke awe and wonder. In the Catholic Christian tradition, a theophany is equated with 'revelation'—where God discloses His divine nature and mission to humanity.

Throughout salvation history, certain key events—known as theophanies, or manifestations of God—reveal different aspects of Christ's

---

[3] Luke 2:1-20
[4] Matthew 2:1-12
[5] Matthew 3:13-17
[6] John 2:1-11
[7] Matthew 17:1-9

identity and mission. In the Nativity and the Baptism of Jesus, we encounter "nature theophanies" in which it is revealed that Jesus is both fully human and fully divine. In contrast, the Epiphany, the Transfiguration, and the Wedding at Cana serve as "mission theophanies." The Epiphany shows that Jesus' mission is universal; the Transfiguration fulfills the visions of the prophets; and the Wedding at Cana, through the first miracle, reveals Jesus' partnership with the Holy Spirit in transforming us through sacramental grace.

Although it is philosophically possible to distinguish between the nature and mission of Christo-theophany, this distinction is primarily symbolic rather than literal. Fundamentally, when discussing the nature and mission of the Holy Trinity, one comprehends that their mission reflects their intrinsic identity, and their identity inherently encompasses their mission. An exemplary illustration of this invisible differentiation between Christ Jesus' nature and mission is exemplified in today's Gospel Reading from Luke 3:15-16, 21-22, which states, "After all the people had been baptized and Jesus also had been baptized and was praying, heaven was opened and the Holy Spirit descended upon him in bodily form like a dove. And a voice came from heaven, "You are my beloved Son; with you I am well pleased."

While the theophany of the Epiphany uniquely revealed Christ Jesus' mission towards those who visited Him, the theophany of His Baptism also conveys that reality concerning those whom He visited. In stating that "after all the people had been Baptized," Jesus is with all who have repented of their sins, and those who have repented now share a solidarity with Jesus through Baptism. Therefore, in the place where humanity has confessed its fallenness, neediness, and helplessness, the theophany of help also descended as a sign of solidarity in the form of a human body, the Holy Spirit, to commence His joint mission with them—especially with Jesus Christ, who is announced from the heavens above as the beloved Son of God.

Although the Baptism of the Lord occurs decades after the Nativity and Baptism, the words of the prophet in today's First Reading from

Isaiah 42:1-4, 6-7—that "Here is my servant whom I uphold, my chosen one with whom I am pleased, upon whom I have put my spirit; he shall bring forth justice to the nations"—and the Second Reading from Titus 2:11-14; 3:4-7, which states that "Jesus Christ, who gave himself for us to deliver us from all lawlessness and to cleanse for himself a people as his own, eager to do what is good," remind us of the shared challenge inherent in these events. Our aid is akin to one of us—He is a helpless and needy infant, Immanuel—God with us—perhaps a startling sight for the wise men who traveled from afar, and perplexing to those who witnessed His baptism, which was similar to theirs, yet the Heavens declared Him also to be akin to God.

That day, Jesus gently stepped into the murky waters of the Jordan, feeling the soft riverbed under His feet as the brown waters swirled around His ankles. The crowd gathered along the banks grew quiet, their eyes fixed on Him with curiosity and admiration. Sunlight peeked through the leaves, creating gentle patterns of light and shadow on the scene, while soft whispers floated among the onlookers like distant echoes. Every step He took seemed to carry the weight of many stories, with the muddy water symbolizing the depths of humanity He was willing to embrace. Mud also symbolized humanity, who was created from dirt, but now redeemed through the sacred water of Baptism. It was here that John the Waymaker's eyes met Jesus' with a sense of reverence and awe, understanding the importance of this moment. Indeed, the air was thick with anticipation, as if the heavens were leaning in to hear the first stanza of a divine symphony.

As a matter of human pride, we often resist the notion that our assistants are akin to us. We derive comfort when those undertaking menial tasks appear to be of a lower social standing or when those aiding us with complex issues seem to be our equals or superiors. For example, affluent individuals often feel uncomfortable when their housekeepers drive identical luxury vehicles or vacation at the exact same exotic locations as they do.

This sense of solidarity with our helpers has historically been considered a social taboo, and collectively, we have all agreed to uphold it. However, this norm of polite society sharply contrasts with the essence of every Christo-theophany, liturgy, and sacrament of the Church. These sacred spaces and times reveal that Jesus, in His likeness to us, can genuinely assist us because He lowered Himself to comprehend our human experience.

Moreover, more profoundly, while He lowered Himself to share in our humanity, He elevated the human condition to the destiny of our true selves by transforming us to be like Him—both human and divine.

# 2nd Sunday in Ordinary Time

| | |
|---:|:---|
| First Reading | Isaiah 49:3, 5-6 |
| Responsorial Psalm | Psalm 40:2, 4, 7-8, 8-9, 10 |
| Second Reading | 1 Corinthians 1:1-3 |
| Gospel Acclamation | John 1:14a, 12a |
| Gospel Reading | John 1:29-34 |

# You Have Been Called to the Liturgy of the Holy Mass

After the Feast of the Baptism of the Lord, Years A and C in our Sunday liturgical calendar use readings from Isaiah for the first reading and from the first chapter of John for the Gospel. Year B features readings from First Samuel and the second chapter of John, which recounts the Theophnay of the Wedding Feast at Cana. Despite the different cycles, the message for the Second Sunday in Ordinary Time remains consistent: that God has called us to serve Him and fulfill His holy will in the world. This reminder is especially meaningful following Christmas and Epiphany, which celebrate Christ's arrival into the world and the Magi's visit from the East. It underscores that we, too, have a calling on our lives and that we won't fully realize our true selves or who we were created to be unless we respond rightly to that call.

In the First Reading from Isaiah 49:3, 5-6, we observe the first of three oracles by Deutero-Isaiah concerning the Suffering Servant. While it is not as explicitly identified in this oracle that the Suffering Servant refers to the future Messiah as it is in subsequent oracles,[8] certain clues within these verses suggest such an identification. In verse one, the oracle addresses the coastlands and distant peoples; consequently, the message appears to transcend Judea and Israel. Additionally, in verse one, the oracle shifts to the first person, stating, "Before birth the Lord called me, from my mother's womb he gave me my name," which bears a resemblance to Jeremiah 1:5, where it is said, "Before I formed you in the womb, I knew you …" Furthermore, in verse five, it is written, "For now the LORD has spoken who formed me as his servant from the womb, That Jacob may be brought back to him and Israel gathered to him." In verse two of this chapter, the phrase "He made my mouth like a sharp-edged sword," echoes the depiction in the book of Hebrews of

---

[8] Isaiah 50:4-11 and 52:13-53:12

the Word of God as "... living, and powerful, and sharper than any two-edged sword." Lastly, in verse six, the statement "I will make you a light to the nations, that my salvation may reach to the ends of the earth," emphasizes the universal scope of this oracle; it signifies that God's call extends to a worldwide community of His people. In the Gospel of John, Jesus refers to Himself as "the Light of the world," through whom salvation is attained.[9]

The Second Reading from First Corinthians 1:1-3 today underscores, with amplified emphasis, the significance of our calling. It states that "Paul, called to be an apostle of Christ Jesus by the will of God," was summoned, along with "Sosthenese our brother," and that those "of the Church of God that is in Corinth" have been "called to be holy." Furthermore, it affirms that "all those everywhere who call upon the name of our Lord Jesus Christ, their Lord and ours," are encompassed. I appreciate Paul's wordplay here, illustrating that those who have been called are those who invoke the name of Jesus Christ, establishing a vital connection between the elect and Christ Jesus, the Elect. For we possess nothing without Him, who brings forth creation from nothingness. Even our calling in life relies upon Him, who delivered the Word of eternal life. It is through Him and His grace that our calling is sustained, enriched, propelled, and strengthened. There exists no genuine calling in this existence outside of Him, who was sent to those whom He calls to attain true life in Him.

In today's Gospel Reading from John 1:29-34, John the Waymaker demonstrates a profound understanding of this necessity greater than anyone else. He recognizes that the calling on one's life cannot be fully understood or realized until one acknowledges that it is dependent upon the coming of Christ into the world. "John the Waymaker saw Jesus approaching and proclaimed, "Behold, the Lamb of God, who takes away the sin of the world. He is the one of whom I said, 'A man is coming after me who ranks ahead of me because he existed before me.'"

---

[9] John 8:12.

The Liturgical Season of Ordinary Time begins in a beautiful and meaningful way. We walk alongside the Magi, heading east toward Mount Calvary, where we will arrive on the Easter Vigil. Today's message is full of hope and clarity: you are warmly called to follow Christ Jesus wherever He leads. The Holy Mass is such an important part of our life as a Church — a gentle reminder every day, especially on Sundays and special days, of what it truly means to be obedient to that call.

Whether we are moving, sitting, kneeling, chanting, or singing, we are constantly engaged in prayer, confession, and listening — these are the ways liturgy shapes us, guiding us in the key skills of discipleship, friendship, and service. Plus, the liturgy patiently helps us trust in our walking and waiting — because we are not on this journey alone or on our own schedule. He who called us will lead us closer to perfection, guiding us through every suffering, trial, and blessing. The most important thing we can do is keep returning to the place He calls us, where we find nourishment with the food that sustains us on this beautiful, ongoing journey.

# 3rd Sunday in Ordinary Time

First Reading    Isaiah 8:23-9:3
Responsorial Psalm    Psalm 27:1, 4, 13-14
Second Reading    1 Corinthians 1:10-13, 17
Gospel Acclamation    Matthew 4:23
Gospel Reading    Matthew 4:12-23 or 4:12-17

# The Liturgy of the Catholic Mass: A Journey from Darkness to Light and Back Again

Concerning the readings for the Third Sunday in Ordinary Time of Year A, we shall proceed with another selection from the Prophet Isaiah and First Corinthians, and commence our examination of the Gospel of Matthew.

Today's First Reading from Isaiah 8:23 - 9:3 likely concludes the section of Isaiah's 'Immanuel/Virgin birth Oracle' in which a successor to King Ahaz was foretold. Here, the prophet narrates the events surrounding the arrival of Immanuel. The phrase, "land of Zebulun and the land of Naphtali," indicates that God permitted the kingdom of Assyria to subjugate the Israelites into despair, gloom, and darkness. This event is contrasted at the conclusion of today's reading with the account in the Book of Judges (Chapter 7), where God delivered Midian and the entire camp into His power, enabling Gideon and his men to achieve victory over their enemies.

The Gospel of Matthew consistently aims to identify Jesus of Nazareth as the fulfillment of the prophecies. It records in our Gospel reading today from Matthew 4:12-23 that "When Jesus heard that John had been arrested, he withdrew to Galilee. He left Nazareth and went to live in Capernaum by the sea, in the region of Zebulun and Naphtali, so that what was spoken through Isaiah the prophet might be fulfilled: 'Land of Zebulun and land of Naphtali, the way to the sea, beyond the Jordan, Galilee of the Gentiles, the people who sit in darkness have seen a great light, on those dwelling in a land overshadowed by death light has arisen.' From that time onward, Jesus began to preach, saying, 'Repent, for the kingdom of heaven has drawn near.'" The early readers of this text would have perceived the connection between these passages; that if Jesus is Immanuel, and we are presently experiencing the era of the new Midian where God delivered His people from "the yoke that burdened them, the pole on their shoulder, and the rod of their taskmaster," then this call to repentance and the imminent kingdom of heaven must be inherently linked to warfare. Additional context regarding this deliverance is provided later in Matthew, such as in Matthew 11:29-30, where Christ Jesus replaces the yoke of Assyria with His own, stating, "Take my yoke upon you and learn from me, for I am meek and humble of heart; and you will find rest for yourselves. For my yoke is easy, and my burden is light."

In our post-Christian and post-Truth world today, everyone wants to follow something or someone other than the Lord of God. They want us to follow the latest diet trends, fashion trends, news stories, the newest episode of a television or streaming series, or the latest comment from a billionaire or politician. Even in the Church, we are expected to follow the newest evangelization program or the trendiest celebrity priest. Indeed, the world always seeks what is new, rather than Him who came to renew the world.

This pattern was also the case in the Church in Corinth, as recounted in today's Second Reading from First Corinthians 1:10-13, 17. It was reported to the Apostle Paul that a spirit of factions and divisiveness had taken root in the Church. "For it has been reported to me about you, my brothers and sisters, by Chloe's people, that there are rivalries among you. I mean that each of you is saying, "I belong to Paul," or "I belong to Apollos," or "I belong to Cephas," or "I belong to Christ." The people seem to be dealing with personality cults, perhaps based on preferences in teaching methods, the newest evangelization program, or how Peter, Paul, and Apollos related to them personally.

Perhaps Peter connected more effectively with those who were traditionally Jewish, while Apollos preached more eloquently, and Paul related better to those who preferred straightforward Christian teaching. We do not know for sure what caused these factions, but what is clear is that they were the latest trends on people's minds. Saint Paul addresses this in the opening of his letter, asking, "Is Christ divided? Was Paul crucified for you? Or were you baptized in the name of Paul? For

Christ did not send me to baptize but to preach the gospel, and not with the wisdom of human eloquence, so that the cross of Christ might not be emptied of its meaning."

If the Gospel of Matthew, chapter & verse, were in everyone's hands at that time, the Apostle Paul might have pointed to 4:12-17 from our Gospel Reading today to teach us that we are only obligated to respond to the call of Christ Jesus because He is the only one who calls us to our eternal purpose and destination. We are called to follow only Christ Jesus because He is the only One who can lead us to our true home. The Apostle Paul might also have referenced the book of Ecclesiastes to remind us that responding to the call of anyone other than Christ, or following anyone other than Christ, is mere vanity.

The readings today beautifully highlight an essential truth about the Divine Symphony—something many Catholics might not always reflect on. It's the meaningful act of stepping into the sacred space —a conscious choice to leave behind the darkness of the world and embrace the light of Christ Jesus. Afterward, we are sent back into the world, now carrying that light—the Holy Eucharist living within us—so we can shine as the light of Christ for others. It's through true faith and the Church, established by God Himself, that we receive this incredible blessing and gift almost every day of the year. For this reason, Christ Jesus is the only man born of a woman worthy of our following.

# 4th Sunday in Ordinary Time

| | |
|---:|:---|
| First Reading | Zephaniah 2:3; 3:12-13 |
| Responsorial Psalm | Psalm 146:6-7, 8-9, 9-10 |
| Second Reading | 1 Corinthians 1:26-31 |
| Gospel Acclamation | Matthew 5:12a |
| Gospel Reading | Matthew 5:1-12a |

# The Liturgy Forms the Spirit of Humility in the Hearts of God's Remnant People

Today's First Reading for the Fourth Sunday in Ordinary Time – Year A is taken from the Book of Zephaniah, 2:3 and 3:12-13. An interesting aspect of the Book of Zephaniah is that it is among the shortest books in the Bible, and there is limited knowledge regarding the prophet himself, aside from his lineage and the fact that he prophesied during the reign of Josiah, the sixteenth king of Judah.

The prophetic message of Zephaniah follows approximately seventy-five years after the prophecies of Isaiah and Micah. Zephaniah's oracle is delivered with the immediacy of divine speech, beginning in verse one with, "The word of the Lord which came to Zephaniah," and concluding in chapter 3, verse 20, with the phrase, "says the Lord." As an Old Testament prophet, Zephaniah aligns with the prophetic tradition of his predecessors by announcing the imminent arrival of the 'day of the Lord',[10] thereby reminding us that divine purification involves destruction.

Furthermore, he challenges us with the truth that, despite God's promise to Abraham and Isaac that their descendants would be as numerous as the stars in the sky, only a remnant of God's people will ultimately remain.

According to Zephaniah's oracle in the present passage, this remnant may be diminutive because humility appears to be increasingly rare in contemporary society. The prophet Zephaniah exhorts, "Seek the LORD, all you humble of the earth, who have observed his law; seek justice, seek humility; perhaps you may be sheltered on the day of the LORD's anger." He further declares, "But I will leave as a remnant in your midst a people humble and lowly, who shall take refuge in the

---

[10] Zephaniah 1:7 and 1:14.

name of the LORD: the remnant of Israel," emphasizing divine mercy and hope amid judgment.

Whereas Zephaniah referred to the remnant of God's people as the humble ones, the Apostle Paul, in his first letter to the Church at Corinth in 1:26-31, regarded them as the foolish, the weak, and the lowly. He wrote, "Consider your own calling, brothers and sisters. Not many of you were wise by human standards, not many were powerful, not many were of noble birth. Rather, God chose the foolish of the world to shame the wise, and God chose the weak of the world to shame the strong, and God chose the lowly and despised of the world, those who count for nothing, to reduce to nothing those who are something."

Then, in today's Gospel Reading from Matthew 5:1-12a, Jesus, in His Sermon on the Mount, refers to this remnant of the humble, foolish, weak, and lowly as the blessed ones. This revelation is a consistent theme throughout the sacred Scriptures: that those believed to be cursed are actually blessed; that those considered poor are actually rich; and that those deemed forsaken have been chosen. Individuals such as Joseph, Ruth, Moses, the young David, the Virgin Mother Mary, her cousin Elizabeth, the Apostle Paul, and numerous others are examples of persons whom God has raised up.

When you reflect on the world we live in today, where very few people would choose mercy over killing their enemy, peace over chaos, righteousness over sinful pleasure, persecution over making friends with the world, and poverty of spirit over having everything, you must believe that we are living in the day of the Lord's return. Maybe we are, or perhaps we are not. It hardly matters for those who live lives of repentance and pursue Christ Jesus. Nor is it the concern of the liturgy of the Divine Symphony, which forms in us a humble heart.

Humble people are those who recognize their shortcomings and openly confess their sins, as we do during the Rite of Penance in the first movement of the Mass. They also listen attentively to the word of God so that it may shape their hearts to Him, as we do during the Liturgy of the Word. Furthermore, humble people make their lives a sacrifice for God, as we promise when we lift our hearts to Him during the Sursum Corda. They acknowledge that this life is not about themselves but about God, as we demonstrate through our actions during the Liturgy of the Holy Eucharist when we receive Him to unite our bodies with His. Finally, humble people serve God, as we do when we are sent out during the Concluding Rite.

Even in our ancient liturgical traditions, we are being formed to be humble people—to kneel, to pray, to confess, and to be in union with those in worship with us. Show me a humble heart, and you've shown me a person who would crawl on their knees for miles to receive the Holy Eucharist, not in their hand, but on their tongue. Assassins take and snatch, while those of humble hearts receive their gifts with patience and humility.

It is the tragedy of our current generation that we have a Church today that aims to cultivate pride rather than humility, teaching us to stand before our King rather than kneel. It teaches priests to make the liturgy about themselves rather than about God entirely. It is evident that pride, rather than humility, is the mission of the Church today, and this is precisely why we are increasingly seeing a lack of the blessings Jesus promised—those for the meek, the hungry, the merciful, the pure of heart, the peacemakers, and the persecuted.

Yet, the remnant of God's people has never been part of the religious establishment or their machinations. We have always been outside their networks. We have always faced persecution from them, and that is how we recognize who they are. They find it easy to persecute us because they know exactly who we are and how to locate us, thanks to Zephaniah's oracle. We are the ones who speak no lies and harbor no deceit on our tongues. They recognize us from the Apostle Paul, who wrote that we do not boast in ourselves but in the Lord, and from the promise of Christ Jesus that we are the saints—those who will be rewarded in Heaven.

# 5th Sunday in Ordinary Time

First Reading   Isaiah 58:7-10
Responsorial Psalm   Psalm 112:4-5, 6-7, 8-9
Second Reading   1 Corinthians 2:1-5
Gospel Acclamation   John 8:12
Gospel Reading   Matthew 5:13-16

# In the Liturgy, we Consume the Light of the World, thereby Becoming the Light of the World

There are just a few keywords that the Holy Spirit inspired man to write so that He might create a seamless quilt out the written word. In the absence of recognizing these keywords, the sacred Scriptures could appear at times to be just a patchwork of different fabrics of conflicting colors that was haphazardly put together in a poorly managed sweatshop. One such keyword that relates to today's readings for the Fifth Sunday in Ordinary of Year A is 'light', which, in the sacred texts, represents, symbolizes, and serves as a central and governing motif throughout the Catholic Bible.

For example, in Genesis 1:3 we read "Then God said, 'Let there be light,' and there was light." The light that God creates here is אוֹר (Heb. *'owr*), which means simply 'light'. This light of day one is different from the light He created on day five, which is מָאוֹר (Heb. *ma'owr*), which means illumination. There are three essential things to take note about *'owr* for our purposes here. The first is that God created *'owr* in the beginning for the well-being of creation. The second is that *'owr* was taken away from the world when the Lord struck down Egypt with the Ninth Plague. Exodus 10:21-23 says that there was dense darkness throughout the land of Egypt; "Men could not see one another, nor could they move from where they were, for three days, while all the Israelites had *'owr* where they dwelt." The final thing to note is that the Ninth Plague was the only plague that God set for a specific number of days. The three days that Egypt was without *'owr* correspond to the three days between Christ Jesus' crucifixion and resurrection.

For John, now transitioning to the Greek φῶς (*phōs*) for light, Jesus is the light that shines in the darkness, which the darkness cannot overcome.[11] Also, according to Christ Jesus' self-testimony about Himself, He is the light that entered the world.[12] Here, John uses the motif of light to play off Genesis 1:3-5, where God separates *owr* from the darkness, and to play off the *owr* that dwelt among the Israelites while the Egyptians were groping around in darkness for three days. This is why John writes, "He was in the world, and the world came to be through him, but the world did not know him. He came to what was his own, but his own people did not accept him."[13] Now, the true light, which was taken away from the world, because Pharaoh would not accept Moses' testimony and stop persecuting the Israelites, has returned to the world to "enlighten everyone."

While the twenty-fifth chapter of the Gospel of Matthew clarifies that today's First Reading from Deuteronomy, Isaiah 58:7-10, serves as a prophetic indication of the coming Messiah, it is imperative to recognize that, within the context, there existed a prior understanding within the Jewish tradition that one could attain a likeness to God through acts of service to others. This notion stands in stark contrast to Eve's attempt to be like God. The passage begins: "Thus says the LORD: Share your bread with the hungry, shelter the oppressed and the homeless; clothe the naked when you see them, and do not turn your back on your own. Then your light shall break forth like the dawn, and your wound shall quickly be healed; your vindication shall go before you, and the glory of the LORD shall be your rear guard. Then you shall call, and the LORD will answer, you shall cry for help, and he will say: Here I am!" Once again, if these acts are performed, then your light shall break forth like the dawn.

---

[11] Cf. John. 1:5
[12] Cf. John. 8:12
[13] v. 10-11

It is noteworthy that the Hebrew word for 'light' here is *owr*, the same as that used in the creation account. Consequently, an early prophetic understanding emerges that serving the marginalized draws us closer to God and grants us access to divine favor. Later in Matthew 25:31-46, Jesus expands upon the positive message of Deutero-Isaiah by stating that those who feed the hungry, shelter the oppressed and homeless, and clothe the naked are, in fact, nourishing, sheltering, and clothing Him. Such individuals will be blessed with eternal inheritance. Furthermore, Jesus emphasizes the seriousness of neglecting to serve those created in God's image, declaring, "And these will go off to eternal punishment ..."

In today's Gospel reading from Matthew 5:13-16, Jesus emphasizes this teaching from the prophets—that we possess the potential to resemble God; stating, "You are the light of the world." Naturally, the relationship between human nature and divine nature is further clarified in John's Gospel, where Christ Jesus refers to Himself as the Light of the World, because He embodies the glory of mankind, the transfigured individual, the light that entered the world as man. However, the primary message of the Sermon on the Mount is that we were created to be like God—to serve as His light in the world, enabling others to discover and perceive God, even amid the darkness. Therefore, it is crucial that "your light must shine before others, that they may see your good deeds and glorify your heavenly Father." To clarify, the manner in which the light is illuminated upon us is through our acts of service—good deeds—toward those who are wounded and lost.

Such a man as this was the Apostle Paul, who the light of God had shone upon so brightly that many came to follow Christ through his good deeds, and many came to persecute him for that very same reason. It is easy to get lost in the Apostle Paul's writings, especially those in today's Second Reading from First Corinthians 2:1-5. There goes Paul again with all those "I" statements and being all self-deprecating. Still, in saying things like, "I did not come with sublimity of words or of wisdom," and "I resolved to know nothing ... except Christ crucified," and

"I came to you in weakness and fear and much trembling," the Apostle is telling us the most important thing about the light of Christ that we need to know. That is, we cannot control the light; we do not shine upon the light; instead, the light shines upon us; the light doesn't need us; rather, we need the light, and we were created for the light, because we are children of the light.

Truly, the works of self-indulgence are numerous and easy to fall into, and there is no light in them. We even have those in our community who never stop turning the liturgy into something that falsely illuminates human effort and vanity. This legacy of dark liturgy is now facing God's wrath, but that was not its original purpose. How jealous would the prophets be of us Catholics, who have the chance actually to receive the Light of the World into our bodies, thus becoming the light of the world instantly upon worthy reception of Him? Then, we are dismissed by the Priest, who embodies the Light of the World – in *Persona Christi* - to go into the darkness and do good deeds in His name and power - to be the Light we have just received.

God, in His mercy, made it very simple for us to attain Heaven. Every day, around the world, a valid Catholic Mass brings Light into the world, except on Good Friday; yet, humanity continues to choose darkness. We may lament this truth, which is understandable, or we can commit ourselves even more diligently to serve in the darkness so that God's light shines more brightly through us. If the world darkens, it shouldn't be because they failed to see Christ's light shining through us. It should only be because they saw it and deliberately turned away.

# 6th Sunday in Ordinary Time

| | |
|---:|:---|
| First Reading | Sirach 15:15-20 |
| Responsorial Psalm | Psalm 119:1-2, 4-5, 17-18, 33-34 |
| Second Reading | 1 Corinthians 2:6-10 |
| Gospel Acclamation | cf. Matthew 11:25 |
| Gospel Reading | Matthew 5:17-37 |

# The Liturgy and the Law Share the Same Source and Purpose

The First Reading for the 6th Sunday in Ordinary Time, Year A, is from the Book of Sirach 15:15-20, although it should have commenced at verse 14, as it is in that verse that the author Ben Sira articulates his interpretation of Genesis, stating, "God in the beginning created human beings and made them subject to their own free choice."

Some scholars of the sacred text suggest that Ben Sira engages in an argument with other Old Testament passages, such as Exodus 11:10, which states that Pharaoh sinned because God had hardened his heart against Moses and the Israelites, and that David sinned against God by taking a census, as God had incited him against the Israelites. However, Ben Sira dismisses the notion that God has a role in causing humans to sin; rather, each individual possesses within their own capacity the free will and the ability to determine their own destiny.

According to Ben Sira, "If you choose you can keep the commandments, they will save you; if you trust in God, you too shall live; he has set before you fire and water to whichever you choose, stretch forth your hand. Before man are life and death, good and evil, whichever he chooses shall be given him." Here, Ben Sira aligns with other sacred Scriptures, such as Matthew 5:19 in today's Gospel Reading, where Jesus states, "... whoever obeys and teaches these commandments will be called greatest in the kingdom of heaven," which bears a striking resemblance to Ben Sira's assertion, "If you choose you can keep the commandments, they will save you."

Ben Sira also aligns with the Book of Wisdom 11:24, which states, "For you love all things that are and loathe nothing that you have made; for you would not fashion what you hate." Additionally, Ben Sira shares the perspective of James in 1:13, asserting, "No one experiencing temptation should say, 'I am being tempted by God'; for God is not subject to temptation to evil, and he himself tempts no one." Furthermore, Romans 1:18-32 attributes to the Apostle Paul the idea that God permits those who desire impurity, lusts, and degraded passions to persist in their free choice of the punishment they deserve.

God's gift of free will would be meaningless, even cruel, if He had not also provided us with guidance, standards, and the help we need to consistently make choices that honor Him rather than ourselves. Catholic Christianity teaches that God assists us on our journey by inscribing the natural law into our hearts—an innate awareness of good and evil. Beyond this, He has given us explicit commands, beginning with the original mandate to "be fruitful and multiply," followed by the enduring command to observe the Passover, first instituted on the night of the Exodus and later renewed by Christ Jesus in the New Covenant, freeing us from sin and death. The Ten Commandments, too, were engraved by God's own finger and delivered to Moses on Mount Horeb, then reaffirmed by Jesus in the Sermon on the Mount.

This profound reality is powerfully affirmed by the Catechism of the Catholic Church, which teaches that the moral law—written by God in the depths of every human heart—is far more than a set of external rules. It is, in fact, a profound invitation to communion with Him. As paragraph 1955 states:

> The natural law expresses the original moral sense which enables man to discern by reason the good and the evil, the truth and the lie: 'The natural law is written and engraved in the soul of each and every man, because it is human reason ordaining him to do good and forbidding him to sin... But this command of human reason would not have the force of law if it were not the voice and interpreter of a higher reason to which our spirit and our freedom must be submitted.'" [14]

Thus, the Catechism makes clear that God's law, inscribed within us, not only guides but also empowers us, ensuring that we are never left in confusion or error. Instead, we are equipped with both the light

---

[14] Cf. Romans 2:14-15; Gaudium et Spes 16.

of reason and divine revelation, so that our freedom is always directed toward goodness and, ultimately, the glory of God. In faithfully following this law, we become—as the Church teaches—"co-workers in the truth" and heirs to the blessings God promises to those who love Him.

Most importantly, we are never left to our own devices, for God Himself dwells within us through the Holy Spirit. As the Apostle Paul writes in 1 Corinthians 2:6-10, the Spirit "scrutinizes everything, even the depths of God." Because of this indwelling, we are able to speak God's mysterious, divine wisdom—ordained for our glory before time began—a wisdom the rulers of this world failed to grasp, or else they would not have crucified the Lord of glory. Thus, through God's law written in our hearts and the Spirit who guides us, we are continually led toward the fullness of life and the blessings God desires for us.

In today's Gospel Reading from Matthew 5:17-37, considerable attention is often directed to the "But I say to you" statements from Jesus' Sermon on the Mount. It is indeed powerful how God, who incarnated in the flesh, elevates His commandments given in the Old Covenant to a higher standard—an elevated expectation that we, as the People of God, are prepared for, and a higher standard that the Holy Spirit, now dwelling within us, is capable of helping us achieve. It is commendable and admirable that we serve a God who sets lofty expectations for us, rather than one who merely accepts the minimum effort. Such a God desires us to excel in Him.

Some within the Church today hold a misguided belief that the practice of the Catholic faith should be made simpler and more accommodating. They suggest fewer fasting days, more casual attire at Mass and among the religious, less emphasis on penitence, and support for individuals in their sins. Discussions tend to focus less on sin and obedience to commandments and more on inclusion and acceptance. This approach—centered on minimal effort and a relaxed attitude toward holiness—contradicts Christ Jesus's teachings, who said, "unless your righteousness surpasses that of the scribes and Pharisees, you will not enter the kingdom of heaven, and whoever breaks one of the least of these commandments and teaches others to do so will be called least in the kingdom of heaven."

So, what is the relationship between law and liturgy? Of course, we could point out how the liturgy helps us obey the law. That is true, but let us focus on the ultimate purpose of both the law and the liturgy. Since both originate from the Holy Trinity, they share the same goal: our good. This revelation is evident in the blessing linked to the Fourth Commandment, which promises that obeying our parents will lead to long life. Psalm 119 celebrates all the blessings of the law, and Jesus begins His Sermon on the Mount with the Beatitudes—'blessed are you' statements—and blessings for following all commandments. For example, our First Reading says, "If you choose, you can keep the commandments; they will save you." These verses demonstrates that God gave us the law so we would obey it, and through obedience, we receive blessings.

Likewise, the Church teaches in paragraph 1082 of the Catechism that "in the Church's liturgy, the divine blessing is fully revealed and communicated. The Father is acknowledged and adored as the source and goal of all blessings, created and salvation-related. In His Word—who became incarnate, died, and rose for us—He fills us with blessings. Through His Word, He pours into our hearts the Holy Spirit, the Gift that contains all gifts." Even James 1:17 affirms that the law, unlike the liturgy, remains unchangeable, stating, '... all good giving and every perfect gift is from above, coming down from the Father of lights, with whom there is no alteration or shadow caused by change."

There is one final point I would like to share with you. If the law and the liturgy are given to us to be our blessings, then it naturally follows that the further the world moves away from divine law and the more it drifts from living the liturgy, the less blessed it will be. Truly, we have more work to do in this world to reveal its beauty and blessedness through God, and that work always begins with us becoming a liturgical people.

# 7th Sunday in Ordinary Time

| | |
|---:|:---|
| First Reading | Leviticus 19:1-2, 17-18 |
| Responsorial Psalm | 103:1-2, 3-4, 8, 10, 12-13 |
| Second Reading | 1 Corinthians 3:16-23 |
| Gospel Acclamation | 1 John 2:5 |
| Gospel Reading | Matthew 5:38-48 |

# The Liturgical Teaching on the Imago Dei

The fundamental and unchangeable rationale for why humans should love themselves and one another is rooted in the belief that they were created in the image and likeness of God. The human species embodies the Imago Dei, and as articulated in today's readings for the Seventh Sunday in Ordinary Time, our identity as the Imago Dei is the basis for our call to holiness. Specifically, because God is holy and we are made in His image and likeness, we inherently possess the potential for holiness within our capacities.

The First Reading today, derived from Leviticus 19:1-2, 17-18, belongs to a genre of post-exilic social legislation conveyed by Moses to the community of God's People concerning the Decalogue, or a delineation of laws designed to prevent violations of the Ten Commandments. This genre of social laws is predominantly documented in Exodus 21 and 22, Leviticus 19, and Deuteronomy 24, with a primary focus on the manner of treatment towards one another. The most distinctive and arguably most profound aspect of the Leviticus 19 mandates is their introduction in verses 1 and 2, which provide the rationale for obedience by stating, "The LORD said to Moses, 'Speak to the whole Israelite community and tell them: Be holy, for I, the LORD, your God, am holy.'" It is remarkable that God communicates with us in this manner, indicating that, because of a likeness to Him within us, we possess the capacity to emulate His holiness.

Truly, everyone He has created possesses His breath of life within them. When the immortal soul departs from the body, the body ceases to have life. This command section in Leviticus begins with a reference to the Imago Dei from Genesis 2:26 and often ends 15 of 34 commands with either "I, the Lord, am your God" or "I am the Lord." This phrase also concludes section 19:37, encompassing these statutes and decrees. These notes act as a reminder from God as Father, saying, 'You can do this because you are like me'—'Yes, you are capable of holiness because I, your Father, am Holy, and I created you in my likeness,'

According to Christ Jesus, Leviticus 19:17-18, "You shall not hate any of your kindred in your heart. Reprove your neighbor openly so that you do not incur sin because of that person. Take no revenge and cherish no grudge against your own people. You shall love your neighbor as yourself. I am the LORD," together with Deuteronomy 6:5, ". . . and you shall love the Lord your God with all your heart, and with all your soul, and with all your might," combine to make the Greatest Commandment and sum of the whole of the Law and the Prophets.[15]

In today's Second Reading from First Corinthians 3:16-23, the Apostle discusses the Imago Dei, writing, "Do you not know that you are the temple of God, and that the Spirit of God dwells in you? If anyone destroys God's temple, God will destroy that person; for the temple of God, which you are, is holy." This revelation is a common theme throughout Paul's writings: because we belong to Christ rather than the world, we are different, and we must embrace that difference. In this case, "If any one among you considers himself wise in this age, let him become a fool, so as to become wise. For the wisdom of this world is foolishness in the eyes of God."

God has revealed Himself to us through His only begotten and beloved Son, Christ Jesus, and through His Church, the Holy Spirit is revealing more and more about God's plan for salvation. However, all of this remains what we call the Mystery of our Faith, because we do not even fully understand what we know; our knowledge of what has been revealed is so shallow that the word 'shallow' cannot adequately describe the complexity of our ignorance.

This lack of discernment is why those who see themselves as wise often work tirelessly to destroy the Imago Dei wherever they find it—from in the womb to on death row, and even within the Catholic Church

---

[15] Cf. Mt 22:34–40; Mk 12:28–34; Lk 10:25–28; cf. Mt 19:19; Rom 13:8–10; Gal 5:14

itself, the Body of Christ with Christ as its Head. Because they despise themselves, they also hate the Image of God whenever they encounter it. Their lack of humility, along with their refusal to admit and confess their sins, leads them to harm other sinners. This attitude extends to the Catholic Mass liturgy as well. Anyone who hates the Imago Dei also hates the liturgy, since it is the only place on earth where God's image is revealed to humans—created in His image—to help them become their true supernatural selves, holy as God himself is holy.

In today's Gospel reading, we continue to hear from Jesus' Sermon on the Mount. For this Seventh Sunday in Ordinary Time, the passage is taken from Matthew 5:38-48, where Jesus addresses his disciples: "You have heard that it was said, An eye for an eye and a tooth for a tooth. But I say to you, offer no resistance to one who is evil. When someone strikes you on your right cheek, turn the other one as well." It has been observed that some interpret this teaching of Jesus as a stern guidance against vengefulness. The concept of Lex Talionis is particularly unusual for those who believe in the Imago Dei. What kind of individual desires to live in a society where justice is meted out with retribution, "an eye for an eye and a tooth for a tooth"? Nonetheless, the principle of Lex Talionis has been cited throughout history as a justification for inflicting revenge upon others, who are created with the same divine breath. The Lex Talionis surpasses what could be termed childish conduct, since even children are not inherently vengeful; rather, such tendencies are learned behaviors.

Conversely, Lex Talionis is merely an expression of animalistic conduct. Inflicting harm upon others as retribution for their wrongdoing is akin to a natural instinct observed within the animal kingdom. It can be likened to marking one's territory through urination along its boundary. Jesus proceeds with His critique of Lex Talionis, stating, "You have heard that it was said, You shall love your neighbor and hate your enemy. But I say to you, love your enemies and pray for those who persecute you, that you may be children of your heavenly Father, for he makes his sun rise on the bad and the good, and causes rain to fall on the just and the

## Seventh Sunday in Ordinary Time

unjust. For if you love only those who love you, what reward do you have? Do not the tax collectors do the same? And if you only greet your brothers, what is unusual about that? Do not the pagans do the same? So be perfect, just as your heavenly Father is perfect. Additionally, Jesus' call to receive children in His name and to visit the imprisoned stands in stark contrast to our animalistic instincts to kill or harm them. These acts of humility and mercy reflect a divine calling that transcends our base instincts, emphasizing love and kindness rather than violence and retribution.

On the contrary, this is not a difficult teaching at all. Moreover, the Divine Symphony repeatedly demonstrates what our neighbor deserves, what justice they are owed, and what their rightful due is—namely, to be united with Him in whose image they were created. The greatest sign of justice we have is when the priest celebrant elevates the consecrated Imago Dei above the altar. Although the wise of the world reject it, the Imago Dei, under the guise of bread and wine, constantly reminds us that if dead bread and wine can be made holy, then so can we.

All that is asked of us is to truly obey God—an obedience rooted in love and a desire to mirror His goodness in our lives. Part of that obedience calls us to earnestly seek the good of our neighbor—the same good we earnestly desire for ourselves. Yet, as God's people, we have not always lived up to this calling. We have, at times, condoned vengeance in many forms—through unjust wars, discrimination, slavery, or the death penalty—failing to truly see and honor the Imago Dei within each person. Ironically, it has often been easier for us to recognize the divine image in consecrated bread and wine than in our fellow human beings. While worldly wisdom may fall short, the unwavering truth of the liturgy remains our anchor.

In a world hurtling toward destruction and death, the altar before us proclaims a different reality: eternal life offered through sacrifice. Let us desire this life—not just for ourselves, but fiercely and foolishly for the least among us. May this aspiration challenge us to be better, to stand unapologetically for justice, compassion, and love. Through such commitment, we will truly become a Eucharistic People—vessels of divine life in a broken world, shining light where darkness seeks to prevail.

# 8th Sunday in Ordinary Time

First Reading    Isaiah 49:14-15
Responsorial Psalm    Psalms 62:2-3, 6-7, 8-9
Second Reading    1 Corinthians 4:1-5
Gospel Acclamation    Hebrews 4:12
Gospel Reading    Matthew 6:24-34

# The Liturgy of the Catholic Mass Draws Us into the Divine Reliance

The readings for the eighth Sunday in Ordinary Time – Year A, from Isaiah 49:14-15, 1 Corinthians 4:1-5, and Matthew 6:24-34, convey a compelling message of divine providence, trust, and the abundance of grace bestowed upon us. Today, the Holy Spirit prompts us to consider, 'What do you have to worry about based on what you have been given?' This question functions as a foundational point and perspective through which we can examine or reevaluate the richness of the sacraments, the completeness of truth within His Church, and the divine presence within us, which reassures us that our spiritual journey towards Him remains secure.

The First Reading from Isaiah 49:14-15 today serves as a vital reminder of God's enduring love and dedication to His people. The passage begins with Zion (the people of Israel) lamenting, "The Lord has forsaken me; my Lord has forgotten me." In response, God employs the gentle analogy of a mother's love for her child to exemplify His devotion: "Can a woman forget her nursing child, or show no compassion for the child of her womb? Even these may forget, yet I will not forget you."

This passage reassures us that God's love is more enduring and dependable than even the strongest human bonds. In light of the Holy Spirit's question today, it emphasizes that we have nothing to worry about because we are surrounded by God's infinite love and faithfulness. We are not left with just scraps; instead, we have been given the fullness of His love, which surpasses all human understanding. This divine love is a cornerstone of our faith, providing a foundation on which we can build our lives free from fear or anxiety.

In the second reading, Paul addresses the Church in Corinth in 1 Corinthians 4:1-5, urging them to see themselves as "servants of Christ and stewards of God's mysteries." He warns against rushing to judgments, reminding them that the ultimate judgment belongs to the Lord.

This passage calls us to humility and trust, recognizing that our worth and success are measured not by worldly standards but by our faithfulness to God's calling. Paul's message aligns seamlessly with the question we have been asked.

As stewards of God's mysteries, we have been entrusted with the full truth and the responsibility to pass down the faith and traditions through the Sacraments. If anyone considers this divine stewardship a burden, the Apostle reminds us that God has given us this charge as a privilege, one that should ease our worries rather than increase them. The sacraments, especially the Holy Eucharist, are tangible signs of God's grace, nourishing our spiritual journey and strengthening us against life's trials. In the sacraments, we receive not just a taste but the fullness of God's presence, ensuring that we lack nothing on our path to eternal life.

The Gospel reading from Matthew 6:24-34 presents a compelling and solemn exhortation from Christ Jesus directed to His disciples, emphasizing the importance of not being preoccupied with material concerns. He states, "No one can serve two masters," underscoring that "for a slave will either hate the one and love the other, or be devoted to the one and despise the other. You cannot serve God and wealth." Jesus advocates that His disciples should "seek first the kingdom of God and His righteousness," offering reassurance that "all these things will be given to you as well."

This teaching answers our question by contrasting the anxiety caused by material concerns with the peace found in trusting God's provision. Jesus' words remind us that our main focus should be on our relationship with God and His kingdom. When we prioritize this divine connection, everything else aligns accordingly. We receive more than we can imagine through God's kingdom and His righteousness. The sacraments act as channels for us to access grace and strength, enabling us to fulfill this divine calling.

Today's readings passionately call us to embrace a worry-free life, firmly rooted in God's abundant grace. The prophet Isaiah boldly reassures us of God's unwavering love, inspiring confidence and hope. The Apostle reminds us of our sacred responsibility as stewards of His mysteries, challenging us to live purposefully and faithfully. Christ our Lord urgently beckons us to seek His kingdom above all else, promising that in doing so, we will find true fulfillment and peace. Let us respond wholeheartedly to this divine invitation.

In the sacred liturgy of the Catholic Mass and the Sacraments, we encounter the divine fullness of God's truth and presence—a profound invitation to experience His boundless love. Baptism welcomes us into the divine family, affirming our place in His eternal embrace. Confirmation empowers us with the Holy Spirit, igniting our courage to live boldly in faith. The Eucharist sustains us with the Body and Blood of Christ, nourishing our souls for the journey ahead. Reconciliation restores our broken relationships with God, our neighbor (the Church), and ourselves, bringing healing and renewal. Anointing of the Sick provides comfort and grace in times of illness. Holy Orders entrusts ministers to serve the Church's mission with humility and love. Matrimony unites couples in a sacred bond, reflecting Christ's love for His Church. Each Sacrament reveals a greater gift—God's infinite grace that removes worry, awakens trust, and invites us into a deeper reliance on Him.

This divine abundance surpasses worldly riches, which often lead us away from true dependence on God and foster self-centeredness. The readings for the Eighth Sunday in Ordinary Time remind us to cherish and respond to God's generous gifts. Through His eternal love, divine stewardship, and kingdom, we possess all we need for our ultimate journey home. Let us live with confident faith, trusting fully in the God who provides abundantly and unceasingly. Embrace this divine gift, and step forward boldly into the life He offers.

# 9th Sunday in Ordinary Time

First Reading   Deuteronomy 11:18, 26-28, 32
Responsorial Psalm   Psalms 31:2-3, 3-4, 17, 25
Second Reading   Romans 3:21-25, 28
Gospel Acclamation   John 15:5
Gospel Reading   Matthew 7:21-27

# The Phylactery is Fulfilled in Liturgy and the Sacraments of the Church

In Matthew 23:5, Jesus admonishes the Pharisees for their ostentatious displays, stating, "All their works are performed to be seen. They widen their phylacteries and lengthen their tassels." Phylacteries, also known as 'tefillin', are small black leather boxes containing sacred scriptures. These are bound to the forehead and wrists, deeply rooted in the First Reading from Deuteronomy 11:18, 26-28, 32, where Moses exhorts, "You shall put these words of mine in your heart and soul, and you shall bind them as a sign on your hand, and fix them as an emblem on your forehead."

Phylacteries, crafted from the hide of a kosher animal, typically a cow, hold verses from the Torah, including the Shema prayer from Deuteronomy 6:4-9 and 11:13-21, as well as Exodus 13:1-10 and 13:11-16. These sacred items, while not meant for consumption, symbolize the profound connection between the divine word and the hearts of the faithful.

This Mosaic law is ultimately realized in Christ Jesus, the living Word of God. As stated in today's Second Reading from Romans 3:21-25, 28, "manifested apart from the law, though testified to by the law and the prophets," Christ exceeds the external observance of traditions such as phylacteries. Instead, his presence is regarded as transformative for individuals. In this context, Christ is described as the Word that nourishes, symbolized by the Holy Eucharist, fulfilling the divine promise in a significant and personal way.

Through His presence, we are genuinely transformed from within, surpassing any external symbol or ornament. Christ Jesus is not confined to a mere forehead or wrist, but resides deeply in our hearts and souls, continuously enriching our lives with His grace. This divine indwelling serves as a powerful reminder of the sacredness and beauty of our faith.

While we might criticize the performative aspect that the phylactery became, it still served as an essential lesson from Moses, urging the Israelites to keep a visible reminder of the consequences of sin and the rewards of virtue. Today, many of us wear crucifixes, Miraculous Medals, and scapulars to serve as similar reminders. These external symbols, rich with our tradition, are more than mere accessories; they are signs of our faith and devotion, guiding us toward a life of grace and holiness.

Likewise, the Sacraments of the Church serve as visible signs of Christ's active presence among His people. More importantly, the grace conveyed through the Sacraments works within us and through us, transforming us into the Imago Dei—God's image—in the world. This transformation enables us to share Christ Jesus more fully with others, allowing His love to flourish within all of us.

Whereas Moses commanded the Israelites, "I set before you this day a blessing and a curse: a blessing for obeying the commandments of the Lord, your God, which I enjoin on you today; a curse if you do not obey," Jesus echoes this in a positive affirmation in today's Gospel Reading from Matthew 7:21-27, stating, "Everyone who listens to these words of mine and acts upon them will be like a wise man who built his house on rock. The rain fell, the floods came, and the winds blew and buffeted the house. But it did not collapse; it was firmly established on rock. Conversely, everyone who listens to these words of mine but does not act upon them will be like a fool who built his house on sand. The rain fell, the floods came, and the winds blew and buffeted the house. And it collapsed and was completely ruined." Indeed, as Psalm 128 proclaims, the goodness of God showers upon those who fulfill His will: "Blessed are all who fear the LORD, and who walk in his ways. What your hands provide, you will enjoy; you will be blessed and prosper."

Together, today's readings call us to a deep contemplation: the divine fulfillment expressed through Moses' teachings, exemplified flawlessly in Christ Jesus, is not merely a matter of tradition but a transformative force that demands our active response. While adornments and symbols of faith can inspire and uplift, their true power lies in the sincerity with which we embody their deeper meanings—meanings that beckon us to live out our faith with conviction and purpose. Christ Jesus has poured out His very Self into us through the Holy Eucharist, cultivating within our hearts qualities that, when genuinely nurtured, can flourish to bring healing, hope, and salvation to a broken world.

This is not a call for passive observance; it's an urgent summons to embrace Christ's words fully—not simply as divine obligations, but as a radical, life-changing testimony of our unwavering commitment. When we accept this challenge, we become living witnesses to His divine work, following the trail worn down by the saints who walked I before us—a trail of faith that transforms lives and fulfills the principal purpose of the liturgy—to boldly proclaim His presence through our actions, our words, and our very being.

# 10ᵗʰ Sunday in Ordinary Time

First Reading    Hosea 6:3-6
Responsorial Psalm    Psalms 50:1, 8, 12-13, 14-15
Second Reading    Romans 4:18-25
Gospel Acclamation    Luke 4:18
Gospel Reading    Matthew 9:9-13

# Liturgy and the Ite, Missa Est is the Activity of Knowing and Loving God

The most striking pattern inherent in human relationships is our frequent failure to love as we should. It is not a matter of lacking genuine interest or the capacity to love another person, but rather, the deficiency is found in our base desire. Deficient desire in love, in this context, refers to a superficial curiosity or transient attention towards someone or something, which does not necessarily encompass a transcendent connection.

Interest refers primarily to engagement or intrigue, rather than comprehensive understanding. Conversely, desire signifies a profound longing or aspiration for an objective. Desire represents an active and living commitment—typically motivated by emotional or personal significance—to go beyond ordinary experiences and pursue exceptional outcomes.

When it comes to our relationship with God, many of us resemble the Israelites described in Hosea's prophecy from today's First Reading, Hosea 6:3-6. We express an interest in returning to God, acknowledging that our sins have created a debt greater than we can ever repay, and recognizing that our judgment day is approaching. We cry out in trust to the God who loves us unconditionally, despite our shortcomings, saying, "Let us know, let us strive to know the Lord; as certain as the dawn is His coming. He will come to us like the rain, like spring rain that waters the earth."

The imbalance in our relationship with God should be unsettling to us: while God is always honest with us, He must search deeply within our hearts to uncover the truth about why we are so duplicitous at times. In this moment, God exposes the stark reality of our flawed nature, saying, "Your loyalty is like a morning mist, like the dew that disappears early." Indeed, our wounded nature inclines us to waver between desires and superficial interests. Even when we strive to love

God, we are hampered by our limited understanding of Him. We may offer sacrifices and burnt offerings, yet what He truly seeks is our unwavering loyalty and genuine love—steadfast and unwavering, not just ritualistic compliance.

If only we could be like Abraham, who, in today's Second Reading from Romans 4:18-25, the Apostle Paul recounts that his faith was so strong and enduring, and his loyalty to God was so committed that he hoped against hope. Even in the face of human experience, he still believed in God's promise that he would become "the father of many nations," even in his and his wife Sarah's old age.

In today's Gospel Reading from Matthew 9:9-13, it is observed that Matthew, the tax collector, is engaged in his duties at his customs post, meticulously counting coins and maintaining records. The vibrant activity of the marketplace surrounds him, with the sounds of merchants and townsfolk engaged in lively conversation. Matthew is familiar with the disapproving glances and whispered insults from those who perceive him as a collaborator with the Roman authorities. Nevertheless, amidst this routine, his heart secretly yearns for something greater—something supernatural, surpassing mere mundane labor and transactional interactions.

As he sat there, a sudden hush spread through the crowd, and Matthew looked up to see what was causing the disturbance. It was Jesus of Nazareth, a man whose teachings and miracles had begun to stir waves of interest, curiosity, and hope among the people. Jesus walked with an air of authority and compassion, His presence commanding attention.

Upon approaching Matthew, Jesus fixed his gaze upon him, a look that appeared to penetrate the layers of guilt, regret, and superficiality obscuring Matthew's spirit. At that moment, Matthew experienced an overwhelming sense of being truly known and understood, as though Jesus perceived not merely his occupation but his real self—who he truly is. Subsequently, with a voice that conveyed both authority and invitation, Jesus proclaimed, "Follow me."

The simplicity of that call invites us to contemplation and a renewed sense of conversion. In those two words, Matthew sensed a summons to leave behind his old life and step into a new journey—one rooted in love, service, and faith. It calls us to loyalty and unwavering commitment. It also reminds us of Abraham's steadfast faith—trusting in God's promises even when the path was uncertain. This call challenges us to listen more attentively, to respond with openness, and to embrace the transformative power of God's love.

Without hesitation, Matthew stood up from his seat, leaving behind his booth and the life he was familiar with. The coins and ledgers that once captivated him now appeared insignificant. He followed Jesus, venturing into the unknown with a heart full of renewed purpose.

Later, while dining at Matthew's house, Jesus ate with tax collectors and sinners, which scandalized the Pharisees. They asked, "Why does your teacher eat with tax collectors and sinners?" Jesus responded, "Those who are well do not need a physician, but the sick do." Then Jesus references Hosea's prophecy, saying, "Go and learn the meaning of the words, 'I desire mercy, not sacrifice.' I did not come to call the righteous, but sinners."

Matthew's response to Jesus' call exemplifies the loyalty that God seeks—loyalty grounded in mercy, love, and a willing heart. Similar to how Abraham's faith was regarded as righteousness, Matthew's readiness to follow illustrates the profound transformation that takes place when an individual sincerely responds to God's calling. In that pivotal moment, Matthew's life served as a testament to the transformative power of divine love and the persistent call to lead a life characterized by faith and dedication.

Today's readings invite us to become not passive observers but bold participants in God's transforming love, much like Abraham who hoped against hope, and Matthew who left everything behind at Jesus' call. In the Mass, we are summoned to repentance, intimacy, and conversion: we lay down our failures in the Penitential Rite and are confronted by

Hosea's prophetic challenge, Abraham's radical trust, and Jesus' merciful invitation. The Holy Eucharist draws us into Christ's heart, and the dismissal—*"Ite, Missa Est"*—commissions us to carry His mercy and faith to the world, living with such unwavering love and conviction that our loyalty to God is unmistakable, our faith contagious, and our lives a radiant testimony that needs no explanation.

# 11th Sunday in Ordinary Time

First Reading   Exodus 19:2-6a
Responsorial Psalm   Psalm 100:1-2, 3, 5
Second Reading   Romans 5:6-11
Gospel Acclamation   Mark 1:15
Gospel Reading   Matthew 9:36-10:8

## How the Liturgy Communicates God's Mercy of Remembrance and Mission

Leading up to the awe-inspiring Great Theophany, the inaugural encounter between Moses and the People of Israel at Mount Sinai is vividly depicted in today's First Reading at Mass for the 11$^{th}$ Sunday in Ordinary Time, derived from Exodus 19:2-6. It narrates that this historic event transpired in the third month following their miraculous departure from Egypt. On the initial day of their arrival in the wilderness of Sinai, after passing through Rephidim, they encamped before the sacred mountain. It was there that God, in His infinite mercy and sovereignty, reminded the Israelites of His mighty deeds—how He delivered them from the Egyptians, carried them on eagle's wings, and brought them close to Himself. God's voice resonated with a divine summons: "You have seen for yourselves how I treated the Egyptians and how I bore you up on eagle wings; I brought you here to myself. If you listen to my voice and keep my covenant, you will be my treasured possession, more dear to me than all other peoples—though the whole earth is mine. You will be a kingdom of priests, a holy nation."

God's tendency to remind us of all He has accomplished and how far we have come is not for His benefit but ours. He offers us this mercy to help us stay focused and humble, especially when life's challenges tempt us to forget both our progress and the One who has brought us here. More importantly, forgetting our belonging to God can cause us to lose trust in Him as we journey toward becoming who He has designed us to be. This gracious act of remembrance is beautifully woven into the observance of the Passover meal of the Old Covenant, where the Israelites recall their deliverance from Egypt, and into the Passover meal of the New Covenant, where believers attend to the memorial feast of their salvation from sin and death through the sacrifice of the Lamb of God.

Also, in both instances, reminder is connected to mission. God says, 'I have saved you, now go do what I saved you for.' In the Divine Symphony, this mercy of reminder is conveyed to us through the readings of the sacred Scriptures during the Liturgy of the Word and the call to "Do this in memory of me," during the Liturgy of the Holy Eucharist. These are then linked to the mercy of mission communicated to us at the dismissal of the Concluding Rite, where it says, "*Ite, Missa est,*" meaning go, you are dismissed, or another of the four beautiful variations found in the Ordinary Form. With this temporary mission-farewell, we are called to carry God's mercy into the world, to become living witnesses of grace and compassion in our daily lives. In this divine pattern, we are lovingly reminded of who we are and inspired to fulfill the mission entrusted to us: to serve, to love, and to proclaim the Kingdom of God to all we meet.

This act of mercy, encompassing both reminder and mission, is also evident in today's Second Reading from Romans 5:6-11. Here, the Apostle Paul offers a succinct exposition of Catholic doctrine concerning justification by faith in Christ and the call to embody this faith through missionary service rooted in His love. In reminding us of our former state and the magnitude of God's grace, the Apostle states, "For Christ, while we were still helpless, yet died at the appointed time for the ungodly. Indeed, only with difficulty does one die for a just person, though perhaps for a good person, one might even find the courage to die. But God demonstrates His love for us in that, while we were still sinners, Christ died for us."

For the Apostle Paul, transforming memory into mission entails leading a life that proclaims faith, hope, and love in Christ Jesus. That is, since we now possess a faith that justifies us, we consequently have a hope in which we boast "of the glory of God," and because we now hold a hope that "does not disappoint," we have also received the love of God "poured into our hearts through the Holy Spirit."

This love that has been poured into us is not just any love. For, in verse eight, the Apostle writes that this is the same love that God proved "His love for us in that while we were still sinners Christ died for us." Therefore, if by this love God proved His love for us through the sacrifice of Christ, now dwelling within us, how closely are our missions connected to that same love?

The Gospel reading for today, from Matthew 9:36 to 10:8, should have been preceded by verse 9:35, which begins the narrative concerning the reminder that Christ Jesus imparted to the people. It states, "Jesus went around to all the towns and villages, teaching in their synagogues, proclaiming the gospel of the kingdom, and curing every disease and illness. At the sight of the crowds, his heart was moved with pity for them because they were troubled and abandoned, like sheep without a shepherd."

This passage invites us to reflect on the journey of Christ Jesus and those He encounters. Like the Israelites in the wilderness, we may find ourselves seeking divine encounter and guidance. Christ, the new Great Theophany, reveals Himself not in thunder or smoke but through His presence within us and among us. His call to the twelve apostles to proclaim the kingdom, heal the sick, and serve without cost reminds us of our own mission to embody compassion and divine love. May this reflection inspire us to seek Christ in our midst and embrace our calling to serve with humility and faith.

In other words, He sent out His apostles to find the lost, sick, and troubled, and to heal them so they can start their journey and mission into the Kingdom of God. The Apostles of Christ Jesus and the ordained priests who participate in their ministry still carry out that same mission today. Through His love, Christ Jesus has given us His Church and His Sacraments to remind us daily of His mercy and to continue His mission.

Another word for the mercy of reminder is 'tradition,' for it is tradition that continually forges and unites us, anchoring our souls in the grandeur of God's mighty deeds for His People. Through the Sacraments, this sacred tradition blossoms into a living, grace-filled chorus that intimately binds us not only to God but to the entire community of believers across eternity and space. Though each of us feels God's love in a personal way, His divine nature assures us that through Baptism, Confirmation, and the Holy Eucharist—these divine invitations—we are forever intertwined with Him. The divine reminder pounds on the human soul with clarity: God's love for us knows no end, and our sacred duty is to pursue holiness with uncompromised hearts and steadfast resolve.

As we depart from this liturgy, may we refuse to let the mercy and mission entrusted to us remain mere words or fleeting memories. Let us allow the voice of God—echoing through Scripture, tradition, and sacrament—to stir us from complacency and propel us into action. Each of us is summoned, not just to recall with gratitude the wonders God has worked, but to become living witnesses who carry His love and compassion to the wounded, poor, forgotten, and searching world around us. The challenge before us is urgent: Will we dare to let Christ's boundless love define our lives, embolden our witness, and transform our communities? Empowered by the Spirit, let us embrace this sacred call with courage and conviction, determined to bear the light of God's Kingdom wherever we go.

# 12th Sunday in Ordinary Time

| | |
|---:|:---|
| First Reading | Jeremiah 20:10-13 |
| Responsorial Psalm | Psalms 69:8-10, 14, 17, 33-35 |
| Second Reading | Romans 5:12-15 |
| Gospel Acclamation | John 15:26B, 27A |
| Gospel Reading | Matthew 10:26-33 |

# In the Liturgy of the Catholic Mass, Divine Justice and Peace Kiss

The world often struggles to reconcile justice and mercy, seeing them as opposite principles. Justice is often viewed as harsh, strict, and punitive, with decisions that impose severe consequences, like the death penalty or abandoning someone during their darkest moments. Conversely, mercy is sometimes misunderstood as weakness, a brief act of kindness that is perceived as weakening one's strength and resolve.

However, these worldly views overlook the deeper truth about these virtues. In the liturgy of the Catholic Mass, justice is seen not as a cold decree, but as a flame that purifies and restores. Mercy, far from being fragile, shines as God's limitless generosity, lifting the fallen and welcoming the repentant. Together, justice and mercy reveal a divine harmony that calls us into the fullness of grace—a union the world struggles to fathom but finds fully expressed in God's steadfast care for humanity.

Chapter 20 of Jeremiah constitutes a segment of a comprehensive narrative in which the prophet elucidates the significant personal sacrifice associated with delivering God's frequently unwelcome messages during a particularly turbulent period in Judah's history. Verse seven of this chapter is among the most revered passages within sacred Scripture. In this verse, Jeremiah laments the internal turmoil and crisis he endures regarding his divine calling: "You seduced me, LORD, and I allowed myself to be seduced; you were too powerful for me, and you prevailed. All day long, I am an object of derision; everyone mocks me. . . I resolve not to mention Him, nor to speak in His name any longer. However, it is as if fire burns within my heart, confined within my bones; I grow weary of restraining myself, and I cannot!"

This lamentation subsequently directs our attention to the First Reading from Jeremiah 20:10-13 for the 12th Sunday in Ordinary Time

— Year A. In this passage, the prophet transitions from a profound and emotional lament to an even more fervent and emotional act of imprecation (Latin for 'to invoke evil'), stating, "LORD of hosts, you test the just, you see mind and heart, Let me see the vengeance you take on them, for to you I have entrusted my cause."

The Psalms are renowned for containing verses of imprecation, as exemplified in 35:1: "Oppose, O LORD, those who oppose me; war upon those who make war upon me." Similarly, Psalm 109:6-7 states: "Appoint an evil one over him, an accuser to stand at his right hand, that he may be judged and found guilty, so that his plea may be in vain." This verse reflects the conventional understanding of divine justice. The concept that God's justice and wrath are distinct represents an enduring perspective on how divine retribution operates within the moral framework of the world.

The Old Testament clearly illustrates instances of God's justice, including the expulsion of Adam and Eve from the Garden of Eden, the destruction of Sodom and Gomorrah by fire, and the earth swallowing Korah, Dathan, Abiram, and the 250 others. God's justice exemplifies His wrath.

Nonetheless, in the absence of contraction, God's justice also embodies His mercy, and His perfect expression of justice and mercy was bestowed upon us through the name of His beloved begotten Son, Christ Jesus. As articulated in the Second Reading from Romans 5:12-15, the Apostle states, "But the gift is not like the transgression. For if by that one person's transgression the many died, how much more did the grace of God and the gracious gift of the one person, Jesus Christ, overflow for the many." A few verses later, he writes more succinctly, saying, "Where sin increased, grace overflowed all the more."

The Divine Symphony exemplifies, par excellence, the fact that sin can neither prevail against nor approach the magnitude of God's mercy and grace. It is evident that sin is increasing and proliferating throughout the world. Nevertheless, the words of the prophet Malachi have been fulfilled in the Catholic Mass, where it is stated, "From the rising of the sun to its setting, my name is great among the nations; incense and offerings are made to my name everywhere, and a pure offering." [16]

In today's Gospel reading from Matthew 10:26-33, Jesus reveals the inseparability of divine justice and mercy. First, He reassures the disciples not to fear, explaining that God's justice will expose all hidden things and hold the world accountable. However, entwined like a polyphony, in God's justice, His magnanimous mercy is a mere melody of His intimate care for creation: "Even all the hairs of your head are counted… You are worth more than many sparrows." These words remind us that God's justice is not cold or detached but is knit together in His tender love for each person.

Secondly, the heart of the passage is centered on Jesus's proclamation: "Everyone who acknowledges me before others I will acknowledge before my heavenly Father. But whoever denies me before others, I will deny before my heavenly Father." Once again, God's utmost compassion is demonstrated through the gift of His Son, granting salvation to all. Nonetheless, this compassion necessitates a response. Those who accept Christ receive the complete measure of His grace, whereas those who reject Him encounter divine justice. This teaching aligns with Paul's words in Romans 5:12-15, where sin and grace are contrasted: "Where sin increased, grace overflowed all the more."

Finally, Jesus's words compel us to proclaim Him boldly, even in the face of trials, mirroring the unwavering faith of the prophet Jeremiah, who entrusted his cause to God despite persecution. Today's Gospel offers a powerful reflection on the divine harmony of justice and mercy, inspiring hope and grace for those who accept Christ, while also highlighting the justice owed to those who reject Him.

In the sacred liturgy of the Catholic Mass, we are invited to encounter the living reality of God's justice woven inseparably with His mercy. As the celebration begins with the Penitential Rite, we humbly recog-

---

[16] Malachi 1:11.

nize our faults and ask for forgiveness, opening our hearts to God's healing grace. In the Eucharistic sacrifice, Christ's mercy is revealed most vividly; through the consecrated bread and wine, His Body and Blood become present to us, a gift of love beyond measure. Each part of the liturgy—whether in the Readings and Homily that call us to honest self-examination, or the prayers and intercessions that surround us with comfort and hope—asks us to reflect deeply on our relationship with God.

At the altar, heaven and earth meet, and we are drawn into a divine symphony where justice and mercy are not distant abstractions, but living truths that invite transformation. Are we embracing the fullness of God's compassion and truth, or are we hesitating to live out justice and mercy in our daily lives? The Mass calls us to respond with courage and love, singing with our hearts and actions these virtues as disciples committed to God's eternal promise.

Altogether, today's readings encourage us to live boldly and fearlessly as a liturgical people, flourishing and trusting in God's boundless mercy and honoring His flawless justice.

# 13th Sunday in Ordinary Time

| | |
|---:|:---|
| First Reading | 2 Kings 4:8-11, 14-16a |
| Responsorial Psalm | Psalm 89:2-3, 16-17, 18-19 |
| Second Reading | Romans 6:3-4, 8-11 |
| Gospel Acclamation | 1 Peter 2:19 |
| Gospel Reading | Matthew 10:37-42 |

# The Fulfillment of the Liturgies of Shunem and Zarephath

In today's First Reading for the Thirteenth Sunday in Ordinary Time from 2 Kings 4:8-11, 14-16, we hear about a woman living in the quiet village of Shunem, whose home was known for its warmth and hospitality. The text doesn't give her name but describes her as "a woman of influence." One day, the prophet Elisha passed through town, and she persuaded him to dine with her family. This circumstance started a routine—whenever he traveled that way, he stopped at her home to eat. Sensing the holiness of this man of God, she said to her husband, "Let us build a small room on the roof and furnish it with a bed, table, chair, and lamp, so that when he comes to us, he can stay there." Her hospitality was more than courtesy; it was an invitation for the presence of God to dwell in her home.

Elisha, moved by her kindness, asked how he could help her. Although she hadn't shared her situation with the prophet, his servant noticed that she had no children and that her husband was old. Elisha called her to the doorway and prophesied: "This time next year, you will be holding a baby son." Yes, in making space for the prophet, she had made room for God, and He, who fills every generous corner with grace, blessed her with the very gift her heart had longed for.

Across the sweep of Israel's story, two women stand as mirrors of divine generosity. In Shunem, a lady of means carved out a humble chamber on her roof for the prophet Elisha—its stone walls warmed by the sun, its simple bed and lamp a testament to sacrificial welcome. In distant Zarephath,[17] a destitute widow pressed out her last handful of meal for Elijah, risking all on God's promise—and found her jar of flour and jug of oil overflowing throughout the famine. Though one home

---

[17] 1 Kings 17:8-16.

was richly furnished and the other barely held scraps, both women unlocked the same truth: by making room for God's messenger, they opened their lives to His abundant blessing.

Therefore, when Jesus cites these ancient examples in today's Gospel Reading from Matthew 10:37-42, "Whoever receives a prophet because he is a prophet will receive a prophet's reward," He harvests this teaching from living tradition and further extends the promise to the righteous and even to the smallest act of kindness toward "these little ones," showing that the grace poured out in Shunem and Zarephath remains unchanged. This is not a new morality but the everlasting light of covenantal love. In other words, wherever Christ is welcomed, whether in hidden rooms or a humble kitchen, He transforms hospitality into a channel of mercy, and He delights in rewarding every open heart.

In the subsequent Second Reading from Romans 6:3–4, 8–11, the Apostle Paul employs the well-known blessing-formula "whoever does x will receive y" to illustrate that through baptism, we have died with Christ and now partake in His resurrected life. By being buried into His death, we acknowledge that we have made space for God within our hearts, and in return, God welcomes our elevating human frailty into His own risen Body. In this manner, we are united in an intimacy surpassing that of the Shunammite woman who merely provided a simple room for Elisha, for Christ Himself has assured us: "In my Father's house there are many dwelling places. If there were not, would I have told you that I go to prepare a place for you?"

Reading this sacred narrative through the liturgical sense reveals the Catholic Mass as the most beautiful "room" God has prepared for His people. Here, heaven descends to earth, and we are invited to share the peace and joy of His presence. In this Divine Symphony, God—who once entered the humble homes of Elijah and Elisha—now welcomes us into the Father's household, making Himself both our companion and our nourishment. Each Mass is not merely a gathering; it is Christ Himself inviting us to His table, where we receive His Word, partake in His Body and Blood, and unite our lives to His perfect offering.

As we make space for Him in our hearts, He draws us deeper into His own dwelling. The ancient promise rings true: "Whoever receives a prophet because he is a prophet will receive a prophet's reward." In Christ, we are called not only prophets, but also priests, and kings.[18] Therefore, in the Holy Eucharist, this blessing is fulfilled—hospitality is transformed into holiness, and every open heart becomes a sanctuary for divine love. The Mass is an everlasting banquet, where doors are opened wide and every soul is called to enter the mystery of God's mercy, goodness, and joy.

---

[18] This threefold Christian identity is rooted in Scripture and Catholic teaching. See 1 Peter 2:5, 9; Revelation 1:6; 5:10; Acts 2:17–18; Matthew 5:14–16; Romans 5:17; and Catechism of the Catholic Church 783–786.

# 14th Sunday in Ordinary Time

First Reading Zechariah 9:9-10
Responsorial Psalm Psalm 145:1-2, 8-9, 10-11, 13-14
Second Reading Romans 8:9, 11-13
Gospel Acclamation Cf. Matthew 11:25
Gospel Reading Matthew 11:25-30

# How the Liturgy Participates in the Call of Christ Jesus for the Conversion of Jews

The First Reading for the 14th Sunday in Ordinary Time today is from Zechariah 9:9-10. This passage is part of a section within the prophet's writings, comprising chapters 9 through 14, which biblical scholars have identified as two collections of oracles.

The early Christian Gospel writers identified key benchmarks that the Messiah would need to fulfill—criteria they believed Christ Jesus embodied. First, the Messiah would be an anointed King of Israel. Second, as King, he would enter Jerusalem riding "an ass, on a colt, the foal of an ass," as prophesied by Zechariah. Third, he would inaugurate a reign of peace that extended over all the earth. The peace Zechariah envisions is not merely spiritual or metaphorical, but corporeal—a cessation of physical warfare. "He shall banish the chariot from Ephraim, and the horse from Jerusalem; the warrior's bow shall be banished, and he shall proclaim peace to the nations." His dominion, Zechariah writes, "shall be from sea to sea, and from the river to the ends of the earth." Echoing Psalms 72:8, this phrase evokes not only geopolitical breadth but a symbolic restoration of creation—a catholic (universal) dominion marked by peace, justice, and the undoing of violence.

The response from Jewish apologists regarding Christian utilization of this verse is intriguing because, in their critique of Christian prophecy, they end up highlighting its beauty, akin to how a pinch of salt enhances the sweetness of a substance. The Jewish critique of the second benchmark is that entering Jerusalem on a donkey 2,000 years ago was a common practice, as riding a donkey was the primary mode of transportation. They further emphasize that the author of the Gospel of Matthew interpreted Zechariah's parallelism literally, writing, "on a colt, the foal of an ass," with Matthew 21:7 stating, "They brought the ass and the colt and laid their cloaks over them, and he sat upon them." The Jewish apologist is likely correct in this regard, which explains why Mark and

Luke, despite not emphasizing the Messianic fulfillment as strongly as Matthew to a Jewish audience, only mention Jesus riding into Jerusalem on a single animal.

Biblical parallelism is evidently a frequent characteristic throughout both the Old and New Testaments. A well-known example of biblical parallelism appears in the Rite of Purification during the Catholic Mass liturgy from Psalm 51:2, "Wash me thoroughly from my iniquity, and cleanse me from my sin." This repetition emphasizes the desire for purification, possibly reflecting Zechariah's intended meaning in this context.

Apart from his valid critique of Matthew, the Jewish Apologist extends the limitations of his argument by asserting that Jesus did not fulfill the other two criteria because He was neither Israel's King nor the inaugurator of a utopian era of universal peace. Indeed, this is a conclusion that every Apologist should logically arrive at. Through the inherent constraints of logic and reason alone, the Apologist is confined to conclusions derived solely through sense perception. Conversely, it was through faith and divine revelation that Simon Peter was able to declare, "You are the Messiah, the Son of the living God."

Today's Second Reading from Romans 8:9, 11-13 also addresses the shortcomings of the Jewish Apologist's expectations. Certainly, the Jewish person is justified in one aspect of their expectations; they ought to have anticipated that the Messiah would resolve the issues of the flesh through flesh—addressing corporeal problems through a corporeal body. However, they were mistaken not to expect that God Himself would incarnate to resolve the problem of the flesh by healing and regenerating human nature beyond mere passions. The ontological condition of human nature, wounded by the fall of our first ancestors, explains the presence of sin in the world, which in turn causes violence. Consequently, only a divine remedy could truly remedy the root cause of our sins.

The Apostle Paul describes the coming of the Messiah in this way: "If the Spirit of the one who raised Jesus from the dead dwells in you, the one who raised Christ from the dead will give life to your mortal bodies also, through his Spirit that dwells in you. For if you live according to the flesh, you will die; but if by the Spirit you put to death the deeds of the body, you will live." Truly, as we should all recognize by now—though the Jewish Apologist may not—it is impossible to find peace solely within the flesh. As long as we are not genuinely united with God, we remain at war with Him. Humanity has always received the king their hearts' desire; this is why Christians have found their eternal King in Christ Jesus, and why the Jewish people have yet to find a king in the world.

In today's Gospel Reading from Matthew 11:25-30, Christ Jesus responds to the opposition He received from the Jews with mercy, affirming that their rejection of Him is a matter of their lack of humility. He states, "I give praise to you, Father, Lord of heaven and earth, for although you have hidden these things from the wise and the learned, you have revealed them to little ones." However, a potential tension arises in Jesus' words: He suggests that the wise and learned lack the humility and beatitude necessary to believe, yet also states that "no one knows the Father except the Son and anyone to whom the Son wishes to reveal Him."

Thus, the question emerges—is the capacity to know the Father a matter of human disposition or divine choice? The answer is both—a gift and a cooperation. This revelation is consistent with the Apostle Paul's teaching in Ephesians 2:8-9: "For by grace you have been saved through faith, and this is not from you; it is the gift of God; it is not from works so that no one may boast." Likewise, Saint Augustine's words are pertinent: "The God who created you without your cooperation will not save you without your cooperation." This interplay underscores the divine generosity and the human response in salvation.

The gift of faith from God is activated and becomes alive through our desire to believe. All can believe, and that is why all are called, as Christ told us in today's reading, saying, "Come to me, all you who labor and are burdened, and I will give you rest." Yes, we respond to the Jewish Apologist. Christ calls you to believe that He is your King. You have been summoned to your King, who is the King of Peace. For peace is not something humans can achieve on their own, for they might boast about their accomplishments if they could. Rather, peace is a person named Christ Jesus.

For this reason, we Roman Rite Catholics have, in various arrangements of words, prayed since as early as the 3$^{rd}$ century in our Good Friday liturgy for the conversion of the Jews, saying:

> Let us earnestly pray for the faithless Jews, that the Almighty God may reveal His mercy by lifting the veil from their hearts. May He open their eyes to recognize Jesus Christ, our Lord and Savior. O God, who in His infinite mercy does not exclude even those who are in spiritual blindness, hear our heartfelt prayers for the Jewish people. Enlighten their minds with the truth that is found in Christ, and free them from darkness and ignorance. Through Jesus Christ our Lord, who lives and reigns with you in the unity of the Holy Spirit, forever and ever. Amen.

# 15th Sunday in Ordinary Time

First Reading   Isaiah 55:10-11
Responsorial Psalm   Psalm 65:10, 11, 12-13, 14
Second Reading   Romans 8:18-23
Gospel Acclamation   Cf. Mark 4:14, Luke 8:11, John 6:37, 40
Gospel Reading   Matthew 13:1-23

# The Liturgy of the Catholic Mass is the Rich Soil, and We are the Seeds

The Deutero-Isaiah canon of Scripture, beginning in chapter forty and concluding in chapter fifty-five, can be organized in various ways. However, one of the simplest approaches is to consider it as comprising two distinct parts: the first being the 'Book of Comfort' (spanning from chapters 40 to 55), so named due to the initial words spoken by the prophet in verse forty, which state, "Comfort, give comfort to my people, says your God." This phrase establishes the prophet's mission and mandate throughout that section. The second part is referred to as the 'Book of Struggle for the New Temple and the New Jerusalem' (encompassing chapters 56 through 66). The reading for the Fifteenth Sunday in Ordinary Time — Year A — is drawn from the concluding chapter of the Book of Comfort, specifically verses 10 and 11.

It is a compelling use of similitude here, where God likens the word that He says, "goes forth from my mouth," to "the rain and snow [that] comes down." The satisfaction point of the rain and snow, says the Lord, is that it waters the earth, and the fruit of that satisfaction point is that it makes fertile and fruitful the things needed for the human condition to survive — like the seeds of wheat that become bread. Then He says, "So shall my word be that goes forth from my mouth; It shall not return to me empty, but shall do what pleases me, achieving the end for which I sent it."

Yet, if we explore this similitude further, we might note how water deeply penetrates and infuses the soil. In the same way, the Word of God does. We could observe that rain has no choice but to fall, yet it will rise again in another form—either as gas or as part of the life it merges with. Similarly, Christ Jesus descended so that we might ascend with Him within us; that is, God became man so that man might become like God. Finally, we might notice how rainwater partners with carbon dioxide as it enters the soil, helping plants thrive by releasing micronutrients such as zinc, copper, and iron. In the same way, the divine partnership of Christ and Holy Spirit blesses us with the gifts of the Spirit to help us more fully share in the divine nature.

Chapter eight of the Apostle Paul's Letter to the Church of Rome commenced with arguments addressing the vulnerabilities of our wounded flesh and its inherent hostility towards the Holy Trinity. In today's Second Reading from Romans 8:18-23, Paul transitions to elaborating that humanity's Original Sin not only inflicted wounds upon human nature but also affected all of creation; he states that creation "is groaning in labor pains even until now," and expresses hope to "be set free from slavery to corruption and share in the glorious freedom of the children of God."

Therefore, there is not only a similarity between the order of humans and the order of nature as stated in the First Reading, but also a real relationship that has existed since the beginning when the Creator made us from earth and gave us the responsibility to have dominion over all other living things on the planet. In other words, if the material from which our nature was formed is now wounded, it makes sense that the nature of our planet is also wounded. This fact explains why we have seen that humans, governed by their slavery to sin, are also those who are most inclined to cause harm to nature. At the same time, those seeking to be holy in Christ Jesus are more likely to avoid taking more from the planet than they actually need.

The compilers of our lectionary continued this theme of nature and humanity in the Gospel Reading from Matthew 13:1-9, where we are privileged to hear Jesus' Parable about the Sower, who was indiscriminately sowing seeds along the path he was traversing, passing by rocks and thorns, and into rich soil. The question of what type of seed the Sower was casting—whether wheat or mustard seed—was not disclosed, as the inquiry of 'what' holds no significance in this context; likewise, the personal name of the Sower was not provided, emphasizing that the question of 'who' is also irrelevant here. Instead, the primary concern is the question of 'where,' to which there is only one correct answer, as articulated by Christ Jesus: "... the seed sown on rich soil is the one who hears the word and understands it, who indeed bears fruit and yields a hundred or sixty or thirtyfold." Additionally, this parable cannot be viewed in isolation from the First Reading, which taught us that the Word of God is akin to rain and snow that make the soil rich, fertile, and fruitful, thereby enabling the seed to fulfill its purpose according to His divine design.

Through the Liturgical Sense, the readings at Mass today reveal a profound truth: the liturgy of the Catholic Mass is more than just ritual—it's the fertile soil where God's divine plan unfolds. Imagine ourselves as seeds planted by the Divine Sower, nourished by His Word, His grace, and His very Body, Blood, Soul, and Divinity.

Over two thousand years of divine visitation in the liturgy—His presence in our worship and our response in return—have been infused and empowered by the Holy Spirit, guiding us to bear abundant fruit. This sacred rhythm transforms us, making us active participants in God's divine symphony. When we sit, we are planted in rich soil; when we kneel, we drink deeply from His Word; and when we stand and process, we long more intensely for the Son of God. Embracing this truth calls us to an active and trusting engagement, allowing us to participate in God's transformative grace fully and to become fruitful in our lives, our neighbors, and the Church. We are not merely spectators but vital seeds in God's eternal, life-giving harvest.

# 16th Sunday in Ordinary Time

| | |
|---:|:---|
| First Reading | Wisdom 12:13, 16-19 |
| Responsorial Psalm | Psalm 86:5-6, 9-10, 15-16 |
| Second Reading | Romans 8:26-27 |
| Gospel Acclamation | Cf. Matthew 11:25 |
| Gospel Reading | Matthew 13:24-43 |

# The Liturgy of the Mass is the Best Evidence of God's Loving Patience

Today's First Reading for the 16th Sunday in Ordinary Time, derived from the Book of Wisdom 12:13, 16-19, is extracted from a more comprehensive homily that begins in 11:6 and concludes in 19:12. The preface of this homily, found in 11:1, describes it as a narrative or illustrative account of events through which the Israelites' enemies, such as the Egyptians and the Canaanites, during their Exodus, were punished but ultimately benefited God's chosen people. Addison G. Wright, in his *The Structure of the Book of Wisdom,*[19] termed this illustrative sequence 'Five Antithetical Diptychs'.

The second of these Antithetical Diptychs is designated as 'Quail instead of the Plague of Little Animals,' wherein our designated readings for today, the author elucidates that God's justice and mercy towards the enemies of Israel stem from the fact that God is not subservient to His omnipotent might. He states, "For your might is the source of justice; your mastery over all things makes you lenient to all. For you demonstrate your might when the integrity of your power is disbelieved; and in those who recognize you, you rebuke arrogance. Yet, although you are master of might, you judge with clemency, and with great mercy, you govern us; for whenever you will, power accompanies you. Moreover, you have taught your people, through these deeds, that those who are just must be kind; and you have provided your children with a solid hope that repentance for their sins will be permitted." This segment of the homily follows verses 11:17 – 12:8, in which the author of Wisdom expounds that God is merciful because He loves.

In its own manner, the liturgy of the Mass functions as a form of diptych, serving as an evolving illustration. On one side, it depicts the

---

[19] Addison G. Wright, "The Structure of the Book of Wisdom," *Biblica* 48, no. 2 (1967): 165–184.

congregation being prepared to receive Christ Jesus, while on the adjacent side, it shows the community in communion with Christ Jesus. The link binding these two representations is the love of God. Furthermore, the homily of Wisdom regarding God's just lenience, exemplified through the concept of a diptych, is also supported by the understanding that God's treatment of us is rooted in His patience. In essence, God's mercy, goodness, and lenient justice must be gradually revealed to us, much like a diptych, owing to our fragile condition—a wounded state that occasionally inclines toward rebellion against God. However, this condition has the potential for improvement over time through exposure to His patience, presence, and love.

Suppose our Eternal Father's love is patient with us, as the Apostle Paul describes. Likewise, the love of the Holy Spirit is always patient with our weakness and searches deeply within us to bring us back home. In today's Second Reading from Romans 8:26-27, it states, "The Spirit comes to the aid of our weakness; for we do not know how to pray as we ought, but the Spirit himself intercedes with inexpressible groanings. And the one who searches hearts knows what is the intention of the Spirit because he intercedes for the holy ones according to God's will." In this way, knowing that we are wounded and sometimes unable to pray and confess as we should, the Divine Symphony steps in to put words in our mouths, confessions on our tongues, and songs on our lips to show God that we need His help, His mercy, His justice, and His leniency in our lives.

For if the Church, which is the Temple of the Holy Spirit, were to come to our aid and teach us how to pray and worship, we would not be able to call ourselves abandoned or orphans. Yet, here the promise from God is again fulfilled in the words of Christ Jesus, who said, "I will not leave you orphans; I will come to you"[20] and "I will ask the Father, and he will give you another Advocate to be with you always."[21]

---

[20] John 14:18
[21] John 14:16

If our Eternal Father's and the Holy Spirit's love is patient with us, in accordance with the Gospel Reading today from Matthew 13:24-43, Christ Jesus likewise exhibits patience towards us, akin to the man in the parable "who sowed good seed in his field," who demonstrated patience with weeds growing alongside the wheat until the appropriate time for harvest. His love is enduring with regard to our wounded condition, as illustrated by the parable of the mustard seed sown in the field. The Lord states, "... yet when full-grown, it is the largest of plants." Christ Jesus' love demonstrates patience with our weaknesses, paralleling the woman in the parable who patiently waited for the fermentation of the yeast to cause the wheat dough to rise.

Truly, the Liturgy of the Catholic Mass stands as the most compelling evidence on earth that God is infinitely patient with us. It is through this sacred time with Him that He grants us the extraordinary privilege to worship Him—not just once, but repeatedly—despite our frequent sins and shortcomings. This revelation is a testament to His boundless mercy and enduring love. The liturgy not only welcomes us back, time and again, but also offers us forgiveness for venial faults, invites us to confess and seek atonement, and empowers us to use our bodies—gifts from Him—to praise His holy name.

Through the priest, acting in the person of His Son, Christ Himself speaks to us, forging a genuine communion with the Real Presence of Jesus. Ultimately, in a powerful act of divine patience and mercy extended to the entire world, God sends us forth with the Holy Spirit dwelling within us—calling us to be vessels of His grace, shining light into darkness, and bringing hope to those lost in sin. The Mass, therefore, is not just a ritual; it is a profound expression of God's unwavering patience, love, and desire for communion with all of us.

As you reflect on the depth of God's unwavering patience and mercy toward you, let that divine example compel you to extend the same patience and mercy to yourself today. Do not settle for passively receiving His Word—embrace it, let it transform your very thoughts and actions, and become a radiant, living testament to His love. The liturgy is not merely forming you for ritual worship and participation, but for a life of divine purpose: to be a vessel through which God's patience, forgiveness, and compassion shine forth into the world. Allow His grace to challenge you—rise above past shortcomings, open your heart to continual growth, and strive to embody His love with renewed courage and conviction. This is the calling the liturgy is shaping you for; step into it boldly and make His patience visible through your life.

# 17th Sunday in Ordinary Time

|  |  |
|--:|:--|
| First Reading | 1 Kings 3:5, 7-12 |
| Responsorial Psalm | Psalm 119:57, 72, 76-77, 127-128, 129-130 |
| Second Reading | Romans 8:28-30 |
| Gospel Acclamation | Cf. Matthew 11:25 |
| Gospel Reading | Matthew 13:44-52 |

# The Liturgy of the Mass Creates in Us a Servant's Heart

King Solomon humbly asked God to make him a more faithful servant, seeking not wealth or power, but the wisdom to serve God's people well. Because his request sprang from a genuine desire to serve, God blessed him abundantly—granting him wisdom beyond compare.

Today's First Reading for the 17th Sunday in Ordinary Time – Year A, from 1 Kings 3:5, 7-12, brings us a powerful example from sacred Scripture that invites us to reflect deeply. Through the story of young King Solomon, the Holy Spirit calls each of us to open our hearts, inspiring us to seek not just blessings for ourselves, but the grace to become instruments of God's love and service. In Solomon's humble prayer, we are encouraged to examine our own desires and to let God teach us how to serve others with a generous and understanding heart.

If God appeared to you in a dream at night, as He did with Solomon, and said, "Ask something of me, and I will give it to you," what would you ask for? Remember that God's pleasure with Solomon's request stemmed from the fact that Solomon was a very young man when he was anointed King over a vast people, a people he did not find for himself but whom God had chosen. All Solomon asked for was "an understanding heart to judge your people and to distinguish right from wrong." However, since he only requested the gift of understanding, God also granted him the gift of wisdom—he asked for one thing, and the Lord gave him two, saying, "I do as you requested. I give you a heart so wise and understanding that there has never been anyone like you up to now, and after you, there will come no one to equal you."

We can draw a few other insights from this exchange between God and King Solomon. First, we might compare Solomon with Eve, the first woman who succumbed to the temptation of selfishness and the desire to be like God by gaining knowledge of good and evil, acting on that temptation by sinning against God. In fact, selfish people can't truly serve others because they are too focused on serving themselves. In this way, Eve was not unusual at all; rather, she was quite like most people, so ordinary as a fallen sinner that her life's outcomes were also quite common. Now, consider Solomon, whose humility before God caused him to seek knowledge of good and evil solely so he could govern rightly as King of God's people. Because of this, God made Solomon unique among all humans, before or after him.

While gifts of wisdom and understanding may have filled the capacity of Solomon to such an extent that there has never been another one like him who was as wise and understanding, it is also true that we are greater than Solomon because the promise from God in this New Covenant is that we do not have to wait for Him to come to us in a dream and ask us what we need from Him to help us be better servants, because Jesus taught us in John 14:13-14, ". . . whatever you ask in my name, I will do, so that the Father may be glorified in the Son. If you ask anything of me in my name, I will do it." In other words, the teaching is that we were called to serve God so that God might be glorified, and that teaching is affirmed in today's Second Reading from Romans 8:28-30, with the Apostle Paul writing, "We know that all things work for good for those who love God, who are called according to his purpose. For those he foreknew, he also predestined to be conformed to the image of his Son, so that he might be the firstborn among many brothers and sisters. And those he predestined he also called; and those he called he also justified; and those he justified he also glorified."

Furthermore, although we will not attain our glorified body in this earthly life, we are nonetheless called to undertake the work that glorifies God, which in turn leads to our own glorification. The gifts of the Holy Spirit—wisdom, understanding, counsel, fortitude, knowledge, piety, and fear of the Lord—equip us to fulfill our divine calling effectively. These gifts are what Solomon was compelled to pray for, and they are also the focus of the liturgy of the Catholic Mass, which prepares us and guides us to emphasize them more fully. While Solomon received only two gifts of the Holy Spirit, those who have been baptized and confirmed have received the fullness of the Holy Spirit— the third Person of the Holy Trinity dwelling within them— and, in union with the Second Person of the Holy Trinity, Jesus Christ, in the Holy Eucharist, for those who have worthily received Him.

In the Gospel reading from Matthew 13:44-52, our Lord presents three distinct parables, illustrating that the kingdom of heaven is akin to a treasure hidden in a field, a merchant seeking fine pearls, and a net cast into the sea. Indeed, our earthly journey is as straightforward and effortless as an analogy. We are fundamentally individuals created by God to seek Him; however, it is the simplest game of hide and seek we will ever engage in, as the object of our pursuit is concealed in plain sight.

We are a chosen people who are not accidentally, but actively searching for the objective good, and, for this reason, we know it when we find it. Just as the men who were actively in the field looking for a treasure, a pearl, and a catch of fish, rejoiced when they found that for which they sought, so too do those who have discovered the essence of the liturgy of the Catholic Mass abound in joy. We know the immutable essence of the liturgy is objectively good because it is a person named Jesus Christ, and we know He has called us to the liturgy according to His purpose to fill us with the gifts of service to His Father so we might glorify Him, and that He might find us worthy to be glorified at our resurrection.

# 18ᵗʰ Sunday in Ordinary Time

| | |
|---:|:---|
| First Reading | Isaiah 55:1-3 |
| Responsorial Psalm | Psalms 145:8-9, 15-16, 17-18 |
| Second Reading | Romans 8:35, 37-39 |
| Gospel Acclamation | Matthew 4:4B |
| Gospel Reading | Matthew 14:13-21 |

# The Liturgical Teaching on How to Avoid Separation from God

Today's Gospel Reading from Matthew 14:13-21 begins, "When Jesus heard of the death of John the Baptist, he withdrew in a boat to a deserted place by himself. The crowds heard of this and followed him on foot from their towns. When he disembarked and saw the vast crowd, his heart was moved with pity for them, and he cured their sick. When it was evening, the disciples approached him and said, "This is a deserted place and it is already late; dismiss the crowds so that they can go to the villages and buy food for themselves." Jesus said to them, "There is no need for them to go away; give them some food yourselves.""

The feeding of the five thousand is one of the instances in Christ Jesus' ministry where today's First Reading from Isaiah 55:1-3 was fulfilled: "You who have no money, come, receive grain and eat . . . Heed me, and you shall eat well, you shall delight in rich fare. Come to me heedfully, listen, that you may have life. I will renew with you the everlasting covenant, the benefits assured to David."

Reading the Miracle of the Multiplication of the Loaves and Fishes as a type of Sacrament of the Holy Eucharist, and the calling of all in need of grace and mercy as a type of liturgy of the Catholic Mass, is a proper use of the liturgical sense of sacred Scripture. However, we would have to contend with the fact that the key distinction between the type and the reality is that while all are called, not all may worthily receive the bread of the everlasting covenant.

The Apostle in today's Second reading from Romans 8:35, 37-39 asks the question, "What will separate us from the love of Christ?" and goes on to answer his question in saying that no form of suffering, "neither death, nor life, nor angels, nor principalities, nor present things, nor future things, nor powers, nor height, nor depth, nor any other creature will be able to separate us from the love of God in Christ Jesus our Lord." Paul, here, is not saying that nothing can separate us from God, because in other places he clearly teaches that transgressions and sin do separate us from God and lead us to death.[22] On the contrary, it is not external pressures that can separate us from God, but it is how we respond to our environment that either leads us to virtue or into sin.

From the perspective of eschatological theology, separation from God is understood as Hell itself—the state in which a person is deemed unworthy to dwell in the presence of God for all eternity. This ultimate separation is the consequence of being unfit for eternal communion with God.

In a similar way, liturgical theology teaches that separation from God renders us unworthy to receive Holy Communion. In this context, unworthiness means that, during our earthly pilgrimage, we are not prepared to welcome God to dwell within us through the sacrament of the Eucharist. Thus, while eschatological separation refers to the eternal loss of communion with God, liturgical separation refers to the loss of the privilege of receiving Christ in the Eucharist during our journey toward our eternal destination.

Rooted in another teaching from Paul in 1 Corinthians 11:27-29, the Church affirms in paragraph 1385 of the *Catechism of the Catholic Church*, saying, "Anyone who is conscious of a grave sin must receive the sacrament of Reconciliation before coming to communion." And for venial sins, the liturgy offers a series of prayers, such as the Confiteor, for people to pray to God asking for His forgiveness for their sins. Then, after the Confiteor, the priest intercedes on our behalf, praying, "May almighty God have mercy on us, forgive us our sins, and bring us to everlasting life." Similarly, during the Divine Liturgy of the Byzantine Rite, while the choir sings, the priest prays silently the *Prayer of the Cherubic Hymn*:

> "No one who is bound by carnal desires and pleasures is worthy to approach, draw near, or minister to You, O King of Glory… Yet because of Your ineffable and immeasurable love for man-

---

[22] Cf. Romans 3:23, 6:23, and Ephesians 2:1-3

kind, You became man without change or alteration... and entrusted to us this priestly ministry... Do You Yourself, O Master, make me, Your sinful and unworthy servant, worthy to offer gifts to You... for You are the Offerer and the Offered.

The surest way to avoid separation from God is the Divine Symphony. The liturgy calls us into communion with God, offering a pathway to transformation and renewal. In blessing us through liturgical worship, the liturgy demonstrates that it cherishes our original value, contrasting the world, the flesh, and the devil, which seek to diminish the imago Dei within us. While sin may steal our value, the grace of God and the sacraments of the Church restore us, uplifting us to our intended splendor. Like God's love, the liturgy seeks far greater blessings for us than we often imagine for ourselves, inviting us to embrace our true value and the purpose for which we were created.

# 19th Sunday in Ordinary Time

| | |
|---:|:---|
| First Reading | 1 Kings 19:9a, 11-13a |
| Responsorial Psalm | Psalm 85:9, 10, 11-12, 13-14 |
| Second Reading | Romans 9:1-5 |
| Gospel Acclamation | Psalm 130:5 |
| Gospel Reading | Matthew 14:22-33 |

# The Liturgy of the Catholic Mass is Forming Us to Have No Fear of the World

The Catholic Mass promises that whenever we attend to the liturgy, the Real Presence of the Lord is there with us. No matter how we are feeling, no matter what time it is in our life; whether it is a time of trouble, a time of distress, a time of anxiety, a time of joy, or a time of peace, the promise remains the same; that from the rising of the sun until its setting, as long as we have priests we will be able to visit the Real Presence of our Lord and worship Him and He will condescend to commune with us.

Such a blessing as this was not always the case in God's covenant with His people. For example, in today's First Reading for the 19th Sunday in Ordinary Time – Year A, from 1 Kings 19:9, 11-13, the Prophet Elijah was running in fear for his life after Jezebel had promised to end his life for having killed all her false prophets. Albeit for different reasons, the imagery of Elijah fleeing from Samaria to Beer-sheba, which was in the opposite direction of Damascus, where God would send him, reminds us of Jonah, who fled to Tarshish, which was in the opposite direction of Nineveh, where God was directing him to preach.

Elijah's forty-day and forty-night journey to Mount Horeb serves as a reminder of Moses, who ascended Mount Sinai (likely the same mountain as Horeb) and stayed there for forty days and forty nights. Similarly, just as Christ Jesus' temptation in the wilderness occurred after fasting for forty days and forty nights, Elijah fasted for the same duration until he arrived at a cave on Mount Horeb, where God tested him by asking, "Why are you here, Elijah?" In this context, the Lord suggests that Elijah should be elsewhere, indicating that Elijah is out of place due to his fear of the world. Elijah's response to the divine inquiry, stating, "I have been most zealous for the LORD, the God of hosts, but the Israelites have forsaken your covenant. They have destroyed your altars and murdered your prophets by the sword. I alone remain, and they seek to take my life," exemplifies a typical human reaction. Like Elijah, we often believe that God is indebted to us for fulfilling our divine calling. Yet, we fail to consider why a servant or an enslaved person should demand anything from their master, who supplies all their needs. Furthermore, in times of distress, we tend to doubt or forget that the Presence of the Lord is always with us.

The response from God to Elijah's doubt was to ask, 'What do you need to know so I can show you I'm with you and you're not alone in this?' How about I give you a test? The text reads, "Then the LORD said: Go out and stand on the mountain before the LORD; the LORD will pass by. There was a strong and violent wind rending the mountains and crushing rocks before the LORD—but the LORD was not in the wind; after the wind, an earthquake—but the LORD was not in the earthquake; after the earthquake, fire—but the LORD was not in the fire; after the fire, a light, silent sound." Ah ha. There it was. Sometimes, we look for these big, magnificent signs of awe and wonder to prove that God is with us. Still, sometimes, it is just the appearance of a small wafer of bread and a drop of wine, or in Elijah's case, a light, silent sound.

When Elijah heard the presence of God, out of reverence and perhaps a little shame and embarrassment because of his doubt, he "hid his face in his cloak and went out and stood at the entrance of the cave." Then the question comes again, "Why are you here, Elijah?" To which the prophet responds as he did before. Now the Lord is ready to show mercy to this poor prophet who has served him well by commanding him to go back through Samaria, where Jezebel was seeking his life, and then to Damascus, where he is to complete his final three assignments. First, to anoint Hazael as king of Aram, second, to anoint Jehu as king of Israel, and third, to anoint Elisha as his successor. The prophet Elijah would only carry out the last of these three assignments.

The theme of overcoming fear through trust in the Presence of the Lord continues in today's Second Reading from Romans 9:1-5, which serves as a preface to the Apostle Paul's lamentation for the Jews. In this epistle to the Church of Rome, he states, "I have great sorrow and constant anguish in my heart" because he experiences profound distress over the plight of his former brethren and kinsmen who have rejected Jesus, the Messiah of God. Nonetheless, he persists in conveying the truth to them because, he asserts, "my conscience joins with the Holy Spirit in bearing me witness."

Today's Gospel Reading from Matthew 14:22-33 also upholds the theme of overcoming fear by trusting in the Presence of the Lord, exemplified by Simon Peter stepping out of the boat and beginning to walk on water toward Jesus. Peter surmounted his fear, and as he began to sink, he cried out, "Lord, save me!" The Lord responded by extending His hand to rescue him from sinking further. Truly, there are countless fears that can hold us back, but through unwavering trust in the Lord our God, we can conquer every fear.

The Church and her Sacraments do more than invite us—they summon us into a life of divine courage, fearlessness, and transformative grace. We are not called to reject sin merely out of fear of losing Heaven or suffering the torments of Hell. Instead, we are challenged to rise above mediocrity and embrace a bold, unwavering love and trust in God that compels us to live daringly, unafraid of the world's storms.

Each time we hear or pray for another person, "Peace be with you," recognize that it is far more than a simple greeting; it is Christ Himself extending the gift of His peace—a peace that shatters chains of anxiety, doubt, and hesitation. Dare to let this peace set your soul ablaze. Let it propel you beyond your comfort zones, embolden your faith, and inspire you to acts of radical love and mercy. Step forward each day with conviction, knowing that you are empowered by the living God who dwells in you to walk in faith, love, and a courage that conquers every fear. The world will test you, but united with Christ, who has united with you, and you will not be shaken. Say yes to this divine invitation—and let your life become a testament to faith that refuses to cower, love that never fails, and courage that overcomes every darkness.

# 20th Sunday in Ordinary Time

| | |
|---:|:---|
| First Reading | Isaiah 56:1, 6-7 |
| Responsorial Psalm | Psalm 67:2-3, 5, 6, 8 |
| Second Reading | Romans 11:13-15, 29-32 |
| Gospel Acclamation | Cf. Matthew 4:23 |
| Gospel Reading | Matthew 15:21-28 |

# The Liturgical Teaching on the Catholicity of God

Today's First Reading for the 20th Sunday in Ordinary Time – Year A is derived from Isaiah 56:1, 6-7, and introduces the theme of today's readings by emphasizing God's universality and inclusiveness. Chapter 56 of Isaiah marks the beginning of the final section of the Book of Isaiah, often referred to as Trito-Isaiah (i.e., the Third Isaiah). The historical context of this segment is immediately post-exile. Following the Babylonian captivity from 587 to 516 BCE and the subsequent scattering throughout neighboring nations, Israel's prophets exhorted the exiles to return to their homeland. For Isaiah, the prophecies conveyed to him for this gathering after the Second Exodus encompass not only Israel's ultimate redemption but also herald a significant transformation in Israel's ecclesiology. While the Torah afforded foreigners residing within Palestine certain protections,[23] those previously excluded from full participation in the community of God's chosen people—such as Eunuchs and foreigners—are now being welcomed into the House of God and its walls. Furthermore, their sacrifices and offerings are to be accepted at His altar.

The essential thing to note in the Old Covenant is that God has not changed the criteria for membership in His community. On the contrary, the requirements remain the same for foreigners as for the Jews. The text states, "The foreigners who join themselves to the LORD, ministering to him, loving the name of the LORD, and becoming his servants—all who keep the sabbath free from profanation and hold to my covenant, them I will bring to my holy mountain and make joyful in my house of prayer; their burnt offerings and sacrifices will be acceptable

---

[23] Cf. Exodus 22:20; Deuternomy. 10:19.

on my altar, for my house shall be called a house of prayer for all peoples." In other words, the body of the ecclesia has not yet expanded, but what has been extended to all peoples was the mercy of God.

Similarly, in the Gospel reading from Matthew 15:21-28, we witness a significant moment in Jesus' ministry where He initially demonstrates reluctance in responding to the plea of a Canaanite woman whose daughter is tormented by demons. When the woman appeals to Jesus for help, His response, "I was sent only to the lost sheep of the house of Israel," clarifies His primary mission focus. This statement, however, is not a contradiction of the message in Isaiah, nor is it a commentary on the broader inclusion of Gentiles into the Kingdom of God. The woman is not asking to become part of the Jewish community; she is simply seeking mercy for her suffering child.

Jesus' words serve to identify who the "lost sheep" are—specifically, the people of Israel—rather than excluding the Canaanite woman from His compassion. What is remarkable is the woman's understanding and faith; she knows exactly where to seek help, recognizing Jesus as the source of mercy. In response to her persistent faith, Jesus ultimately extends His mercy to her, healing her daughter at that very hour. This encounter exemplifies the boundless nature of Christ's mercy, which reaches beyond traditional boundaries when met with genuine faith.

Now, after the resurrection, ascension, and descent of the Holy Spirit, something about the ecclesia of God's People changes because the nature of the ecclesia changes. It shifts from being a mere cooperative covenant to becoming an actual person. In other words, the Old Covenant community could not expand because it was based upon the finite limits of Abraham's seed, which could only be as numerous as the stars in the sky.[24] That is not the case in the glorified and infinite Body of Christ; God does not have a capacity limit in His Body. Therefore, God has not only come for all and can save all because He has the capacity

---

[24] Genesis 26:4.

for all, but according to the Apostle in today's Second Reading from Romans 11:13-14, 29-32, the motive for God's extension remains the same, writing, "Just as you once disobeyed God but have now received mercy because of their disobedience, so they have now disobeyed so that, by virtue of the mercy shown to you, they too may now receive mercy. For God delivered all to disobedience, that he might have mercy upon all."

The expansion of God's community into the Body of Christ is explained in our liturgical theology in two ways. First, while in the Old Covenant there was only one priesthood with one sacrifice to offer, and only in one place, in the New Covenant, there remains only one priesthood with one sacrifice, but it occurs in as many places as there are Catholic priests. Second, because Christ's sacrifice was for all of humanity, so are the sacraments of His Church for everyone, through which many will be saved. Paradoxically, through this explanation, God even accommodates the human tendency to make Him small. We tend to reduce God so that He is easier to understand, control, and manipulate.

Although it is stated that divine mercy is boundless, it is also true that we may not fully understand its nature or may feel undeserving of such compassion. Therefore, God presents Himself as small as a baby, a teacher who walks with fishermen, a humble king, a criminal sentenced to the death penalty, a piece of bread, or a drop of wine, so as not to overwhelm our senses or sensibilities. In this way, God encounters us through His mercy.

God's universality—His true Catholicity—means that His love extends to all people, yet He boldly calls each of us to a higher standard: to enter His Kingdom, we must embrace His commandments and allow ourselves to be transformed. This is not an easy path to comprehend, and it challenges our hearts and minds until we truly encounter His mercy and grace. It is in that encounter, through the transforming power of His Spirit and the life-giving sacraments, that we are empowered to respond—no longer by mere human strength but by the indwelling presence of the Holy Spirit. Through this gift, we are not only commanded to be holy but also equipped to become so.

How extraordinary it is that the infinite God, utterly unlike us in His holiness, would lower Himself to our level—not only sharing in our humanity but doing so without sin. He does this to draw near, to be present in every era and every place, ensuring that no one is excluded from His reach. The challenge before us is clear: God invites us to overcome our doubts, our limits, and our excuses, daring us to believe that He is truly accessible and that, through His mercy, we can become like Him. Let us not settle for anything less than striving to respond to this immense love with our whole lives, trusting that His grace will do in us what we could never do alone.

# 21ˢᵗ Sunday in Ordinary Time

|  |  |
|--:|:--|
| First Reading | Isaiah 22:19-23 |
| Responsorial Psalm | Psalm 138:1-2, 2-3, 6, 8 |
| Second Reading | Romans 11:33-36 |
| Gospel Acclamation | Matthew 16:18 |
| Gospel Reading | Matthew 16:13-20 |

# The Liturgical Teaching on the Two Types of People

Today's Readings for the 21$^{st}$ Sunday in Ordinary Time inspire us to reignite the fire within—renewing our understanding of who our true Master is and committing ourselves wholeheartedly to His divine will. This powerful message is conveyed through the contrast between two kinds of people: those who are unaware of God's love and serve only themselves, and those who have embraced His truth and dedicate their lives to serving Him. As we reflect on these words, let us open our hearts to recognize our calling and to strive fervently to follow His path, setting the stage for a deeper journey of faith and purpose.

The First Reading today from Isaiah 22:19-23 and the Gospel Reading from Matthew 16:13-20 are verses that Catholic apologists frequently leverage to defend the dogmas of Apostolic Succession and the Primacy of Peter. While we acknowledge that the three oracles concerning the Fall of Babylon and all human glories, found in chapters 21, 22, and 23 of Isaiah, must be recognized in their historical fulfillment, we also interpret them as having future fulfillments. Specifically, Isaiah 22:22 states, "I will place the key of the House of David on his shoulder; what he opens, no one will shut, and what he shuts, no one will open," which appears to be prophetic in light of Matthew 16:19, where Christ Jesus tells the newly renamed Cephas, "I will give you the keys to the kingdom of heaven. Whatever you bind on earth shall be bound in heaven; and whatever you loose on earth shall be loosed in heaven." Furthermore, just as Isaiah 7:14 is prophetic in foretelling the virgin who would give birth to a son named Emmanuel, an event fulfilled in its immediate historical context, it is also understood as a prophecy concerning the Blessed Mother Mary and her son Jesus. Similarly, while the name Emmanuel, meaning 'God is with us,' relates to the meaning of

Jesus' name, "God saves," the name Eliakim, meaning "God has established,' corresponds to the significance of Jesus establishing His Church on Cephas.

According to Isaiah 22:15-25, Shebna served as the royal steward, or the chief minister of state, wielding considerable power and influence. However, he exhibited arrogance and pride, constructing a lavish tomb in a high place for himself. The prophet Isaiah reproved him for his vanity and prophesied that God would punish him by removing him from his office and exiling him. Isaiah further stated that he would be succeeded by Eliakim, another servant of the king, who would demonstrate faithfulness and humility. Some non-biblical Jewish texts also mention Shebna but provide different accounts of his fate. The Talmud (Sanhedrin 26a) indicates that Shebna repented after Isaiah's prophecy and assumed the role of Hezekiah's scribe or secretary. He may be the same individual as "Shebna the scribe" mentioned in 2 Kings 18:18, 26, 37; 19:2; Isaiah 36:3, 11, 22; 37:2, where he appears as one of the messengers sent by Hezekiah to negotiate with the Assyrian envoy. According to the Midrash (Pirke De-Rabbi Eliezer 10), Shebna did not repent and perished during the Assyrians' siege of Jerusalem. His body was thrown over the city wall and landed on a large stone, which then split into two and crushed him.

Eliakim was a high-ranking official in the court of King Hezekiah of Judah, who lived in the 8th century B.C. He is referenced in the book of Isaiah and various non-biblical Jewish texts. According to Isaiah 22:20-25, Eliakim was the son of Hilkiah, and God designated him to succeed Shebna as the royal steward or chief minister of state. He was bestowed with the key to David's house, symbolizing his authority and responsibility. Isaiah also commended him as a faithful and honorable servant of God and the king, who would serve as a paternal figure to the inhabitants of Jerusalem and Judah. Nonetheless, Isaiah also issued a warning that Eliakim would bear a significant burden and that his family would rely heavily on him for support. Similar to Shebna, some non-biblical

Jewish texts acknowledge Eliakim, though they present differing accounts of his role and destiny. The Talmud, in Sanhedrin 26a, equates Eliakim with Joah, the son of Asaph, who served as a recorder or historian during Hezekiah's reign. He may also be identified as the same "Joah the son of Asaph the recorder" mentioned in 2 Kings 18:18, 26, 37; 19:2; Isaiah 36:3, 11, 22; 37:2, as one of the messengers dispatched by Hezekiah to negotiate with the Assyrian envoy. According to the Midrash, in Pirke De-Rabbi Eliezer 10, Eliakim was slain by Shebna, driven by jealousy of his position and power. Shebna allegedly employed two assassins to eliminate Eliakim; however, they were apprehended and executed by King Hezekiah.

This juxtaposition of Shebna and Eliakim should not lead us into a superficial exploration of similes and contrasts between Martha and Mary. Instead, let the lives of Shebna and Eliakim serve as embodiments of the fundamental question, "Who do people say that the Son of Man is?" For there are fundamentally two types of individuals in this world: the humble and those who are about to be humbled. In essence, some know Christ Jesus, while others do not; some are familiar with their master and, consequently, are granted the authority to serve Him within the office bestowed upon them, whereas others do not know their master and, as a result, succumb to the slavery of self-indulgence.

One of the most awe-inspiring and transformative truths about the Divine Symphony is that it holds the ultimate answer to our most profound and persistent questions. The liturgy of the Mass is far more than a mere ritual—it is a divinely inspired journey that invites each of us into the fullness of life, offering a living testimony and enduring memorial to God's boundless sacrifice and His infinite mercy. From the rising of the sun until its setting, the Mass continuously unfolds the mystery of Christ Jesus, revealing not only His true identity but also inviting us to discover our own in Him.

If you have ever doubted the reality of God or longed for an encounter with the living Jesus, come to the Mass. Here, in the sacred gathering, the divine revelation is made manifest—tangible, accessible, and deeply personal. Do not let uncertainty or hesitation hold you back; step into the Mass and let your heart be awakened to the truth that God is real, that His love is present, and that Jesus awaits you with open arms.

Through the sacred Sacrament of the Holy Eucharist, the Mass offers the most compelling evidence in the universe—evidence of God's reality, His boundless love, and His yearning to dwell within us, uniting us with Him in a divine dance of love. This profound truth echoes the words of the Apostle Paul to the Church at Rome: "Oh, the depth of the riches and wisdom and knowledge of God! How inscrutable are his judgments and how unsearchable his ways!" Yet, such an unfathomable mystery is unveiled simply and powerfully through the humble appearance of bread and wine—food for the humble, a divine moment of conviction for those ready to be humbled—and exalted as the divine gift that transforms us all.

# 22nd Sunday in Ordinary Time

First Reading  Jeremiah 20:7-9
Responsorial Psalm  Psalm 63:2, 3-4, 5-6, 8-9
Second Reading  Romans 12:1-2
Gospel Acclamation  cf. Ephesians 1:17-18
Gospel Reading  Matthew 16:21-27

# How the Liturgy Trains Us to Make Ourselves a Living Sacrifice

There is a remarkable quality we can all admire in the prophet Jeremiah: his unwavering honesty with God. Despite his struggles and doubts, Jeremiah never hesitated to express his true feelings to the Lord. Today's First Reading from Jeremiah 20:7-9 reminds us that Jeremiah's candidness was not new; earlier in his prophetic journey, he called God a deceiver, lamenting, "Why is my pain continuous, my wound incurable, refusing to be healed? To me, you are like a deceptive brook, waters that cannot be relied on!" Yet, amidst his anguish, Jeremiah's faith shines through.

Even when Jeremiah felt betrayed and ridiculed, he did not run from his pain—he faced it head-on. His words lay bare a man struggling with darkness and doubt, yet they also reveal a soulful honesty and a relentless determination to stay true to God. There's something deeply moving about Jeremiah's vulnerability; his willingness to pour out his heart, no matter how raw, reminds us that genuine faith is not about perfection—it is about showing up, even when it hurts. As we journey deeper into Jeremiah's story, let us ask ourselves: what might happen if we brought our unfiltered struggles to God? Could our honesty become the doorway to resilience and renewed hope in our own spiritual lives?

If you are anything like me, you probably know someone like Jeremiah who never hesitates to share exactly how they feel—especially if they have been hurt. Maybe you've even rolled your eyes and thought, "Just calm down!" (I know I have.) But the truth is, we all need to be heard, especially in moments of pain. I have to confess, with God, I'm often that person: the one who brings every messy, complicated feeling to Him without holding back.

The ministry God has given me often feels more like the mission of Jeremiah or John the Baptist—a voice crying out from the margins—

than the steady, measured approach of Saint Dominic de Guzmán, whom I have always admired. Sometimes, being that voice in the wilderness is exhausting. It can feel as if my cries echo into emptiness, unheard and unnoticed. Yet, I am learning that God welcomes my honesty, my doubts, and even my outbursts. Maybe, just maybe, it is in the wilderness of our hearts and the honesty of our prayers that we encounter God most deeply.

Reflecting on today's readings, I see myself in Jeremiah's honest conversations with God—especially during the moments in my youth when I would come to Him with raw, unfiltered emotions, sometimes several times a year. Jeremiah taught me the importance of being genuine with God, and I have come to deeply appreciate that God always makes room for my humanity. As I matured and accepted my vocation, those "pity parties" became less frequent, though I sometimes wondered if God missed them, thinking perhaps my outbursts brought Him a little amusement. Eventually, I chose to embrace my calling as a humble, albeit imperfect, servant of His will. I found peace in accepting my place, and now I find true joy in receiving my daily bread and fulfilling the work God sets before me. Even though the path often brings suffering, I feel most alive doing what He desires.

Despite my feelings of misery as a servant, I find it necessary to reflect each night on my spiritual journey. I ask myself whether I have truly carried my Cross that day and followed Christ wholeheartedly. Have I surrendered all that He has entrusted to me? Have I exhausted myself mentally, physically, and spiritually in my service? Have I shown love enough to deny myself? Have I prayed for others adequately? And have I fasted sufficiently? These questions serve as a sincere measure of my service, echoing the words of Christ in today's Gospel from Matthew 16:21-27: "Whoever wishes to come after me must deny himself, take up his Cross, and follow me. For whoever wishes to save his life will lose it, but whoever loses his life for my sake will find it."

The command to "take up our Cross" can seem incomprehensible to many in our generation. The Cross was not simply a symbol—it was an instrument of brutal execution. The crucifix we venerate today represents the state's death penalty inflicted on our Lord. Imagine if someone said to you, "Take up your own future death sentence and follow me to the place where I carried mine"—would you willingly accept that challenge? This is not just a symbolic act; it's a call to a real sacrifice. It requires us to ascend our own Mount Calvary, enduring suffering that tests both body and spirit. Carrying our Cross will humble us and may even break us, yet this is the path Christ calls us to follow. The alternative is to reject this path and, by doing so, to follow the way of darkness. Ultimately, there are only two paths for our lives: one leads to a glorified existence in union with God, the other to spiritual ruin. The choice is ours, but there are only two possible destinations: heaven or hell.

The Apostle reinforces the call to worship through physical sacrifice in today's Second Reading from Romans 12:1-2, stating, "I urge you, brothers and sisters, by the mercies of God, to offer your bodies as a living sacrifice, holy and pleasing to God, your spiritual worship. Do not conform yourselves to this age but be transformed by the renewal of your mind, that you may discern what is the will of God, what is good and pleasing and perfect." Paul's exhortation to present ourselves as living sacrifices is particularly challenging in the modern era, which frequently overlooks our nature as embodied souls. We were created for worship that engages our whole being; we possess bodies precisely so that we might bear the cross of sacrifice and, ultimately, death.

This profound truth is further underscored in the Liturgy of the Catholic Mass, especially during the *Sursum Corda* prayer, when the priest proclaims, "Lift up your hearts." At this moment, the priest invites the congregation to become a living sacrifice, encouraging deep reflection on what it means to elevate our hearts—our very selves—and offer them to our Creator. When we respond, "We lift them up to the Lord," the priest continues, urging us further with the words, "Let us give thanks to the Lord our God." In this liturgical call and response, we recognize that true righteousness and justice consist in offering ourselves wholly to God as living sacrifices—an expectation set forth by God and cultivated through the continual celebration of the Mass.

No one ever said the path would be smooth or simple—true sacrifice is never convenient, and it's rarely clean. Yes, our Lord promised that His yoke is easy and His burden is light, but He also made it clear: you will have a burden, a yoke, and most of all, a cross to bear. He never pretended otherwise. So, pour out your struggles and sorrows—let your lament rise, just as Jeremiah did in his darkest moments, as Paul did amid trials, as every saint and sinner has done throughout history. Your honest cries are not a sign of weakness; they are the heartbeat of authentic faith.

But here is the challenge—a challenge for every disciple hoping to follow Jesus with integrity: When the day is done and silence descends, do not simply let exhaustion sweep you away. Take a moment to kneel before God and courageously ask yourself: Did I truly show up in the world today? Did I live with intention, embracing the purpose for which I was created, the purpose God continues to shape within me—especially through the transforming mystery of the Mass? Did I carry my cross with perseverance and love, letting my faith shine even when it hurt?

Let your daily reflection be both an inspiration and a summons. Allow it to ignite a deeper resolve to give yourself more fully tomorrow, to surrender your comfort and embrace the noble struggle. For Christ calls not just for our prayers, but for our whole selves—offered as a living sacrifice, holy and pleasing in the eyes of God. Let's not settle for surviving the day. Let's dare to rise, to love, and to serve with everything we are, trusting that in our honest sacrifice, God is shaping us for glory.

# 23rd Sunday in Ordinary Time

| | |
|--:|:--|
| First Reading | Ezekiel 33:7-9 |
| Responsorial Psalm | Psalm 95:1-2, 6-7, 8-9 |
| Second Reading | Romans 13:8-10 |
| Gospel Acclamation | 2 Corinthians 5:19 |
| Gospel Reading | Matthew 18:15-20 |

# The Liturgy is Building a Culture and a Community of Mercy, Love, and Healing

Today's First Reading for the 23rd Sunday in Ordinary Time—Year A—comes from Ezekiel 33:7-9 and outlines the prophet's responsibility as a watchman for the house of Israel. Through our Baptism in Christ Jesus, we are called to share in His mission as prophets, priests, and kings; thus, we too are entrusted as watchmen, bearing responsibility for the members of God's flock. This calling is further clarified in Ezekiel chapter three, where verse 17 identifies the prophet himself as the sole watchman. However, in Ezekiel 33:2-6, the general responsibilities of all watchmen during times of conflict are described. Additionally, there is a notable development in the watchman's mandate: while chapter three limits Ezekiel's duty to warning only the wicked, chapter thirty-three expands this obligation to include warning the righteous as well. According to Lawrence Boadt, C.S.P.,[25] this broadening of responsibility was prompted by the imminent threat of Babylon's destruction of Jerusalem, signifying that even the righteous would not be exempt from danger.

The watchman's warning would have meant the difference between life and death if heeded in time, but now it is too late. Here again, the text carries implications for the Christian who actively engages in spiritual struggle against evil and temptation. In the case where God says, "You, son of man, I have appointed watchman for the house of Israel; when you hear me say anything, you shall warn them for me," we Catholics are not only called to echo warnings against evil as outlined in Scripture, but we also may consider echoing the warnings the

---

[25] Lawrence Boadt, C.S.P., "Ezekiel," in *The New Jerome Biblical Commentary*, ed. Raymond E. Brown, Joseph A. Fitzmyer, and Roland E. Murphy (Englewood Cliffs, NJ: Prentice Hall, 1990), 324

Blessed Mother Mary has communicated to us through many of her apparitions.

In today's Second Reading, the Apostle reaffirms the principles of Christ Jesus concerning the greatest commandment and the new commandment,[26] underscoring our duty to admonish both the wicked and the righteous regarding the ramifications of yielding to the snares of the adversary. In his epistle to the Church of Rome (12:8-10), he states, "Owe nothing to anyone, except to love one another; for the one who loves another has fulfilled the law. The commandments, "You shall not commit adultery; you shall not kill; you shall not steal; you shall not covet," and all other commandments, are summed up in this saying, namely, "You shall love your neighbor as yourself." Love does no evil to the neighbor; therefore, love is the fulfillment of the law."

Additionally, in addressing specific instances of misconduct among individuals, today's Gospel Reading from Matthew 18:15-20 precisely delineates how love for members of our community must be expressed. Christ Jesus instructs, "If your brother sins against you, go and tell him his fault between you and him alone. If he listens to you, you have gained your brother. If he does not listen, take one or two others along with you so that every matter may be established by the testimony of two or three witnesses. If he refuses to listen to them, tell it to the church. If he refuses even to listen to the church, then treat him as you would a Gentile or a tax collector."

In the Gospel reading for the upcoming Sunday, Simon Peter inquires of Jesus regarding the number of times one must forgive those within the community who transgress. He suggests, "As many as seven times." Jesus responds, "Not seven times, but seventy-seven times." This exemplifies that, just as God embodies love and is infinite, our love should likewise be unrestricted.

---

[26] cf. Mt. 22:36-40; John 12:34

The liturgy of the Catholic Mass beautifully responds to our call to be vigilant protectors of both the wicked and the righteous, and ambassadors of love within our community. It fosters a sacred gathering where hearts unite in worship, embracing truth and spirit. In these moments of communal worship, we reaffirm a divine truth: there is a higher power beyond ourselves—one who did not create us just to serve as our own gods. Recognizing this, we understand that the fundamental right granted to every human being is the right to life—life that flows from our Creator. Because life is a divine gift, and the divine identifies as the Way, the Truth, and the Life, it follows that every life is called to find its fullness and purpose in Christ, the source of all existence. Let us open our hearts to the divine presence, inspiring us to cherish and uphold the sacredness of each life, and to live in unwavering hope and love.

Therefore, we are called to love one another in a way that opens the door to a deeper, life-changing encounter with God—a moment when each person is truly transformed by meeting the Divine. The miracle of the Holy Eucharist stands as the ultimate witness to this: God became man so that humanity might share in His divine life. This awe-inspiring mystery was made possible because the Father, in His boundless love, sent His Son for the sake of the world. What greater reason could there be for hope and devotion?

This is the very culture that the liturgy strives to nurture—a community sent forth, renewed and filled with Christ, equipped to bring His love to every corner of the world. The very rhythm of the Divine Symphony—the Mass itself—proclaims that God's forgiveness and mercy have no limits. Every time we gather, we are reminded that our mission is not to fall into despair or darkness, but to live as radiant instruments of His compassion and healing. If God's desire were not to restore and heal, the gift of the Catholic Mass would not exist. But because His love is real and unending, we are continually empowered to go forth and become true agents of love and mercy, helping to renew the world in His image.

# Twenty-Second Sunday in Ordinary Time

# 24th Sunday in Ordinary Time

| | |
|---:|:---|
| First Reading | Sirach 27:30—28:7 |
| Responsorial Psalm | Psalm 103:1-2, 3-4, 9-10, 11-12 |
| Second Reading | Romans 14:7-9 |
| Gospel Acclamation | John 13:34 |
| Gospel Reading | Matthew 18:21-35 |

# The Liturgical Teaching on the Relationship Between Sin and Forgiveness

While the Book of Sirach does not have a definitive structure, the selected passage for the 24th Sunday in Ordinary Time (Sirach 27:30–28:7) addresses critical themes such as malice, anger, vengeance, and harmful speech. In these verses, Ben Sira teaches that wrath and anger are manifestations of a sinful nature, stating, "Wrath and anger are hateful things, yet the sinner hugs them tight." He further explains that clinging to these emotions stands in opposition to God's mercy and to the mercy we owe to others, who are made in God's image and likeness. The text urges, "Forgive your neighbor's injustice; then when you pray, your own sins will be forgiven. Could anyone nourish anger against another and expect healing from the LORD? Could anyone refuse mercy to another like himself and then seek pardon for his own sins? If one who is but flesh cherishes wrath, who will forgive his sins?"

Sirach's warnings against vengeance, anger, and wrath not only align with Christ's teachings in the Sermon on the Mount but also resonate in the Lord's Prayer, as found in the Gospels of Matthew and Luke: ". . . forgive us our sins or trespasses as we forgive those who sin or trespass against us." The imperative to forgive our neighbor is central to the teachings of Jesus Christ. Even as He was crucified, Jesus prayed, "Father, forgive them, they know not what they do." Most Christians recognize that receiving God's forgiveness is closely tied to our willingness to forgive others. Yet, many find it challenging to accept forgiveness without exceptions. For instance, some who oppose the death penalty make exceptions for serious crimes, while others who oppose abortion may allow for it in extreme cases. Similarly, the concept of forgiveness is often embraced in principle but resisted when it confronts our deepest wounds.

However, the gravity of the offense should not prevent us from forgiving. Christ forgave those who were actively killing Him—a profound example. If He could forgive under such circumstances, we are surely called to forgive those who wrong us, especially when our lives are not in danger. True Christian forgiveness is not about making exceptions or justifying our refusal to let go of anger; rather, it means following Christ's example and extending mercy even when it is most difficult. By doing so, we embody the heart of the Gospel and open ourselves to the healing and freedom that forgiveness brings.

This theme is also present in the Gospel reading from Matthew 18:21–35. Simon Peter asks Jesus, "Lord, if my brother sins against me, how often must I forgive? As many as seven times?" Peter's suggestion of seven times was generous compared to common standards, but Jesus responds, "I say to you, not seven times but seventy-seven times." This response contrasts sharply with Lamech's boast of vengeance in Genesis, where Lamech declares, "If Cain is avenged seven times, then Lamech seventy-seven times."[27] Here, Jesus replaces the cycle of vengeance with a call to boundless mercy. He then shares a parable about a king settling accounts, in which a servant, forgiven of a great debt, refuses to forgive another. The king, angered by this hypocrisy, delivers the servant to punishment until he repays his debt. Jesus drives the point home: "So will my heavenly Father do to you unless each of you forgives your brother from your heart."

The ability to forgive is itself a gift from God. God offers us the grace of forgiveness, healing our mind, body, and soul, and restoring our relationships with others and with Him. Since forgiveness is God's gift, we should not withhold it from anyone who seeks it. The Holy Eucharist, given to those who are free from sin, serves as a sign of God's forgiveness. We are therefore called to offer forgiveness as generously and frequently as possible.

---

[27] Genesis 4:23-24.

The call to let our lives reflect Christ's life is echoed in the Second Reading from Romans 14:7–9: "None of us lives for oneself, and no one dies for oneself. For if we live, we live for the Lord, and if we die, we die for the Lord; so then, whether we live or die, we are the Lord's. For this is why Christ died and came to life, that he might be Lord of both the dead and the living." This reflects the purpose for which Christ gave the Church the Sacraments—Baptism, Holy Eucharist, Penance and Reconciliation, the Anointing of the Sick, and the liturgy of the Mass.

God desires to forgive and heal us from the wounds of sin. In His abundant mercy, He has provided the four Sacraments and the liturgy of the Mass, making forgiveness accessible. Through the Lord's Prayer, He teaches us how to seek forgiveness beyond the Mass, while during the Mass, the priest prays for the forgiveness of venial sins. Ultimately, He invites us to receive sacramental absolution in Penance and Reconciliation. If God, in His infinite mercy, has made forgiveness so readily available, how much more should we strive to imitate His mercy in our own lives? As long as we live, let us endeavor to be merciful and forgiving, reflecting God's compassion in all we do. In this way, we mirror His love and mercy to the world.

# 25th Sunday in Ordinary Time

| | |
|---:|:---|
| First Reading | Isaiah 55:6-9 |
| Responsorial Psalm | Psalm 145:2-3, 8-9, 17-18 |
| Second Reading | Philippians 1:20c-24, 27a |
| Gospel Acclamation | Cf. Acts 16:14b |
| Gospel Reading | Matthew 20:1-16a |

# The Liturgy is Forming Us to Have a Holy Indifference

The prophet Isaiah extends an invitation for us to seek and call upon the Lord in chapter 55, which concludes the 'Book of Comfort' that commenced in chapter 40. This biblical passage has been designated as 'An Invitation to Grace' because it elucidates God's hope and mercy toward humanity. On the 15th Sunday in Ordinary Time, we heard verses 10 and 11; today, our focus is on verses 6 to 9. In these verses, Isaiah instructs, "Seek the LORD while he may be found, call upon him while he is near," and concludes with the statement, "For my thoughts are not your thoughts, nor are your ways my ways," declares the LORD. Some translations render this as, "For My plans are not your plans, nor are My ways your ways." These verses may seem contradictory if considered in isolation from the broader context of the Old Testament. This prompts an important question: how can we reconcile the perception of a God who is both near and accessible, yet also distant and transcendent? Is this God attainable or not?

Contrary to this, the Old Testament canon contains twenty-nine explicit instances of the phrase "seek the Lord," each of which associates the act of seeking the Lord with worship, sacrifice, or fidelity to the covenant. Numerous examples also link seeking the Lord to the heart, which represents the core of our identity and existence. Consequently, the Old Testament's perspective on our calling to seek the Lord provides a new understanding of Christ Jesus' words when He said, "Seek, and you will find,"[28] and "You shall love the Lord, your God, with all your heart, with all your soul, and with all your mind."[29] Furthermore, Christ Jesus renders the invitation to seek the Lord attainable, as He truly came near to us, lived among us, and continues to be present with us

---

[28] Matthew 7:7.
[29] Matthew 22:37.

and within us through the Liturgy of the Mass and the Sacraments, notably the Holy Eucharist. Therefore, although God remains transcendent, He is also fully human and fully divine, residing within us through the Holy Spirit to guide us into all truth, enabling us to understand His plans and ways and to respond to His grace by following them.

Imagine living a life so entirely devoted to God that, regardless of circumstances, you can confidently echo the courageous words of the Apostle Paul in his letter to the Philippians.[30] Even in prison, facing the threat of the death penalty, Paul proclaimed a powerful truth: he would magnify Christ through his body—whether by life or death. He joyfully declared, "Christ will be magnified in my body, whether by life or by death. To me, to live is Christ, and to die is gain. If I am to go on living in the flesh, that will mean fruitful labor for me; yet I am torn between the two. I desire to depart and be with Christ—what a far better thing!—but remaining in the flesh is more necessary for your progress and joy in the faith." This unwavering fidelity exemplifies the self-abandonment towards and deep trust in God's plan that we are called to abide in as followers of Christ. Let this inspire us to live with bold faith and unwavering hope, knowing that our lives can reflect the glory of Christ no matter the circumstances.

Indeed, every time we participate in the liturgy of the Catholic Mass, we are beautifully reminded that our lives are not our own—they belong to God. In surrendering everything to Him, we discover a profound freedom: when we seek God in all that we do, we become joyfully indifferent to the outcome of our efforts. This is not indifference born of apathy, but a holy trust, knowing that all results are in His hands. This trust fills our hearts with a deep and lasting joy and peace, for we truly belong to God, secure in His love and purpose for us. What a stark and wondrous contrast this is to a life spent chasing after fleeting things and bowing to the world's empty promises—a life that ultimately leaves us restless and dissatisfied.

---

[30] 1:20c-24, 27a.

When we become obsessed with controlling the outcomes of our actions, we open the door to doubt, anxiety, anger, and despair. Such burdens weigh on us only if we believe we are responsible for every success or failure. Yet, imagine the liberating truth: we are not called to possess the outcomes of our labor. Instead, we are invited to offer our best to God and trust Him with the rest. In this surrender, we find true freedom—not only to labor with hope and purpose but to rejoice, knowing that our faithfulness is fruitful in the hands of the One who loves us beyond measure. Let us embrace this holy indifference, confident that God weaves everything together for good, and rest in the peace that comes from entrusting all things to Him.

Imagine ourselves in today's Gospel Reading from Matthew 20:1-16a, in the midst of the vineyard, not as mere bystanders, but as laborers who have committed to a day's work under the sun, carrying the weight of fatigue and expectation. We know the terms; we accepted the usual daily wage with no complaint. Yet, as dusk falls and the wages are distributed, a disquiet stirs among us. To our astonishment, those who arrived just as the shadows lengthened—whose hands barely touched the vines—receive the same compensation. Our hearts flare with indignation, and we cannot help but question the fairness of the master. "These last ones worked only one hour," we protest, "and you have made them equal to us, who have borne the scorching heat and the toil of the day."

But then, the master's reply pierces through our grumbling: "My friend, I am not cheating you. Did you not agree with me for the usual daily wage? Take what is yours and go. Am I not free to give to the last as I give to you? Or are you envious because I am generous?" In this exchange, a deeper truth emerges—one that unsettles our notions of merit and justice. The vineyard, the tools, the labor, and even the wage are not ours by right but gifts from the master, who is free to bestow his generosity as he pleases. The parable reveals that in the kingdom of heaven, our focus is not to be on comparing ourselves with others or measuring what we have earned, but rather on embracing the privilege of working in the master's vineyard at all.

The story calls us to recognize that everything—our calling, our mission, even the results of our efforts—belongs ultimately to God. Our responsibility is not to control outcomes or demand equity as the world understands it, but to enter wholeheartedly into the labor assigned to us, carrying the mission and the cross Christ has entrusted to us. The reward, then, is not merely the wage at the end of the day, but the grace of being invited to participate in God's work, and to witness firsthand the boundless mercy and generosity with which He welcomes all, whether early or late. The last will be first, and the first will be last—not as a rebuke, but as an invitation to trust in the goodness of the master, who sees beyond our calculations and offers us His very self.

For this, we sometimes find it difficult to put our heads down, do the work, and not worry about the outcomes. Perhaps, to move past that concern, we should return to our consideration of the Apostle Paul in his imprisonment and adopt his attitude of holy indifference. Maybe in a world where we are surrounded by the troubles and machinations of evil people, we might discover our much-needed joy and peace if we seek the Lord rather than troubling ourselves with worrying about the outcomes of people's lives who do not seek the Lord, or worrying about the outcomes of people's lives who do not seek to live their lives liturgically. Not that we should be apathetic to their sins, but rather, if we focus on doing our labor well, we can trust that God will use the outcomes of our obedience to be an extension of His mercy towards them.

# 26th Sunday in Ordinary Time

| | |
|---:|:---|
| First Reading | Ezekiel 18:25-28 |
| Responsorial Psalm | Psalm 25:4-5, 6-7, 8-9 |
| Second Reading | Philippians 2:1-11 or Philippians 2:1-5 |
| Gospel Acclamation | John 10:27 |
| Gospel Reading | Matthew 21:28-32 |

# The Liturgy is Us, Taking Personal Responsibility for Our Lives

A quote traditionally attributed to Saint Ignatius of Loyola resonates deeply: "Work as if everything depended on you. Pray as if everything depended on God." This powerful paradox challenges us to embrace our personal responsibility while completely trusting in God's sovereign plan. Sacred Scripture beautifully reflects this delicate balance—Psalm 23 describes us as sheep, with the Lord as our shepherd, guiding and providing for us: "The Lord is my shepherd, there is nothing I shall want." Yet, Jesus also calls us to deny ourselves and take up our cross in Matthew 16:24-26, urging us to actively follow Him and live out our faith through our actions. This divine interplay between reliance on God's grace and our active participation forms the heart of authentic Christian living. It is succinctly encapsulated in the Pater Noster prayer and vividly brought to life in today's Readings for the 26th Sunday in Ordinary Time – Year A, inspiring us to trust in God's providence while dedicating ourselves to living virtuously.

Chapter 18 of Ezekiel, which some collections have subtitled 'Personal Responsibility,' is constructed in a distinctive hypothetical format, featuring several verses beginning with the word 'if' or the phrase 'but if' to illustrate the path of virtue through hypothetical scenarios. In the specific case of today's First Reading from Ezekiel 18:25-28, it is pertinent to include verse 20 beforehand, as it dismisses the notion that punishment for sin is inherited across generations in favor of individual responsibility and accountability, stating, "Only the one who sins shall die. The son shall not bear the guilt of the father, nor shall the father bear the guilt of the son. Justice pertains to the just, and wickedness to the wicked." In verses 21 through 24, the Lord teaches that He rejoices when the wicked forsake their evil ways and turn to Him, asserting that none of their transgressions shall be held against them. Conversely, the righteous who abandon justice to commit evil shall perish, and their righteous deeds shall be forgotten.

Some might think it is unfair that the Lord does not remember the good things the wicked man did before turning evil, or that He forgets the evil acts committed before he turned good. A part of us wants our entire lives to be judged and graded on a cumulative scale and averaged out. We want God to consider that we were excellent students during some periods, while failing in others. However, overall, we were above-average students, and that cumulative grade should matter on our judgment day. To these detractors, the Lord says, "You say, 'The LORD's way is not fair!'" Hear now, house of Israel: Is it my way that is unfair, or are not your ways unfair?" This is a reasonable response from God, given that He has communicated His standards to us from the beginning. Therefore, who are we to ask for personal exceptions to the standard?

In our Gospel Reading today from Matthew 21:28-32, Christ Jesus employs a parable to illustrate Ezekiel's call to personal responsibility, saying to the chief priests and elders of the people: "What is your opinion? A man had two sons. He came to the first and said, 'Son, go out and work in the vineyard today.' He replied, 'I will not,' but afterward changed his mind and went. The man came to the other son and gave the same order. He replied, 'Yes, sir,' but did not go. Which of the two did his father's will?" They answered, "The first." Jesus told them, "Amen, I say to you, tax collectors and prostitutes are entering the kingdom of God before you. When John came to you in the way of righteousness, you did not believe him, but tax collectors and prostitutes did. Yet even when you saw that, you did not later change your minds and believe him." It is truly comforting that we serve a God as magnanimous and merciful as this, that He does not hold our 'no' against us, as long as we get around to saying 'yes' before we die. Again, He is like the landowner who called laborers to his vineyard and paid them the same wage no matter when they arrived.

The reason our call to holiness is personal, why the sacraments are most efficacious in those who freely accept them, and why we stand alone before God on our judgment day is that we are only obedient to God to the extent that we love Him. If we love God, we also love neighbor and self; and if we love self, we take responsibility for our baptismal call to be holy because we have found nothing in this life greater than eternal life with God. This is why we attend the Holy Sacrifice—not because the precepts of the Church oblige us, but because we sense that there is no better outcome for our lives unless we respond to the divine love burning within us, drawing us closer to its source.

When we partake in the Holy Eucharist, we are consuming Christ Himself—His very Spirit and love. The more we receive Him, the more we begin to mirror His divine life in our lives, being made divine. As the Apostle reminds us in today's Second Reading from Philippians 2:1-11, we are called to embrace Christ's attitude of humility and personal responsibility. Think of His incredible sacrifice—though He was in the very nature of God, He chose not to cling to His equality but humbled Himself. He took on human likeness, became a servant, and willingly laid down His life for us—all because of His boundless love. Let us aspire to follow His example, embodying humility, selflessness, and love in our everyday lives.

# 27th Sunday in Ordinary Time

|  |  |
|--:|:--|
| First Reading | Isaiah 5:1-7 |
| Responsorial Psalm | Psalm 80:9, 12, 13-14, 15-16, 19-20 |
| Second Reading | Philippians 4:6-9 |
| Gospel Acclamation | Cf. John 15:16 |
| Gospel Reading | Matthew 21:33-43 |

# The Liturgy is the Fertile Ground, and We are the Harvest

The mercy of God is constantly evident through the methods He uses to teach us. Our Lord constantly interacts with us as if we were children, using familiar things like bread, wine, and water rather than unfamiliar devices. This approach shows His desire to connect with us in ways that are personal and accessible for everyone because He wants a close, personal relationship with all of us. Ultimately, His effort to communicate in a way we can understand was demonstrated, par excellence, by His becoming human—being born of a woman, being fed and protected as an infant, learning our ways as a child, and then living among us—walking, eating, teaching, and healing. All this was so that we might see His worth, but sadly, many failed to do so and accused Him of being just one of us.

We hear two stories concerning a vineyard in the First and Gospel Readings for Mass on the 27th Sunday in Ordinary Time. In ancient Palestine, vineyards, wine production, and wine consumption were integral aspects of daily life. For the Jewish community, these activities were widespread and readily accessible. Grapes constituted a significant agricultural commodity utilized for consumption and wine-making. In sacred Scripture, wine symbolizes life, vitality, joy, blessings, and prosperity. Within the New Covenant, wine embodies the Blood of Jesus Christ, through which He offers the promise of eternal life to all who partake. Sacred Scripture also employs vineyard imagery as a pedagogical tool to elucidate God's promises and warnings. For example, in Isaiah 65:20-22, the promise of a prolonged life is depicted through the image of individuals living long enough to enjoy the fruit of their vineyards. As vineyards and wine hold a significant place in both cultural and religious contexts, as reflected in the sacred Scriptures, it is not surprising that we are presented with parables related to vineyards.

## Twenty-Seventh Sunday in Ordinary Time

Having previously encountered the parable during the 25th Sunday in Ordinary Time concerning the vineyard owner, we are now granted the grace-filled opportunity to reflect upon a similar parable concerning another vineyard owner, as recorded in Matthew 21:31-43. This parable appears to be closely inspired by the vineyard song-parable from the First Reading, Isaiah 5:1-7, where God is depicted as the vineyard owner and Israel as the vineyard. In this passage, God expresses His satisfaction upon discovering fertile soil on a hillside, which He cleared of stones, tilled, and planted with the finest vines. Additionally, He constructed a watchtower and carved out a winepress. In summary, the owner undertook all necessary measures to ensure the vineyard's prosperity, with the reasonable expectation of a fruitful harvest. However, verse two concludes with the statement, "Then he waited for the crop of grapes, but it yielded rotten grapes."

In today's Gospel reading, Jesus presents the parable from a different perspective. Instead of concluding with a vineyard destroyed by rotten grapes, He describes the vineyard owner's actions: "He leased it to tenants and went on a journey. When harvest time approached, he sent his servants to the tenants to collect his fruit. However, the tenants seized the servants, with one they beat, another they killed, and a third they stoned." Subsequently, the vineyard owner dispatched a larger group of servants to gather the produce. Yet, they too were killed. Ultimately, the vineyard owner sent his son, anticipating that they would show him respect. Nevertheless, the text states, "They seized him, threw him out of the vineyard, and killed him." Jesus concludes this parable with a question, which in the Gospel of Mark (12:9) He answers Himself; however, in Matthew, He addresses the chief priests and scribes present, who questioned His authority, with the inquiry: "What will the owner of the vineyard do to those tenants when he comes?" They replied, "He will bring those wretched men to a wretched end, and lease his vineyard to other tenants who will give him the fruit at the designated times." Jesus responded, "Have you never read in the Scriptures: The stone that the builders rejected has become the cornerstone;

by the Lord has this been done, and it is marvelous in our eyes? Therefore, I say to you, the kingdom of God will be taken away from you and given to a people that will produce its fruit."

If you were paying attention, you might have noticed that the difference between these two parables was not just how they ended, but that they involved two different vineyards owned by the same vineyard owner. The owner's first vineyard was expected to have value because of how it was prepared and the choice vines planted there, but it became worthless. This contrasts with the owner's second vineyard, which was so valuable that several men risked their lives trying to gather its fruit. This second vineyard was the one God desired His house of Israel and the people of Judah to become in the First Covenant, or the first vineyard. However, in this parable, the tenants of this new vineyard are now trying to kill the Son of God, who has come for His Father's harvest.

How divinely marvelous is the liturgy of the Catholic Mass as it unfolds these parables within the presentation of the mysteries of Christ. The wine, which is the fruit of Christ's labors, becomes the fruit of eternal life; His Blood we consume and that lives in us as Him with the Holy Spirit. We are also the branches of His vine, which He has protected, surrounded with a hedge, built a watchtower around, and dug a wine press. Without delving into what these symbols might individually represent, we can simply say that God is protecting, watching over us, and preparing us for the harvest. The only thing we need to do is continue to grow in the vine by returning to the liturgy, which is a fertile field, as often as we can, to be fed and pruned with and by the Word of God, who is both the source of our life and our eternal destination.

With the unwavering assurance that God is firmly on our side, we rejoice boldly in the empowering words of the Apostle to the Philippians: "Do not be anxious about anything, but in every situation, by prayer and petition, with thanksgiving, present your requests to God. And the peace of God, which transcends all understanding, will guard your hearts and your minds in Christ Jesus." Let this truth ignite your faith, challenge your fears, and inspire you to walk in divine peace and joy!

# 28th Sunday in Ordinary Time

| | |
|---:|:---|
| First Reading | Isaiah 25:6-10a |
| Responsorial Psalm | Psalms 23:1-3A, 3B-4, 5, 6 |
| Second Reading | Philippians 4:12-14, 19-20 |
| Gospel Acclamation | Ephesians 1:17-18 |
| Gospel Reading | Matthew 22:1-14 |

# The Liturgy Wants You to Invite People to Come Feast with Jesus

Today's Readings at Mass for the 28th Sunday in Ordinary Time are rich with liturgical types, symbols, and imagery. They highlight the importance of reading the sacred Scriptures through the Liturgical Sense, as almost every verse is connected to something in the Catholic Mass.

Beginning with our First Reading from Isaiah 25:6-10a, the repeated phrase "on this mountain" signifies a people ascending or being called to the place where God resides, where He provides His people with a festive banquet of "juicy, rich food and pure, choice wines," symbolizing union with Him, freedom from death, peace, joy, and salvation. This powerful eschatological prophecy is prevalent throughout sacred Scriptures. In today's Responsorial Psalm 23:5-6, David affirms, "You prepare a table before me… my cup overflows… I shall dwell in the house of the Lord forever." Deutero-Isaiah 55:1-2 proclaims, "Come, buy wine and milk without money… listen, and eat what is good." The prophet Ezekiel states, "My dwelling place shall be with them, and I will be their God, and they shall be my people" (37:27). The Prophet Hosea promises, "I shall ransom them from the power of Sheol; I shall redeem them from Death" (13:14). Nevertheless, Isaiah 25:6-10 is unique in that it encapsulates the entire message of God's desire to be our provider and savior "on this mountain," linking provision and salvation with Zion, the liturgical center of worship and divine encounter.

The traditional interpretation of the Parable of the Wedding Feast in the current Gospel reading from Matthew 22:1-14 frequently highlights God's generously abundant invitation. However, for certain individuals, the King's call to his son's wedding might generate a sense of discomfort rather than pleasure. This resonates with the apprehensions of those who may hesitate to participate in Catholic worship, burdened by concerns of judgment for previous transgressions or the sufficiency of external appearances.

The narrative reveals a curious dynamic. The king did not extend a personal invitation; instead, "He dispatched his servants to summon the invited guests to the feast." Ordinarily, the promise of free food and lively company might suffice to draw a crowd, but "they refused to come." Even when a second invitation followed, the response escalated dramatically—some invitees "laid hold of his servants, mistreated them, and killed them." This shocking act of violence suggests that the relationship between the king and his people was steeped in complexity, hidden beneath the surface. The king's reaction was swift and severe: "He was enraged and sent his troops" to destroy the offenders and burn their city.

Finally, the servants combed "the main roads" to gather anyone they could find, "bad and good alike," until the banquet hall brimmed with guests. Yet even here, the story turns unsettling, as the king harshly rebukes a man for his improper attire. Could it be that the original guests avoided the feast not out of indifference, but out of apprehension? That is a real and relatable possibility.

For some, the kingdom of heaven, as Christians describe it, might evoke an image of an uncompromising judge rather than a compassionate host, a figure of stern authority rather than a merciful father. Who would dare attend a celebration or a Catholic Mass hosted by one they perceive as untrustworthy? And yet, the hesitations are familiar: Why does God ask so much—why can He not accept me as I am? Why must I change? What if I answer His call, only to find that I am still unworthy?

This parable, however, challenges us to rise above the burdens of our histories and the distortions of our perceptions. It invites us to consider the possibility of divine love untainted by our fears. It calls us to take the bold and audacious step of trusting in a love that transcends judgment, one that welcomes us to the feast, not as perfect beings but as guests willing to embrace the chance for grace.

This parable is also a profound question from God: When was the last time you truly trusted in the Sacred Heart of Jesus and boldly invited someone to encounter His love in His dwelling place? If fear or anxiety about their response has held you back, remember these powerful truths: First, as the Apostle reminds us in today's Second Reading from Philippians 4:12-14, 19-20, "I can do all things in him who strengthens me." You are fully capable, equipped, and empowered to reach out for the glory of God's goodness. Second, think about this—everyone you invite will remember your invitation. And if you hesitate to invite, they will also remember that you never reached out. So, step out in courage and faith—be the light and the vessel of God's grace. The challenge is before you: will you trust enough to act and transform lives through His love?

# 29th Sunday in Ordinary Time

| | |
|---:|:---|
| First Reading | Isaiah 45:1, 4-6 |
| Responsorial Psalm | Psalm 96:1, 3, 4-5, 7-8, 9-10 |
| Second Reading | 1 Thessalonians 1:1-5b |
| Gospel Acclamation | Philippians 2:15d, 16a |
| Gospel Reading | Matthew 22:15-21 |

# The Liturgy Teaches Us Who Created Us and Why He Created

On this Sunday's First Reading from Deutero-Isaiah's chapter on Prophetic Fulfillment in the New Exodus - Isaiah 45:1, 4-6, we encounter a remarkable prophecy about God's plan for His people. God announces that He will anoint Cyrus, a foreign king, as His instrument to liberate Israel from exile. This is an unprecedented act of grace, since Cyrus is not a believer in the God of Israel, but a worshiper of pagan gods. The text reads, "Thus says the LORD to his anointed, Cyrus, whose right hand I grasp, subduing nations before him, and making kings run in his service, opening doors before him and leaving the gates unbarred: For the sake of Jacob, my servant, of Israel, my chosen one, I have called you by your name, giving you a title, though you knew me not. I am the LORD, and there is no other; there is no God besides me. It is I who arm you, though you know me not, so that toward the rising and the setting of the sun people may know that there is none besides me. I am the LORD, there is no other."

The prophecy reveals that God is sovereign over all nations and history. He can use anyone, even an outsider, to fulfill His purposes. God also shows His love and care for Israel by calling them His chosen ones and His servants. He wants them to know that He alone is God, and there is no other. Given that the Old Testament uses the term 'messiah' only in regard to kings,[31] prophets,[32] and priests,[33] but never to point to the promised one to herald the final age of Israel, and given that the Jewish idea is that every generation has a messiah, the future foreign pagan king Cyrus being a messiah is not insensible.

The prophecy also contrasts the relationship between God and Cyrus with that between Cyrus and his own gods. In the ancient Near East,

---

[31] Cf. 1 Sam. 16:6; 2 Sam. 19:22.
[32] Cf. Ps. 105:15.
[33] Cf. Lev. 4:3; Dan 9:23-26.

kings claimed to have a special bond with their patron deities, often symbolized by holding their hands during coronation ceremonies. For example, the Cylinder of Cyrus, a clay document from the 6$^{th}$ century BC that records his conquest of Babylon, depicts him as a loyal devotee of Marduk, the chief god of Babylon. The cylinder also accuses Nabonidus, the last Babylonian king whom Cyrus defeated, of being a wicked tyrant who neglected Marduk and his temples. However, Deutero-Isaiah tells us that it is not Marduk who empowers Cyrus, but the true God of Israel. God says He will take hold of Cyrus' right hand and guide him to victory over his enemies. He will also give him access to hidden treasures and secret riches as a sign of His favor. However, Cyrus does not acknowledge or worship God or even know His name. He is unaware that he is being used by the Eternal God to bring about His will for His people.

Therefore, the prophecy shows us how God works in mysterious and surprising ways to fulfill His plan for salvation. He can use anyone or anything, even those who do not know Him or love Him, to advance His kingdom. He can also bless those who cooperate with His will, even if they are unaware of it. He is always in control and always true to His promises.

This theme of God calling us according to His purpose and mercy also appears in today's Second Reading from 1 Thessalonians 1:1-5b. In this passage, the Apostle Paul, Silvanus, and Timothy write a letter of encouragement to the church at Thessalonica. He says, "We give thanks to God always for all of you, remembering you in our prayers, unceasingly calling to mind your work of faith and labor of love and endurance in hope of our Lord Jesus Christ, before our God and Father, knowing, brothers and sisters loved by God, how you were chosen. For our gospel did not come to you in word alone, but also in power and in the Holy Spirit and with much conviction." Paul praises the community for responding to their call to conversion from paganism to Christianity. He reminds them that God Himself chose them. He also adds in vv. 6-7, "And you became imitators of us and of the Lord, receiving the word in great affliction, with joy from the Holy Spirit, so that you became a model for all the believers in Macedonia and in Achaia." In this way, he commends them for allowing themselves to be used as examples to non-believers for the glory of God through their imitation of Christ and the apostles, despite their suffering.

In the case of Cyrus, we heard about a future king who would not choose God but instead lean into his culture and tradition of trusting in false gods. However, God chooses him to fulfill His divine and perfect will. Then, regarding the Christian community in Thessalonica, we learned about converts to the faith who were on fire for having been chosen by God and rescued from serving false gods, so that they might be used to accomplish His divine and perfect will. Now, we come to the Gospel Reading from Matthew 22:15-21, where Jesus uses a simple question about census taxes to teach that everything created in the image of God belongs to God alone, asking, "Whose image is this and whose inscription?" They replied, "Caesar's." Then, he said to them, "Then repay to Caesar what belongs to Caesar and to God what belongs to God."

Some of us resemble King Cyrus in our misguided belief that we belong to ourselves, our tradition, or our culture. In that belief, we become slaves to lesser things than God, only to be used by God because His divine and perfect goodness will always be accomplished through us, whether we cooperate or not. Others of us are like the converts in Thessalonica. We genuinely believe in our calling and are thankful for it, and we do our best to be an example of who created us and why He called us.

Inasmuch as the liturgy of the Mass affords opportunities for both of these people to receive the grace of God, only the latter is disposed to witness how the liturgy is constantly showing us who we are and who God is. From the opening procession to every movement throughout the liturgy, we are reminded that we are being called to process towards God. The sacred Scriptures we hear at Mass remind us how much

God loves us, and we respond to Him, saying we love you too, saying, "Thanks be to God," "Praise be to you, Lord Jesus Christ."

The Holy Eucharist stands as a powerful and transformative testament to God's ongoing work within us. Consider this: if God can miraculously change simple bread and wine—mundane elements, symbols of human frailty and mortality—into His living, divine presence, how much more can He renew, enliven, and elevate those whom He has made in His own image and likeness?

The liturgy, like a loving yet challenging spiritual mother, not only teaches us how to walk in faith, speak with love, worship in spirit, pray with confidence, and confess with humility, but also sends us forth, not to be passive onlookers, but to become living witnesses. We are called to be the heartbeat of a genuine culture, the bearers of traditions rooted in truth, and the embodiment of authentic faith—a living answer to the deepest questions: Who made us? Why were we created? The world is waiting for witnesses, not mere words. Will we rise to the challenge, allowing the Eucharist to truly transform us, so that our lives echo the Creator's purpose and love for all to see?

# 30th Sunday in Ordinary Time

| | |
|---:|:---|
| First Reading | Exodus 22:20-26 |
| Responsorial Psalm | Psalm 18:2-3, 3-4, 47, 51 |
| Second Reading | 1 Thessalonians 1:5c-10 |
| Gospel Acclamation | John 14:23 |
| Gospel Reading | Matthew 22:34-40 |

# The Liturgy Equips Us to Love the Least Among Us

The Torah elucidates God's deep compassion for His chosen people and His intention to draw closer to those who are destined to enter the New Covenant. It demonstrates His love by providing a means for the foreigner and the alien to be accepted and embraced by His community, thereby allowing them to partake in the blessings of the future Church. It is His desire that His people do not harbor any resentment or prejudice against them, but instead recall their own history as strangers in Egypt.

The Torah distinguishes itself from other ancient Near Eastern legal codes, such as those of Eshununna, Hammurabi, and Assyria, by explicitly commanding its followers to love the foreigner and the alien as themselves. This directive goes beyond mere avoidance of harm; it encompasses treating them as members of one's own community.[34] In the First Reading for the 30th Sunday in Ordinary time – Year A, from Exodus 22:20-26, God admonishes His people not to oppress or mistreat these individuals but to identify with them, stating, "You shall not molest or oppress an alien, for you were once aliens yourselves in the land of Egypt." Furthermore, He warns of severe consequences if they wrong widows or orphans, emphasizing that if they cause any to cry out to Him as His people did during their own suffering in Egypt, He will respond with wrath: "If ever you wrong them and they cry out to me, I will surely hear their cry. My wrath will flare up, and I will kill you with the sword; then your own wives will be widows, and your children orphans."

This section of social laws further elucidates how specific statutes in today's First Reading exemplify God's compassionate regard for the impoverished members of His populace. These statutes prohibit the accrual of interest on loans granted to the impoverished and mandate the

---

[34] Cf. Lev. 19:33-34

return of their cloak as collateral before nightfall. The rationale behind these statutes is that the impoverished are already situated in a challenging circumstance, and the imposition of interest would merely intensify their difficulties. The cloak constitutes the most valuable possession of the impoverished individual, as it serves as their sole source of warmth during the night. These statutes demonstrate that God intends for lenders not to exploit the impoverished but to treat them with compassion and dignity. Furthermore, these laws resonate with other provisions in Deuteronomy which safeguard the rights of debtors and restrict the authority of creditors.[35]

In today's Second Reading from 1 Thessalonians 1:5-10, we observe how the Apostle Paul commends this community of converts from paganism for exemplifying adherence to the teachings of the Apostles and the Lord, despite facing numerous hardships. Through their steadfast perseverance in the faith, they have become "a model for all the believers in Macedonia and in Achaia." They serve as living testimonies to the power and glory of God; to such an extent that Paul does not find it necessary to preach the word of God elsewhere, as the message in Thessalonica resoundingly proclaims itself. In this manner, the converts' profound love of God significantly influences their neighbors in other cities and nations.

In today's Gospel Reading from Matthew 22:34-40, Jesus underscores the relationship between the love of God and the love of one's neighbor, as outlined in Exodus and 1 Thessalonians. He instructs us that the love of God bestowed upon us should overflow from our hearts and extend to those in greatest need. A Pharisee sought to challenge Jesus by inquiring, "Teacher, which commandment in the law is the greatest?" Jesus responded, "You shall love the Lord, your God, with all your heart, with all your soul, and with all your mind. This is the greatest and the first commandment. The second is similar: You shall love your neighbor as yourself. The entire law and the prophets depend on these

---

[35] Cf. Deuteronomy 24:6, 10-13.

two commandments." Jesus demonstrates that the law of God is not merely a collection of rules, but a way of life that undergoes a transformation from within. If we love God with our whole being, then we shall also love our neighbor as ourselves, because God's love resides within us and enables us to be a blessing to others.

As a living affirmation of today's divine theme, the liturgy of the Catholic Mass beautifully reveals itself as a profound good. It calls us to immerse our entire being into God, so that we may embody His likeness in the world. The liturgy not only enlightens and stirs us to pray and confess with heart, mind, and voice but also shapes our bodies—urging us to stand, sit, and kneel before God as outward signs of the inner transformation He is working within us. Furthermore, God Himself, through the Holy Spirit, dwells within us in the Holy Eucharist, transforming us into what we have received—not in vain, but to prepare us to be blessings to others. As we are sent forth from the liturgy through the sacred "*Ite, Missa est*," our lives become powerful witnesses of God's love and power. This love draws others near and far, inspiring them to recognize that God is real and His love surpasses all understanding. Together, we become living testimonies of His divine grace, shining His light into the world.

# 31st Sunday in Ordinary Time

First Reading   Malachi 1:14-2:2, 8-10
Responsorial Psalm   Psalm 131:1, 2, 3
Second Reading   1 Thessalonians 2:7b-9, 13
Gospel Acclamation   Matthew 23:9b, 10b
Gospel Reading   Matthew 23:1-12

# The Liturgy of the Catholic Mass is Our Way Home

As we approach the glorious Solemnity of Our Lord Jesus Christ, King of the Universe, the final Sunday in the liturgical year, the readings for the next three Sundays invite us to reflect on the joint mission of Christ Jesus and the Holy Spirit. The message for today's reading for the 31$^{st}$ Sunday in Ordinary Time is that we must pay attention to the intimate relationship between sacrifice and example. Indeed, those who are united with the sacrifice of Christ are worthy of following. In particular, His priesthood should serve as an example for us because it represents an extension of His presence among us. Conversely, if someone is not united with Christ, they are not on the path to Christ; instead, they are on the path of vanity, self-indulgence, pride, deceit, and perdition, and following them will only lead us to Hell.

When considering the oracle the Lord gave to the prophet Malachi in today's First Reading from Malachi 1:14-2:2, 8-10, it becomes evident to associate it with the ongoing crisis involving negligent individuals, heretics, and sexual deviants masquerading as priests and bishops that have persisted openly within the Catholic Church for over a century. The oracle states, "And now, O priests, this commandment is for you: If you do not listen, if you do not lay it to heart, to give glory to my name, says the LORD of hosts, I will send a curse upon you and of your blessing I will make a curse. You have turned aside from the way and have caused many to falter by your instruction; you have made void the covenant of Levi, says the LORD of hosts. I, therefore, have made you contemptible and base before all the people since you do not keep my ways but show partiality in your decisions."

The Book of Malachi, the final book of the Old Testament, composed approximately between 537 and 329 years prior to the incident when Jesus overturned the tables in the Temple, encompasses six oracles. These oracles are articulated as disputes in which the Lord responds to inquiries, elucidating the reasons for His anger towards Israel for violating the covenant established with them. In the context of the current passage, specifically in 1:6, the Lord asserts that the priests fail to honor Him appropriately, stating, "O priests, who despise my name." He then assumes their response of, "You say, 'How have we despised your name?'" and proceeds to answer the presumed question with, "By offering polluted food upon my altar. And you say, 'How have we polluted it?' By thinking that the Lord's table may be despised." This initial oracle demonstrates that God is displeased when priests exhibit contempt for the altar by presenting sacrificial offerings that are impure or unworthy of His name, such as blind, lame, sick animals, or animals obtained through violence.

As it was then, so it is today, where priests fall into the trap of believing that sacrifice on the altar belongs to them; that they can do whatever their hearts desire, as if the Lord has no concern for pure and worthy sacrifice. These priests now create their own words of sacrifice and craft self-indulgent liturgies. They display contempt for the sacrifice of the Mass by bringing worldliness into it. They treat the Mass as a social gathering and show no evidence that what we have been called to is a sacrifice in memory of Him who sacrificed His natural life for us so that we might have eternal life through Him.

Several years subsequent to Malachi's prophecy regarding the degraded state of the Mosaic priesthood, Matthew, in today's Gospel Reading from 23:1-12, provides an account of Jesus addressing the decline of the teaching establishment, stating, "The scribes and the Pharisees have assumed the seat of Moses. Therefore, adhere to and observe all that they instruct you, but do not imitate their conduct. For they preach, but they do not practice. They impose heavy burdens that are difficult to bear and place them on people's shoulders, yet they will not lift a finger to alleviate them. All their actions are performed to be seen by others. They enlarge their phylacteries and extend their tassels.

They seek honor at banquets, privileged seats in synagogues, greetings in marketplaces, and the salutation 'Rabbi'." Subsequently, in verses 12 through 16, Christ Jesus describes the scribes and Pharisees as prideful, hypocritical, and blind guides. Therefore, upon His incarnation, God not only found the Temple worthy of cleansing due to its transformation into a den of thieves, but also deemed the teachers of the Law and the Scriptures a curse upon the people.

Nevertheless, it is important to compare the Jewish teaching establishment, which Jesus indicated was unworthy of emulation, with the account of the period during which the Apostle Paul and his associates spent with the Thessalonians. As recorded in today's Second Reading from 1 Thessalonians 2:7-9, 13, the Apostle writes, "We were gentle among you, as a nursing mother cares for her children. With such affection for you, we were determined to share with you not only the gospel of God but our very selves, so dearly beloved had you become to us. You recall brothers and sisters, our toil and drudgery. Working night and day in order not to burden any of you, we proclaimed to you the gospel of God." Even after thousands of years, the love and humility expressed in Paul's words are still readily discernible. The essence of love is the desire for the best for the object of love, and through their exemplary conduct—desiring for others what is greater than themselves—such individuals demonstrate their humility.

In this sacred liturgy, the Catholic Mass stands as the beating heart of our faith, revealing its ultimate purpose: to lead each of us, wholly and without reservation, into communion with the Father, through the Son, in the power of the Holy Spirit. More than a ritual—more than words and gestures—the Mass is a divine summons to awaken from spiritual complacency and let the fire of God's love transform our very souls. Here, we are not passive observers but active participants in the mystery of salvation, invited to leave behind mediocrity and comfort for the radical, self-giving love of Christ. The liturgy challenges us to conform our lives ever more closely to Jesus, who is divine love incarnate; and in doing so, it commissions us to become living vessels of His mercy and compassion in a world aching for hope and healing. We are called not only to receive this love, but to radiate it—fearlessly and tirelessly—so that every life we touch might be drawn into the embrace of God's redeeming grace.

# 32nd Sunday in Ordinary Time

|  |  |
|--:|:--|
| First Reading | Wisdom 6:12-16 |
| Responsorial Psalm | Psalm 63:2, 3-4, 5-6, 7-8 |
| Second Reading | 1 Thessalonians 4:13-18 or |
|  | 1 Thessalonians 4:13-14 |
| Gospel Acclamation | Matthew 24:42a, 44 |
| Gospel Reading | Matthew 25:1-13 |

# The Call to Pursue Wisdom Outside of Liturgical Worship

In the Book of Wisdom 6:12-16, we encounter a passage that speaks to us on the 32$^{nd}$ Sunday in Ordinary Time – Year A. This passage is consistent with the genre of Hellenistic literature to which Wisdom belongs, aiming to instruct and encourage the Jewish community residing in Alexandria, Egypt, during a period of cultural and religious plurality. Distant from their homeland, the Jews of Alexandria faced the challenge of maintaining fidelity to their ancestral traditions and beliefs amidst the influence of diverse ideas and practices that could lead them astray or cause them to question their faith. In the current reading, the admonition is directed not to the kings of Israel but to foreign kings and judges who "rule over multitudes and boast of many nations" (v. 2).

Although these foreign rulers may have a reasonable sense that their rule was won through blood inheritance or conquering their foes, the Lord reminds them in the next verse that "your dominion was given you from the Lord, and your sovereignty from the Most High, who will search out your works and inquire into your plans, because as servants of his kingdom, you did not rule rightly, nor keep the law, nor walk according to the purpose of God." So, before we transition to the admonition in today's reading, the writer points out that God has the right to admonish because He is the source of their authority to rule. He is the judge who judges all; therefore, it is He whom they must obey.

Having established the authority of God to admonish the ruler, the message of mercy is equally elucidated. God demonstrates a compassionate interest in guiding the ruler by imparting wisdom, ensuring that the ruler neither offends Him nor consequently harms His people. This message is further reflected in verse 9: "To you then, O monarchs, my words are directly, that you may learn wisdom and not transgress."

Prior to imparting specific teachings, eight attributes of Wisdom are presented: (1) Wisdom is unfading and resplendent, signifying her enduring value; (2) Wisdom is readily perceived by those who love her, indicating that she is actively sought; (3) Wisdom makes herself known in anticipation of desire, suggesting her eagerness to reveal herself to those who seek her; (4) Those who seek her diligently from dawn will not be disappointed, as earnest pursuit is met with fulfillment; (5) Contemplation of wisdom leads to the highest form of prudence; (6) Maintaining vigilance for wisdom results in freedom from care; (7) Wisdom seeks out those worthy of her, reflecting her discerning nature; and (8) Wisdom graciously appears along one's journey, demonstrating proactive care and concern for seekers.

The sixth principle, regarding how the pursuit of wisdom encourages vigilance and attentiveness, is articulated by Jesus in the parable of the Ten Virgins found in today's Gospel Reading from Matthew 25:1-13. In this passage, Jesus states, "The kingdom of heaven will be like ten virgins who took their lamps and went out to meet the bridegroom. Five of them were foolish, and five were wise. When taking their lamps, the foolish ones brought no oil with them, but the wise brought flasks of oil with their lamps." It is noteworthy that all ten were sufficiently prudent to maintain their virtue and fulfill other necessary preparations; nevertheless, only five anticipated the possibility of the bridegroom's delay. Upon the bridegroom's arrival, the prepared virgins chose not to share their oil, thereby preserving the outcome for which they had diligently planned. While this response may initially appear contrary to specific Christian values—such as self-sacrifice and putting others first—a broader perspective suggests that the core message emphasizes the importance of wisdom in guiding our decisions and actions. Ultimately, the parable underscores the value of remaining prepared and allowing wisdom to inform conduct worthy of one's vocation.

Within the Catholic tradition, wisdom is understood with particular significance in light of Christ. It is recognized as one of the seven gifts of the Holy Spirit, as outlined in Isaiah 11:2-3, received during Baptism and affirmed through the Sacrament of Confirmation. Wisdom also serves as a foundation for hope, as emphasized by the Apostle Paul in today's Second Reading from 1 Thessalonians 4:13-18. This gift enables individuals to discern what is good and true, guiding them to live in a manner that prepares them for the resurrection and an eventual encounter with the Lord.

The liturgy of the Catholic Mass always pedagogically leads us to wisely prepare for the coming of Christ in His Quadruple Presence—through the sacred Scriptures, in each other, in the Priest acting in persona Christi, and in the Holy Eucharist—so that we can reasonably hope to receive Him after our judgment worthily. However, a deeper point is being made here about how we can pursue the gift of wisdom outside of liturgical worship. In the Book of Wisdom 7:26, wisdom is described as, "For she is the reflection of eternal light, the spotless mirror of the power of God, the image of his goodness." That is, wisdom is light from light, true God from true God, true goodness from true goodness.

This fact is why wisdom is an utterly vital pursuit — one that begins with a humble prayer to the Holy Spirit, asking Him to enlarge and fill our hearts with divine wisdom. How can we truly live our lives if not in constant communion with the Holy through liturgical worship? The parable of the ten virgins challenges us deeply: remain vigilant, pursue wisdom above all earthly pursuits, and prepare yourself for the coming of the Lord. Let this be a call to wakefulness, relentless pursuit of divine insight, and steadfast readiness."

# 33rd Sunday in Ordinary Time

First Reading    Proverbs 31:10-13, 19-20, 30-31
Responsorial Psalm    Psalm 128:1-2, 3, 4-5
Second Reading    1 Thessalonians 5:1-6
Gospel Acclamation    John 15:4a, 5b
Gospel Reading    Matthew 25:14-30

# The Liturgy is a Type of Mother Who Instructs Us

The final Sunday in Ordinary Time – Year A invites us to reflect upon the concluding chapter of the Book of Proverbs, which contains a distinguished and exquisite proverb that stands unparalleled within the wisdom literature of sacred Scripture. This passage is unique as it is the sole instance wherein a man shares a lesson learned from his mother. While we acknowledge that Mary, the Mother of God, imparted counsel to her Son during the story of the wedding at Cana in John's Gospel, we observe that Jesus never cites His mother as the source of any of His teachings, either in childhood or adulthood; he never states, 'My mother said this…' Moreover, in today's Second Reading from 2 Timothy 1:5, we learn that Timothy inherited his faith from his grandmother, Lois, and his mother, Eunice, yet neither does he cite their words directly.

Although Proverbs contains numerous verses emphasizing the significance of maternal instruction—such as 1:8, which states, "Listen, my son, to your father's instruction and do not reject your mother's teaching"—it is only in Proverbs 31 where we hear a mother's words articulated by her son. As an individual profoundly influenced by the teachings of his mother and grandmother, and who quotes their words to his children, I find great rejoicing in Proverbs 31.

I never received any positive guidance from my mother or grandmother on how to find or choose a good wife. They only expressed their opinions of the girls I liked or dated in negative ways; for example, saying, 'I don't like this or that about her.' However, they also influenced me through their actions as women and wives. I ended up marrying a woman who is very similar to my mother. So, I cannot relate to the words of wisdom that Lemuel, king of Massa, learned from his mother in the second part of Proverbs 31. My experience was more like the first part of the chapter, where his mother says, "What are you doing, my son!" Furthermore, every son knows that this is not a question but a statement, which does not expect a reply but a reflection.

King Lemuel's mother taught him that a good woman and a worthy wife are resourceful and invest only in things that are good. I relate to this wisdom because I have seen it in the women of my own family. My grandmother, who never had a formal education or financial independence, became a widow in her late fifties and had to figure out how to survive on her own. My mother, who never worked until my stepfather lost his job in the 1980s and then became abusive when he turned to alcohol, left him and raised five sons by herself. So, when I read in verses 13 and 17 of Proverbs 31—that a worthy wife "works with wool and flax ... she holds the spindle in her hand," I think of the hard work, resourcefulness, and resilience of these women. Verse 12, which says a worthy wife "brings him profit, not loss," or "good, not evil," in the lectionary's translation, reminds me that a good wife is a blessing to her husband and helps him avoid temptation. This is an essential lesson from King Lemuel's mother because a man faces many challenges and choices in life, and he needs a woman who is a helper rather than a hindrance.

Moving beyond the practical implications of the sacred text, one aspect of evidence is that these descriptions of a virtuous wife symbolize the motherhood of the Church; she is not only faithful, holy, and skilled, but also, through the liturgy of the Catholic Mass and the sacraments, she brings us good, not evil. We do not lose anything from her gifts; she invests in us. Her worth surpasses pearls, and she is a trustworthy reward. Verse 30, which states, "Charm is deceptive and beauty fleeting; the woman who fears the LORD is to be praised," warns King Lemuel that the world will not appreciate her as you do. The world might judge your wife as unattractive; it may fail to recognize her value or her true identity, but the world's valuation of her is not her real worth. Some may be dazzled by women who seem more charming and beautiful. However, they are not deserving of being your wife or deserving of praise because it is not fleeting qualities in a woman that reflect her eternal worth.

The mother of King Lemuel symbolizes the Church of Christ Jesus, the One, Holy, Catholic, and Apostolic Church that teaches and guides us through liturgy and sacraments. It is her breast, the Bride of Christ, on which we find nourishment and grace. Just as King Lemuel was taught to trust in the wisdom of a worthy wife, we also trust in the wisdom of the Church, for there is nothing harmful to our souls in her dogma.

The warning here is that relying on the wisdom of our mother is not a passive act. As the Apostle Paul wrote in today's Second Reading in 1 Thessalonians 5:1-6, trusting in the Lord is different from sleeping in the Lord, saying, "We are not of the night or of darkness. Therefore, let us not sleep as the rest do, but let us stay alert and sober." In other words, our Eternal Father constantly guides us to truth through His Son, Christ Jesus, and Christ, through the Holy Spirit and His Church, works through us to meet those He loves. Therefore, we pray and remain faithful, staying awake in Christ—always attentive to His call to serve Him, through which He pours His love into us and, through us, into our neighbors.

The Parable of the Talents in today's Gospel Reading from Matthew 25:14-30 shows us how God wants us to use the gifts and abilities He has given us. He has entrusted us with different talents and blessings, and He expects us to use them for His glory and the benefit of others. He does not want us to be lazy or afraid, like the servant who buried his talent in the ground and did not make any profit for his master. Instead, He wants us to be diligent and brave, like the servants who multiplied their talents and received their master's praise.

In this way, the liturgy of the Catholic Mass really nourishes us through its prayers of intercession and the Holy Eucharist, helping us to grow and bear fruit in our lives. We are encouraged not to shy away from the cross, but to face it with love and confidence. God will reward us according to our faithfulness and generosity. Therefore, honor your father and mother so that your days will be blessed.

# 34th Sunday in Ordinary Time (The Solemnity of Our Lord Jesus Christ, King of the Universe)

*Last Sunday in Ordinary Time*

| | |
|---:|:---|
| First Reading | Ezekiel 34:11-12, 15-17 |
| Responsorial Psalm | Psalm 23:1-2, 2-3, 5-6 |
| Second Reading | 1 Corinthians 15:20-26, 28 |
| Gospel Acclamation | Mark 11:9, 10 |
| Gospel Reading | Matthew 25:31-46 |

# The Liturgy is Christ Jesus Taking Responsibility for Us

The Solemnity of Christ the King, established by Pope Pius XI in 1925, celebrates Christ Jesus' sovereignty over all creation. It was created to counteract the rise of secularism and modernism that threatened to undermine the Christian faith and values.

The Apostle articulated that Christ is the creator and sustainer of all things, both visible and invisible, and that He holds supremacy over every power and authority. He also affirmed that Christ is the head of the church and the firstborn from the dead, signifying that He has triumphed over death and sin and has paved the way to eternal life (Cf. Colossians 1:16-18). Additional, Scriptures also bear witness to the kingship of Jesus Christ and His everlasting dominion over all creation, such as 1 Timothy 6:15, where He is referred to as "the King of kings and Lord of lords," John 18:36, where He declares that His kingdom is not of this world, Revelation 1:5, where He is described as "the firstborn of the dead and ruler of the kings of the earth," and Revelation 17:14, where He emerges victorious over His adversaries as "the Lord of lords and king of kings," and where His followers are designated as "the chosen and faithful."

The Solemnity of Christ the King was initially celebrated on the last Sunday in October before the Second Vatican Council shifted it to the last Sunday in November to align with the end of the liturgical year. This change highlights the link between the feast and the Advent Season, during which we anticipate Christ's coming in glory. The feast reminds us of Christ Jesus's universal and eternal reign over all creation, especially at a time when many have turned away from God and adopted the mantra that there is nothing greater than oneself, and they will act accordingly. Today, many trust more in human institutions like government, science, technology, and money than in God's providence. They behave as if they are their own gods, making decisions about life and death, rejecting their God-given identities as male and female, engaging in unnatural sexual acts, and committing many other evils that flow from the mantra of atheism.

In response to the atheist proclaiming that there is nothing greater than me and that I will act accordingly, the Catholic sings that Christ is my Eternal King, and I will act as such. Our song is not based on faith alone but on faith and a divine mountain of evidence throughout salvation history that Christ, our King, provides for us in every way and takes responsibility for having created us. He takes responsibility for our life as a shepherd for his sheep, as He proclaimed in today's First Reading from Ezekiel 34:11-12, 15-17, saying, "I will look after and tend my sheep. As a shepherd tends his flock when he finds himself among his scattered sheep, so will I tend my sheep. I will rescue them from every place where they were scattered when it was cloudy and dark. I myself will pasture my sheep; I myself will give them rest, says the Lord GOD. The lost I will seek out, the strayed I will bring back, the injured I will bind up, the sick I will heal, but the sleek and the strong I will destroy, shepherding them rightly." Therefore, why should we place our faith in things that do not have our best interests at heart, nor take responsibility for us as God does?

Our life is a rejection of the atheist mantra that there is nothing greater than myself, and I will act as such. According to today's Second Reading from 1 Corinthians 15:20-26, 28, everything that the atheist trusts and relies on is a fake sovereignty and an enemy of Christ, who will be destroyed. It says, "Then, at his coming, those who belong to Christ; then comes the end, when he hands over the kingdom to his God and Father when he has destroyed every sovereignty and every authority and power. For he must reign until he has put all his enemies under his feet. The last enemy to be destroyed is death. When everything is subjected to him, then the Son himself will also be subjected to the one who subjected everything to him, so that God may be all in all." Therefore, why should we put our faith in something that will be destroyed?

Christ Jesus is the greatest king of all because He alone became fully human like us; as Hebrews 2:17 says, "He had to become like his brothers in every way so that he could be a merciful and faithful high priest in service to God, and that he might make atonement for the sins of the people." Christ Jesus did not isolate Himself from us; instead, He embraced our human condition and continues to live with us through His word, His priests, His sacrament of the Holy Eucharist, and each one of us. Because Christ shared our humanity and lives in us, He knows us so well that He says that when we serve each other, we serve Him. This is the message of today's Gospel Reading from Matthew 25:31-46 about the judgment of nations where He identifies Himself with the thirsty, naked, hungry, ill, and imprisoned, saying, "Truly I tell you, whatever you did for one of the least of these brothers and sisters of mine, you did for me."

Christ Jesus is the greatest of kings because He cares for us like a good king cares for His people and servants. Instead of merely giving commands and laws to obey, He helps us with grace to follow Him. He is the worthiest king to follow because He is eternal, and where He leads us is eternal life. He is a loving king because He invites us to love as He loves by giving ourselves for others. He shows us how to love through the liturgy of the Mass, where He offers Himself on the altar of sacrifice. He not only calls us to love sacrificially but also teaches us how to do so by guiding all our faculties, senses, passions, and desires toward the altar, so that the bread we break can be shared with those in need and the cup we pour out can flow out to others. Becoming a Eucharistic people through Christ is how the kingdom of God is shared and how His sacrificial love is spread across the earth by those sharing in His sacrifice at the altar.

# The Season of Lent

# First Sunday of Lent

| | |
|--:|:--|
| First Reading | Genesis 2:7-9; 3:1-7 |
| Responsorial Psalm | Psalm 51:3-4, 5-6, 12-13, 17 |
| Second Reading | Romans 5:12-19 or 5:12, 17-19 |
| Verse Before the Gospel | Matthew 4:4b |
| Gospel Reading | Matthew 4:1-11 |

# The Liturgy Teaches Us How to Resist Every Evil Temptation

For the First Sunday of Lent in Year A, the compilers of our lectionary selected three readings intended to remind us that it is relatively straightforward to recognize when the Evil One is tempting us. The fundamental principle is that all temptations are evil whenever they involve an urge to acquire what is not rightfully ours; that is, anything that God has not bestowed upon us. In this context, the work of the Evil One is uncomplicated; his primary objective is to induce us to act contrary to our divine nature by exploiting our emotions and passions to covet what others possess. He tempts us not to desire the gifts bestowed upon us by God, but rather those granted to our neighbors. Consequently, succumbing to temptation essentially reduces us to the level of toddlers who crawl on the ground, grab anything within reach that does not belong to them, put it in their mouths, and then lament when it is taken away.

In my early thirties, I encountered a period in which I succumbed to temptation. My wife subsequently informed me of various remarks made by others, such as, "Why would he do that? He had everything," and, "What else did he need? He had a great life." Such comments overlook the fundamental nature of temptation and the reasons individuals may make regrettable choices. Temptation does not arise from contentment with what one already possesses; rather, it targets perceived deficiencies. The influences of the world, personal desires, and negative forces often convince individuals that they are entitled to things they do not have, thereby making them susceptible to temptation.

Regarding Adam and Eve in today's First Reading from Genesis 2:7-9 and 3:1-7, one might draw a parallel to the remarks made about me; "How could they give up everything?" "How could Adam not be a strong man and protect Eve?" and "God gave them a great life in the garden, what more could Adam and Eve want? Indeed, God breathed into his nostrils the breath of life, and thus man became a living being." Furthermore, God granted Adam paradise—the Garden of Eden. Consequently, when the serpent reappears, he does not tempt Eve with what is below, as God has already bestowed upon them the earth; rather, the serpent tempts her with what is above—what she does not possess. "No, God knows well that the moment you eat of it, your eyes will be opened, and you will be like gods, knowing good and evil." The woman perceived that the tree was good for sustenance, pleasing to the eye, and desirable for acquiring wisdom. Accordingly, she took some of its fruit and consumed it; subsequently, she shared some with her husband, who was present with her, and he ate as well. Once more, the question might be posed: 'What more could they desire?' They already possess knowledge of all that is good; why would they also seek to understand what is evil? It is not that Eve sought to comprehend evil; rather, she aspired to attain what she lacked—the same as what God possesses.

In today's Gospel Reading from Matthew 4:1-11, the Devil employs a consistent pattern similar to that used with Eve in the garden. He is unable to tempt Jesus with what is from above, as everything belongs to Him. Instead, on each occasion, the Devil attempts to exploit Jesus' emotions and passions to tempt Him away from what is from below, and each time, Jesus counters by directing him to what is from above. "If you are the Son of God, command that these stones become loaves of bread," he replied. "It is written: One does not live on bread alone, but on every word that proceeds from the mouth of God." Subsequently, the devil elevates Jesus to higher ground to reveal what is even further below. "Then the devil took him to the holy city, and made him stand on the parapet of the temple, and said to him, 'If you are the Son of God, throw yourself down." "Again, it is written, You shall not put the Lord, your God, to the test." The devil then ascends even higher to tempt Jesus with what lies further below. Then, the devil takes him to a very high mountain to show him all the kingdoms of the world in their splendor, and he says to him, "All these I shall give to you, if you will prostrate yourself and worship me." At this, Jesus responds, "Get away,

Satan! It is written: The Lord, your God, shall you worship and him alone shall you serve." The essence of the Temptation in the Desert event is that Jesus found nothing greater than God the Father Almighty.

That there is nothing greater than God is what the liturgy of the Mass is repetitiously trying to teach us. The Apostle, in today's Second Reading from Romans 5:12-19, encapsulates the fundamental purpose of the liturgy; he writes, "For if, by the transgression of the one, death came to reign through that one, how much more will those who receive the abundance of grace and of the gift of justification come to reign in life through the one Jesus Christ." Truly, it is through the Sacraments of the Church, especially the Sacrament of Baptism and the Sacrament of Holy Eucharist, that the reign of eternal life—manifested through the Holy Spirit and Jesus Christ—truly dwells within us. For if God reigns within us, how can there be any space within us for sin and death to also reign?

Furthermore, the Divine Symphony calls us to mirror the resistance to temptation exemplified by our Lord and Savior. It reminds us that nothing surpasses God in greatness. Anyone who seeks something greater than God treads the perilous path toward eternal damnation. In the liturgy of the Mass, we are continually called to ascend—reminding us that what lies below is never worth our attachment.

The most powerful moments of the Mass are its elevations: the procession to the sanctuary, symbolizing a voyage to Jerusalem; the lifting of the Gospels above the minister's head; the elevation of the consecrated Body and Blood of Christ; and the raising of the Corpus Christi before us. These sacred elevations serve as unwavering signals that our desires must be fixed upon what is heavenly, not earthly. If we align our desires solely with what God wills for us—rejecting temptations and worldly distractions—there is no evil force that can successfully prevail against us. Therefore, let us accept this divine calling to elevate our hearts and minds, resisting temptation with unwavering resolve and steadfast faith.

First Sunday of Lent

# Second Sunday of Lent

| | |
|---:|:---|
| First Reading | Genesis 12:1-4a |
| Responsorial Psalm | Psalm 33:4-5, 18-19, 20, 22. |
| Second Reading | 2 Timothy 1:8b-10 |
| Verse Before the Gospel | Matthew 17:5 |
| Gospel Reading | Matthew 17:1-9 |

# The Liturgy Wants to Make Us Uncomfortably Comfortable

Cooperating with God always sparks a sense of possibility and purpose, inspiring us to live life with passion and faith. It's a beautiful idea—until God gently guides us to face challenges or step into the unknown. Embracing His grace can be easy when it invigorates us, but genuine growth often begins when cooperating with God pushes us beyond our comfort zones. This divine partnership invites us to transform obstacles into opportunities and trials into triumph in Christ for deeper faith and greater testimony.

What I always loved about this First Reading for the Second Sunday of Lent – Year A from Genesis 12:1-4, is how magnanimous God is with His blessings upon Abram. He asked Abram to do one thing, which was not a simple ask, saying, "Go forth from the land of your kinsfolk and from your father's house to a land that I will show you."

I believe that for most people, especially in a time before moving vans, packers, and storage pods, moving when it is something you had planned is difficult enough, but being called to move—suggestively evicted, in a sense, by God—is even more challenging. We cannot underestimate how comfortable Abram's life must have been. He was living in the home he grew up in, surrounded by family; he was already married to Sarai, and he had his brother's son Lot with them.

Genesis 12:5 reveals that Abram and his household had amassed a considerable number of possessions, as well as several individuals who had been acquired from Haran. This fact indicates that Abram's life was bustling with activity and responsibilities, all while he remained unaware of the destination to which God was leading him. Despite this uncertainty, Abram's response is significant and marks a turning point in salvation history. In this passage, God establishes a covenant of promise with Abram, stipulating that if Abram fulfills God's specific command—namely, to leave his homeland and journey as directed—God will grant him two distinct blessings, and extend two additional blessings to those who receive Abram.

The profound aspect of this covenant lies in the personal manner of God's commitment. God declares, "I will make of you a great nation, and I will bless you; I will make your name great, so that you will be a blessing." These promises are given directly to Abram in recognition of his willingness to leave behind the familiar and venture into the unknown. Furthermore, God states, "I will bless those who bless you and curse him who curses you; and in you, all the families of the earth shall be blessed." The passage concludes with the pivotal affirmation: "Abram went as the LORD directed him."

Our lives do not always permit us to witness all of God's blessings; however, when we love God, we collaborate with Him. As the Second Reading from Second Timothy 1:8-10 reminds us today, we work together with God and His grace to attain salvation and holiness. This matriculation in the liturgical life is achieved "not according to our works but according to his own design and the grace bestowed on us in Christ Jesus before time began, but now made manifest through the appearance of our Savior Christ Jesus." The phrase "made manifest" in this context references the life of Jesus of Nazareth, the Messiah, the Son of Man who walked among us. Additionally, this phrase functions as an idiom for the Holy Eucharist—Jesus Christ, who is made manifest through His appearance as bread and wine. Consequently, as long as we remain obedient to God, we will be granted the strength and assistance necessary to endure the hardships associated with our calling. We invoke this divine assurance through prayer, asking God for our daily bread.

In today's Gospel reading from Matthew 17:1-9, the Transfiguration is incorporated into our Lenten journey this season. "Jesus took Peter, James, and John, his brother, and led them up a high mountain by themselves. And he was transfigured before them; his face shone like the sun and his clothes became white as light. And behold, Moses and Elijah appeared to them, conversing with him. Then Peter said to Jesus in reply, "Lord, it is good that we are here. If you wish, I will make three tents here, one for you, one for Moses, and one for Elijah.'" Simon Cephas's response to this profound consolation and blessing received by him, James, and John exemplifies the human tendency to seek comfort. Regardless of the circumstances surrounding us, our primary desire remains to create comfort for ourselves and those close to us. However, this is not the central theme of today's readings.

Lent serves as a period for reflection and contemplation on the fact that God persistently urges us to venture beyond our familiar comfort zones and embrace a liturgy of discipleship, which can often be challenging. For example, in this context, when Simon Cephas was still speaking, a luminous cloud overshadowed them, and from the cloud a voice proclaimed, "This is my beloved Son, with whom I am well pleased; listen to him." Upon hearing this, the disciples fell to the ground in reverence and experienced profound fear.

In processing us through salvation history; from creation to the cross, and by calling us to stand, sit, and kneel—not when we want to, but when the liturgy calls us to do so—praying and confessing, not with our own words, but with what the liturgy prompts us to pray and confess, the liturgy aims to make us uncomfortable in our own space and thoughts. This discomfort helps us become more at ease in God's space and His desires, while also making us more uncomfortable in pursuing our own desires and more comfortable in cooperating with God.

Furthermore, the liturgy processes us through the entire liturgical year, from Advent to Ordinary Time, then Lent, Easter, Pentecost, and back again to Ordinary Time. It reminds us that we are pilgrims, bearing our crosses to Calvary. As a nomadic people, we journey through deserts and valleys toward our inheritance. The closer we approach home, the more uneasy we become in the world, and the longer we travel, the lighter our load from worldly cares becomes.

Let us allow this sacred rhythm to challenge and transform us. Each season beckons us not merely to observe, but to participate fully—to welcome discomfort and uncertainty as the very tools by which God molds our hearts. As we walk this path together, may we retire our desire for ease and instead pursue the deeper courage and faith that true discipleship demands. Let us not shrink back when God calls us to leave behind comfort zones, but step forward with trust, knowing that only by daring to follow Him into the unknown do we discover our truest selves and the fullness of His blessings. In embracing the journey, may we inspire others by our witness, becoming living signs of hope, perseverance, and unwavering love for God. The pilgrimage is not just toward a distant homeland—it is into the heart of Christ Himself. Will you accept the challenge to be transformed, to walk boldly, and to let go of what holds you back so that you might become all that God is calling you to be?

# Third Sunday of Lent

First Reading   Exodus 17:3-7
Responsorial Psalm   Psalm 95:1-2, 6-7, 8-9
Second Reading   Romans 5:1-2, 5-8
Verse Before the Gospel   John 4:42, 15
Gospel Reading   John 4:5-42

# The Teachings of the Liturgy Versus the Quarrelsome Spirit

Reflecting on the readings from the Second Sunday of Lent, we recognize the profound challenge rooted in our human desire for comfort. Yet, amid this challenge, we are invited to listen to the Divine Symphony—an inspiring call to embrace a transformative journey of being comfortably uncomfortable in the world; that is, to be in the world but not of it. As a holy people, we are called to stand firm in a world that often celebrates sin and persecutes righteousness. Today, for the Third Sunday of Lent – Year A, we delve deeper into another compelling human inclination, encouraging us to grow in faith, courage, and unwavering commitment to our divine calling.

From Exodus 17:3-7, "In those days, in their thirst for water, the people grumbled against Moses, saying, 'Why did you ever make us leave Egypt? Was it just to have us die here of thirst with our children and our livestock?" So Moses cried out to the LORD, "What shall I do with this people? A little more and they will stone me!" The more distant we feel from the person whom we wish to love us, the more we tend to act out – the more demonstrations we make, attempting to capture their attention. We express our frustration, our anger, and our displeasure at having believed the narrative we have constructed — that the individual we love does not prioritize us as we desire. If this reflection has reminded you of a relationship with a loved one, you have not missed the point.

The more false narratives that individuals in relationships internalize about one another, the greater the strain on the relationship, as deception inherently causes division. An illustrative example is the self-deception among the Israelites, who falsely claimed, 'Moses, it was you who compelled us to leave Egypt.' However, did not Moses explicitly inform Pharaoh that it was God who commanded the release of His people? Did not God part the Red Sea as recorded in biblical accounts? Furthermore, Exodus 2:23 clearly states, "A long time passed, during which the king of Egypt died. The Israelites groaned under their bondage and cried out, and from their bondage their cry for help went up to God." Nevertheless, the prevailing false narrative today is that Moses coerced them out of Egypt and is now urging them to perish from thirst in the desert.

Whenever God does not provide for us as we expect, the human tendency is to forget about everything He has done for us in the past and start to distrust Him. Myopically, we retreat into asking, 'What has God done for me lately?" Whenever that happens, we either turn away from God by taking matters into our own hands—because we believe we can do everything better and faster—or we start to complain, quarrel, see ourselves as victims, and launch grievances against God. In both cases, we unnecessarily create distance between ourselves and God due to a lack of trust and patience. In this particular situation, God was merciful enough with the Israelites to provide water from a rock.

Regarding the Israelites' dispute with God over their thirst in the desert, the compilers of the lectionary have chosen to juxtapose this narrative with John 4:5-52. In this Gospel passage, a Samaritan woman engages in a disagreement with Jesus at a well located in the city of Sychar, a place forsaken by the Jews spiritually. From the beginning of the story, discrepancies become evident. "There is a woman of Samaria who came to draw water," the text states, and Jesus addresses her, saying, "Give me a drink." Not only does she refuse to comply, but when the disciples return from the town with food, Jesus declares that He does not require sustenance, stating, "I have food to eat of which you do not know. . . . My food is to do the will of the one who sent me and to finish his work." It is clear, therefore, that Jesus does not rely on food or water. Yet, He just asked this woman of Samaria for water; so what is really going on here?

Well, we find out the answer to that question rather immediately. This Samaritan woman is very quarrelsome, and obviously, Jesus knew that. She is also very observant. She clearly identifies Jesus as not only being from outside of Sychar but as a Jew, and rather than just give the man sitting at the well some water to quench His apparent thirst, she decides to launch into the historical grievance between Jews and Samaritans, saying, "How can you, a Jew, ask me, a Samaritan woman, for a drink?"—for Jews use nothing in common with Samaritans, and later she continues with the historical grievance, saying, "Sir, I can see that you are a prophet. Our ancestors worshiped on this mountain, but you people say that the place to worship is in Jerusalem."

Consequently, we begin to comprehend why it was this woman at the well whom Jesus interrupted. The Samaritan woman exhibits a confrontational attitude towards Jesus, stemming from her sense of being broken and her perceived distance from God for various reasons. She is conflicted regarding her traditional worship practices, which acknowledge only the Pentateuch as God's word and involve worship at Mount Gerizim, rather than at the Holy Temple in Jerusalem. Additionally, she is involved in an adulterous relationship, and at every juncture, Jesus corrects the false narratives that have shaped her life. The water for which she approached this cistern at noon is not present here; rather, I am the source of living water, and "whoever drinks the water I shall give will never thirst." It is indeed a misconception that one can worship God on Mount Gerizim; "You people worship what you do not understand; we worship what we understand, because salvation is from the Jews. But the hour is coming, and is now here, when true worshipers will worship the Father in Spirit and truth; and indeed, the Father seeks such people to worship him. God is Spirit, and those who worship him must worship in Spirit and truth."

Notice how it was Jesus' deconstruction of the stories that had defined this Samaritan woman's life that led to her conversion. The text says, "Many of the Samaritans of that town began to believe in him because of the word of the woman who testified, 'He told me everything I have done." When the Samaritans came to him, they invited him to stay with them, and he stayed there two days. Many more began to believe in him because of his word, and they said to the woman, "We no longer believe because of your word; for we have heard for ourselves, and we know that this is truly the Savior of the world."

There is no greater pitfall or human folly than placing hope in a lie; hoping in a false narrative or an imaginative story that we have repeatedly told ourselves. Lies cause harm, particularly the lies we impose upon ourselves. However, when the Second Reading from Romans 5:1-2, 5-8 teaches us that, ". . . hope does not disappoint, because the love of God has been poured out into our hearts through the Holy Spirit who has been given to us," we are reminded that truth itself has made His dwelling within us. Therefore, what is the advantage of residing in the false reality of a lie when truth itself is shaping our nature to align with it?

When Catholics believe that God became man so that man can become like God, that also means believing in the saying that "Truth became man so that man can live in the truth." The Second Reading also points to the liturgy of the Mass itself, saying, "But God proves his love for us in that while we were still sinners Christ died for us." The memorial sacrifice on the altar, as Mass—Christ being crucified for us so that we might have life—is the central truth of the entire universe.

This truth is recapitulated from the rising of the sun until its setting at every Holy Mass, where a true sacrifice is offered to God. If you want to know the truth, go to Mass and then live that truth in your own life. For we are not only commanded to live in that truth of God's love for us, but we are equipped and empowered to live that truth because we have God the Holy Spirit in us—pressing us—awaking us—sanctifying us—propelling us to be a holy people.

Living in this truth means that we have nothing to quarrel with God about because it would be like quarreling with ourselves. However, the dark world that rejects the light of Christ has much to quarrel with us about. That is precisely why the liturgy of the Mass fills us with His peace and grace before we are sent back out into it, so that we might give away to the world what the God who loves the world has given us to share.

# Fourth Sunday of Lent

| | |
|---:|:---|
| First Reading | 1 Samuel 16:1b, 6-7, 10-13a |
| Responsorial Psalm | Psalm 23: 1-3a, 3b-4, 5, 6 |
| Second Reading | Ephesians 5:8-14 |
| Verse Before the Gospel | John 8:12 |
| Gospel Reading | John 9:1-41 |

# The Liturgy of the Catholic Mass Leads Us into a Spiritual Awakening

On Laetare Sunday, the Fourth Sunday of Lent, the Church shifts from its usual focus on penance to celebrate the joy of God's presence among us. During this liturgy, we are invited to awaken and engage all our spiritual senses, recognizing that through the Mass we can truly see, hear, touch, taste, and smell God in our midst. The entrance antiphon's call, "Laetare, Jerusalem," encourages us to set aside our penitential practices for a time, so that we may embrace hope and renewal as we move closer to the joy of Easter.

In the context of today's Mass readings and their liturgical significance, we remember King David, who sang in Psalm 35:9, "Then my soul will rejoice in the LORD, exult in God's salvation." We also recognize the Blessed Mother, who sang in her Magnificat, "My soul proclaims the greatness of the Lord; my spirit rejoices in God my savior."

The tripartite conception of the soul — as explored by Plato and later examined by Saint Augustine and Saint Thomas Aquinas — posits three distinct aspects of the human person: the rational, which governs thought and wisdom; the spirited, which energizes courage and moral resolve; and the appetitive, which responds to bodily desires and needs. Origen articulated the tripartite nature in this manner, stating, "It is the Logos which is at the center of us all, without our knowing, for the center of man is the heart, and in the heart there is the guiding energy of the whole, which is the Logos."[36] In Catholic theology, these dimensions find resonance in the understanding of body, soul, and spirit — not as mere parallels, but as intricately interconnected facets of the person that collectively reflect the imago Dei, the divine image, in which humanity is created.

---

[36] Joseph Ratzinger, *Behold the Pierced One* (San Francisco: Ignatius Press, 1986), 67.

Consider entering a cathedral to anchor Plato's tripartite soul within lived experience. Within this sacred space, your senses perceive the multicolored light through stained glass windows, and your auditory senses discern the echoes of chant or the profundity of silence—responses from the appetitive aspect, attracted to beauty and ambiance. However, your engagement extends beyond mere sensory perception: your rational faculties analyze the architecture and symbolism, contemplating their theological significances, potentially leading to reflections on eternity or sacred Scripture. Subsequently, surpassing mere thought, your spirited aspect may be activated—aroused by sacred art, memory, longing, or awe—responding with reverence and moral resolve. This movement from perception to contemplation to spiritual emotion exemplifies the harmony envisioned by Plato and signifies a soul oriented towards the pursuit of truth.

Building upon this framework, Plato's tripartite soul corresponds significantly with the Catholic Church's teaching that the human person, created in the image of God, possesses a distinctive capacity for communion with the divine. Even through sensory perception, we encounter God — we can genuinely hear, see, feel, smell, and taste His presence in creation and the Sacrament. Because we can perceive God through our senses, we are able to contemplate Him; and because we can contemplate God, we are capable of worship, reverence, response, and obedience toward Him. This ascending matriculation from perception to contemplation to devotion exemplifies the spiritual architecture of the soul, ordered towards an intimacy with the Creator, so that we may know, love, serve, and find happiness in Him both in this life and in the life to come.

Through the liturgy of the Catholic Mass, God reveals His mercy by allowing us to experience Him through our senses: sight, hearing, taste, touch, and smell. However, His greatest gift is not just awakening our senses, but awakening our rationality—our logos—so that we might come to know the Logos of God. In knowing God, our soul grows and is animated by the Holy Spirit, becoming more like Him. In other words, the ability to contemplate God enables us to imagine and pursue a life with Him. Misusing this ability by reimagining God as something He is not—either by reducing Him to meaninglessness or confining Him to the unknowable realm of Gnosticism—is a disordered use of this gift.

All those adopted as sons and daughters of God through baptism into the Body of Christ have received the first part of their inheritance—the Holy Spirit who dwells in us. This Spirit gives us the right to call God our Father and to see His Son. Therefore, those who can see God can see as God. However, this gift is one that grows and matures in us as we work on purification. As Christ Jesus taught, "Blessed are the clean of heart, for they will see God."[37] Indeed, a pure heart comes through prayer, penance, and sacrifice.

In today's First Reading from *1 Samuel* 16:1b, 6-7, 10-13a, this journey from perception to contemplation to devotion finds vivid expression in 1 Samuel 16:1b, 6–7, 10–13a. Samuel, attuned to his capacity to hear God, does not choose Eliab based on appearance or expectation. Instead, he listens beyond the surface, discerning God's desire and anointing David, the least likely candidate in human eyes. Had Samuel relied solely on natural sight, he would have missed the divine call. But by opening himself to God's vision, he was stirred to act according to divine wisdom. As the Lord declares, "Not as man sees does God see." True spiritual discernment requires allowing each part of the soul to be shaped by grace, so that we may respond to God's voice, even when it defies expectation.

In the Second Reading from Ephesians 5:8-14, the Apostle further emphasizes the theme of spiritual awakening, stating, "You were once darkness, but now you are light in the Lord. Live as children of light." This exhortation to transformation reflects the soul's progression from sensory perception to contemplation and ultimately to divine response. Just as Samuel learned to see with God's eyes, Paul encourages us to walk in the light — revealing what is concealed, discerning what pleases

---

[37] Matthew 5:8.

the Lord, and awakening from spiritual slumber to receive Christ's illumination.

The Gospel from John 9 vividly narrates this: a man born blind is healed by Jesus, not merely physically but also spiritually. His journey reflects our own—from blindness to sight, from confusion to confession, from perception to worship. "I do believe, Lord," he affirms, and he worships Him. This sign represents our soul fully awakened, with every aspect—appetitive, rational, spirited—responding in concordance to the presence of God.

Throughout today's readings—from Samuel's insightful gaze beyond Eliab, to Paul's uplifting call to walk as children of light, to the man born blind who comes to see and worship—one powerful truth shines brightly: God does not see as we see, and a misguided heart perceives only itself. While our fleeting senses may grasp surface appearances, the Lord Heavenly perceives the depths of our hearts, recognizing our true needs and gifts. Lent summons us to purify our appetites and hearts, to enlighten our minds, and to awaken our spirits so that every part of us may learn to see through God's divine perspective. On this joyful Laetare Sunday, may grace transform our senses, intellect, and emotions, inspiring us to rejoice in His radiant light and to carry the vision of Easter boldly in our hearts, guiding us every step of our renewed journey.

# Fifth Sunday of Lent

First Reading    Ezekiel 37:12-14
Responsorial Psalm    Psalm 130:1-2, 3-4, 5-6, 7-8
Second Reading    Romans 8:8-11
Verse Before the Gospel    John 11:25a, 26
Gospel Reading    John 11:1-45

# The Liturgy Empowers and Equips Us to Bring the Dead to Life

Our God is a God of life. He bestowed life upon us initially when He exhaled His breath into the nostrils of man, thus qualifying man as a living soul. Prior to God's gift of life, man was lifeless. Subsequently, the Son of God breathed upon the Apostles, stating, "Receive the Holy Spirit. If you forgive the sins of any, they are forgiven; if you retain the sins of any, they are retained," thereby indicating that through the power of the Holy Spirit, the Apostles and their successors possess the authority to deliver us from death and sin, restoring us to life and freedom in Christ. Additionally, when the Apostle Peter describes the sacred Scriptures as "God-breathed" in Second Timothy 3:15, he affirms that true life and freedom are attained through the reception of the Holy Spirit's life, encompassing the written word of God, which He inspired. Therefore, the breath of God can be defined as that which imparts life. In a similar way, the liturgy instructs us in how to speak so that, filled with the Holy Spirit, our words may also bring life to those around us.

For the Fifth Sunday of Lent – Year A, we hear a section of the first of two divine promises communicated to the Prophet Ezekiel concerning the restoration of life to the twelve tribes of Israel. The passage from Ezekiel 37:12-14 is introduced with a vision granted to Ezekiel, depicting a valley filled with dry bones. In this vision, the Lord delivers two prophetic messages to Ezekiel, regarding how He will restore these bones to life through His breath and Spirit. Ezekiel then articulates these divine words to the bones—representing "the whole house of Israel." Subsequently, the Lord imparts a final prophetic instruction: "Therefore, prophesy and say to them: Thus says the Lord GOD: Look! I am going to open your graves; I will cause you to come up from your graves, my people, and bring you back to the land of Israel. You shall recognize that I am the LORD when I open your graves and cause you to come out of them, my people! I will put my Spirit within you so that you may come to life, and I will settle you in your land. Then you shall acknowledge that I am the LORD. I have spoken; I will accomplish this—oracle of the LORD."

In today's Second Reading from Romans 8:8-11, we encounter a portion of the Apostle Paul's words of encouragement to the Church in Rome regarding their calling to live a life guided by the Spirit. He affirms, "... the law of the Spirit of life in Christ Jesus has set me free from the law of sin and death." For Paul, there exists an internal conflict; our minds can be led astray by unchaste emotions and passions, which tempt the flesh to pursue desires that ultimately result in spiritual death.

The higher and true calling for the Christian is to live their life not in accordance with the desires and commands of the flesh, but in alignment with the desires and liberty granted by the Holy Spirit. As it is written, "those who are in the flesh cannot please God. But you are not in the flesh; on the contrary, you are in the Spirit, if only the Spirit of God dwells in you. Whoever does not have the Spirit of Christ does not belong to him. But if Christ is in you, although the body is dead because of sin, the Spirit is alive because of righteousness. If the Spirit of the one who raised Jesus from the dead dwells in you, the one who raised Christ from the dead will give life to your mortal bodies also, through his Spirit dwelling in you." What a wonderful message for us to be reminded of as we approach the anniversary of our Baptisms, when we first received the gift of the Holy Spirit within us.

From the Gospel of John 11:1-45, which recounts the miraculous resurrection of Lazarus by Christ Jesus, the primary message conveyed in today's selection of scriptures concerns how the breath of God imparts life to us. Lazarus was genuinely deceased, having remained dead for four full days prior to the arrival of Jesus and the disciples in Bethany. There was nothing unusual about Lazarus's death; he had apparently fallen ill, and following his death, his relatives prepared his body for burial. This process entailed washing the body and anointing it with costly perfumes such as nard, aloes, and myrrh. Lazarus's body would have been subsequently wrapped in a shroud, with his hands and feet secured by strips of cloth, and his face covered with a specialized cloth. Over the course of the subsequent three to seven days, family and friends would visit to pay their respects and bid farewell.

A Jewish belief also held that the soul remained with, yet detached from, the body for a period lasting from three to seven days after death. Consequently, it was during this interval of visitation and mourning that Jesus arrived and "found that Lazarus had already been in the tomb for four days." Upon Jesus' arrival at the cave where Lazarus was interred, the stone covering the entrance was moved aside, and He deliberately gave glory to His Father for the miracle that the crowd was about to witness, thereby affirming who had sent Him. Jesus expressed, "Father, I thank you for hearing me. I know that you always hear me; but because of the people standing here, I said this so that they may believe that you sent me." After these words, He loudly proclaimed, "Lazarus, come out!" The deceased emerged, bound hand and foot with burial bands, and his face was wrapped in a cloth. Jesus then commanded, "Untie him and let him go." Many of the Jews who had come to Mary and observed what Jesus had done believed in Him." The breath of God, indeed, bestowed renewed life upon Lazarus.

Extensive evidence substantiates that Mary, Martha, and Lazarus were actual historical individuals. They constituted a notable family residing near Jerusalem in Bethany. Martha is cited in the Talmud as a wealthy and influential woman. Given that both Luke and John reference this family, it appears that their story was of significant importance and deliberately preserved within early Christian oral tradition. Notably, aside from the Passion Narrative, John's most extended continuous narrative pertains to the resurrection of Lazarus. Beyond this historical account, Lazarus and the dry bones from Ezekiel can also be viewed as symbolic of contemporary society. It is reasonable to suggest that we encounter Lazarus daily—individuals akin to living tombs, metaphorically, with stones before them. Additionally, we are familiar with Martha and Mary; you may identify as Martha or Mary—persons longing for Christ Jesus to visit them, so that He may restore to life a family member or someone deceased in sin. At various times, all individuals have aspired for the stone to be removed and for Jesus to perform a miracle for someone in need.

Indeed, the liturgy of the Mass teaches us that the same divine power that raised Lazarus from the dead now resides within us. We are not only the Temple of the Holy Spirit, meaning that His breath is our breath, but we also receive the very life of Christ Jesus at the worthy reception of the Holy Eucharist. This teaching signifies that His life dwells within us. The joint mission of the Second and Third Persons of the Holy Trinity now operates through us. However, what actions shall we undertake with the power of God within us, and what shall be our mission with the divine mission of God dwelling in us? Those who were once dead in sin but are now alive in Christ—how shall we proclaim and share this miracle? I believe it is appropriate for us to gather in fellowship, perhaps by sharing donuts and joy with our fellow parishioners, for that is precisely the purpose to which the liturgy of the Mass calls us and empowers us to act.

Conversely, let us endeavor to remove that obstacle and proclaim life-affirming words to these parched bones in the world. If we do not believe that the Holy Spirit, who once communicated through the prophets, now converses through us, then consider yourself like Martha, to whom Jesus asked, "Did I not tell you that if you believe, you will witness the glory of God?"

# Easter Season

# Palm Sunday

|  |  |
|--:|:--|
| First Reading | Matthew 21:1-11 |
| At the Mass – Reading 1 | Isaiah 50:4-7 |
| Responsorial Psalm | Psalm 22:8-9, 17-18, 19-20, 23-24 |
| Second Reading | Philippians 2:6-11 |
| Verse Before the Gospel | Philippians 2:8-9 |
| Gospel Reading | Matthew 26:14—27:66 |

# The Liturgy teaches us that what Belongs to God, Stays with God

"Hosanna to the Son of David; blessed is he who comes in the name of the Lord; hosanna in the highest." All of the Gospel accounts concur in stating that Jesus was greeted by a sizeable crowd that extended this king's greeting and blessing. Luke's account, alone, diverges by not recording that the crowd uttered 'Hosanna' (meaning 'Help' or 'Save/Give Salvation, I pray') as He entered Jerusalem. The message conveyed through this greeting indicates that, as they pay homage to the Messiah King, they are also simultaneously calling out to Him for assistance. Psalm 118:25-26 serves as the source of this exalted greeting, which is still employed in the modern liturgy of the Jewish Passover (Seder) ritual. The phrase "In the highest' refers to the Most High; that is, an appeal for help in the name of YHWH. Mark's declaration—'Blessed is he who comes in the name of the Lord! Blessed is the Kingdom of our Father David that is to come!'—is akin to a passage found in the Didache (10:6). The Synoptic Gospels further emphasize that the crowd participated in welcoming the Messiah King into Jerusalem by spreading their cloaks on the ground before Him. It is noteworthy that an Israelite's cloak was likely their most valuable possession. Consequently, this significant act of sacrifice of their most treasured possession is immediately intertwined with their cry for help.

The one constant theme that unites all the Gospels into a single Mystery is their emphasis on the reality that everything (every 'thing') belongs to God. The colt, the foal of an ass, belonged to God, so He sent His disciples to go and retrieve it. The cloaks that many were wearing in the crowd when He entered the city belonged to Him, so they threw them at His feet, along with the branches that John called palms. The whole city, which was shaken and asked, "Who is this?" belonged to God. The Temple area that He surveyed in Mark and later cleansed belonged to Him. The stones that He said "will cry out" belonged to Him.

The whole world that the Pharisees said "has gone after Him" belonged to God. The blind and the lame that came to be cured belonged to Him. The reason He can drive sellers out of the Temple area, turn over tables, make a whip out of cords, and shut down all traffic is because everything belongs to Him. This divine reasoning is why Jesus encouraged the religious leaders to study the sacred Scripture that always glorifies Him and identifies Him as God. His authority to do and say all these things begins with this truth—everything belongs to God. As Psalm 24:1 reads, "The earth is the Lord's and all it holds, the world and those who live there."

On a natural level, this idea is simple to understand. For example, if you see a woman nursing a child, you instinctively connect nursing with parenthood and assume that the child is being cared for by its mother, who has custody of its well-being. Similarly, if you notice a brand on a cow, you naturally think that the owner of that brand has property rights over the cow. So, how much more do we belong to Christ, who feeds us Himself and places an indelible and unchangeable spiritual mark on our souls at the worthy reception of the Sacrament of Baptism? The true right to ownership first belongs to the one who has the power to create, not to the one who has the power to procreate, distribute, and oversee.

The belief that we truly own anything is a profound deception—one of the greatest lies Satan has ever promoted. In its most extreme and harmful form, this illusion manifests as possession. For example, some parents may convince themselves that they love their children. In reality, they may try to control or possess them. Certain mothers become deeply upset when their adult children make decisions they disagree with. Marrying someone they do not approve of or pursuing a career they consider unworthy are examples. Men mistakenly think they possess their wives, using this belief to justify abusive behavior. Women may believe they possess their husbands, a belief that leads them to undermine or emasculate them. This distorted sense of ownership drives men and women to make devastating choices. Abortion or contraception destroys what they wrongly believe belongs to them. Such actions often appear as genuine love. In reality, these actions perpetuate a cycle of hate and misunderstanding. True freedom arises from recognizing a call to stewardship, not ownership. Many religious people still experience this liberation. Freedom begins with a humble, prayerful attitude. Simplicity and surrender to God mark the path.

No one should ever expect to progress in the ascent to perfection without some success in both giving back and acknowledging what belongs to God, which is first themselves – we belong to God. This revelation is an essential teaching of the Holy liturgy, which the Sursum Corda encourages us to believe through the priest's invitation, "Lift up your hearts," and our response, "We lift them up to the Lord," but do we genuinely lift up our entire hearts – our entire lives – and surrender them to God? Do we sincerely make ourselves the offering that the liturgy of the Mass instructs us to present?

It is imperative that we consistently scrutinize the possessions and attachments within our lives, asking ourselves whether there exists anything from which we would be unable to part. How closely do we mirror Christ in this regard—He who, holding His own life in no undue esteem, did not hesitate for even an instant to surrender it for our sake? This examination must extend far beyond material wealth—though our finances, too, ultimately belong to God. Indeed, everything we claim as "ours" is, in truth, entrusted to us by the divine.

Suppose God were to command you to relinquish your home; would you possess the spiritual fortitude to obey without reservation? Consider the habits that reinforce our sense of ownership—do you inscribe your name in every book you purchase, asserting a claim of possession? Reflect upon your cherished clothing or personal belongings: could you, at this very moment, donate them to someone in need or discard them for the sake of detachment? These questions pierce to the heart of our relationship with worldly goods.

Even those entrusted with sacred duties are not exempt from this temptation to possess. Some priests, for instance, may act as though the liturgy itself is their personal domain, presuming to alter what has been handed down rather than humbling themselves to faithfully read what the missal says in black text and physically perform what the missal says in the red text (i.e., read the black, do the red). Such pride undermines the humility that true spiritual service demands.

Abraham stands as a compelling example of genuine freedom from earthly attachments; he demonstrated his willingness to return even his beloved son to God. How profound this example becomes when we recall that God Himself later offered His only Son for humanity—humanity that, even now, often withholds from Him even a fleeting moment of time, a resource that, like all else, belongs ultimately to the Creator. Consider the extent of human presumption: if it were possible to commodify air, as we already do with water, oil, and other divine gifts, surely it would be done. That which God bestows freely is so often commercialized, hoarded, or abused by man. History bears witness to humanity's willingness to sell even its own kind, and, most grievously, to attempt to "sell" God Himself in myriad forms.

Given these stark realities, on what grounds can we place our trust in those whose souls are corrupted by pride and avarice to be faithful stewards of God's property? The evidence compels us to embrace humility, detachment, and a profound sense of stewardship, recognizing that all we possess is, in fact, merely on loan from the Divine.

Therefore, we cooperate with God—not only through deep self-reflection but also by engaging with the world around us. Our mission is to confront and correct the injustices inflicted upon God's creation. From the very beginning, humanity's first assignment was to exercise dominion over the lower creation—a divine mandate to steward and nurture. This calling remains urgent and essential for all who love God and dare to reclaim their divine inheritance. It is time to rise with courage and unwavering resolve, fulfilling our sacred duty to restore, protect, and honor God's glorious creation.

# Resurrection Sunday

First Reading — Acts 10:34a, 37-43
Responsorial Psalm — Psalm 118:1-2, 16-17, 22-23
Second Reading — Colossians 3:1-4 or
1 Corinthians 5:6b-8
Gospel Acclamation — cf. 1 Corinthians 5:7
Gospel Reading — John 20:1-9

# The Great Sunday, Our Day of Remembrance, Our Day of Life

From East to West, this sacred day has been called many names: Easter, the Feast of Feasts, the Great Sacrament, the Sacrament of Sacraments, Resurrection Sunday, and the Passover of Christ. In 329 A.D., Saint Athanasius, Bishop of Alexandria, described Easter in his Festal Letters as "the Great Sunday." The multitude of titles ascribed to this day demonstrates its extraordinary importance. No achievement has ever been more victorious than the one commemorated today, and no act of human malevolence has been more heinous than the effort to extinguish the divine light. Indeed, this Great Sunday stands as the most consequential moment in human history, embodying both the utmost grace granted to humanity and the profound darkness of human sin.

If one were to reduce the liturgy of the Catholic Mass to a mere description or categorize it simply as a ritual, it would fail to capture the transcendent significance that compels the faithful to participate. The Mass is far more than a routine or an event to be observed—it is a living encounter with a person, Jesus Christ Himself. Our worship is not centered on an abstract 'what,' but on the living 'Who' at the heart of our faith. By affirming that the liturgy of the Catholic Mass stands as the highest form of prayer, we boldly profess that the entirety of salvation history is made present and accessible within its sacred rites. At its very heart, the liturgy is nothing less than Christ Jesus—His life, death, and resurrection—offered to us so that we may, in turn, be transformed into what the liturgy intends us to become. As the liturgy is Christ Himself made present, it actively shapes and forms us to be united with Him, calling us to participate fully in the divine mystery that it embodies.

With all the liturgical splendor and beauty witnessed during the Easter Vigil and Easter Sunday, it is easy to become captivated by God's new work in our lives and the life of His Church. However, when the lights are turned on or our gaze returns to the altar, the Crucifix of

Christ's Passion remains present—the Roman death sentence given to God two millennia ago.

Upon the Cross, we see both the best and the worst of ourselves. At the Cross, there are two men: the one nailed to the Cross and the man who gazes at His wounded, beaten, and bloodied body. The man He beholds is wounded in heart, divided in mind, jealous, a taker-an assassin, angry, selfish, prideful, and full of wrath. The man on the Cross, however, is humble, obedient unto death, wounded by the sins of others but not broken, beaten by sin but whole, poor in spirit but rich in grace, offered as a sacrifice yet not a victim. The man looking at the One on the Cross cannot stop contemplating Him, perplexed at how someone who seemingly has lost everything possesses more than himself.

The mystery of the Crucifix of Christ's Passion lies in its power to transform something so gruesome and evil into an image that makes us say, "I want to be like Him." Unlike statues or busts of great people that might inspire us to achieve their goals, the Crucifix evokes a deeper prayer—it calls us to desire that Christ's Sacred Heart take possession of our own.

At every Catholic Mass, we are called to remember all of salvation history, but especially on this day, we reflect that our lives are not about us, but about what God did for us through His Body and Blood now shared with us in the Sacrament of the Holy Eucharist. Through His limitless love, He feeds and pours His life into us so we may have life in joyful abundance.

Resurrection Sunday made a joyful life possible. Sown into salvation history is the story of everything God has created, including our journey to Heaven or Hell, and each thought we had and every action we took along the way. In His infinite mercy, God has granted us the grace of having the knot of those sins we have sown forgiven through sacramental and liturgical non-sacramental absolution, so that we might share in the joyful life God has called us to through His Son.

In rising from the tomb, Jesus Christ shattered the bonds of sin and death, opening the door to a radiant new era of life—more glorious and fulfilling than even the paradise of Eden. This is a life overflowing with joy and perfection, rooted in Him, the very heart of our liturgical journey. Let this resurrection remind us that hope, renewal, and divine love transform every moment into eternity.

# Second Sunday of Easter (Divine Mercy)

| | |
|---:|:---|
| First Reading | Acts 2:42-47 |
| Responsorial Psalm | Psalm 118:2-4, 13-15, 22-24 |
| Second Reading | 1 Peter 1:3-9 |
| Gospel Acclamation | John 20:29 |
| Gospel Reading | John 20:19-31 |

# The Liturgy of the Church and Her Sacraments are God Being Merciful with Us

On April 30, 2000, Saint Pope John Paul II canonized Faustina Kowalska and officially designated the Sunday after Easter as the Sunday in the Divine Mercy in the General Roman Calendar. On the first anniversary of that proclamation, Pope John Paul II re-emphasized his message within the context of Easter's resurrection, stating: "Jesus said to Sr Faustina one day: "Humanity will never find peace until it turns with trust to Divine Mercy". Divine Mercy! This is the Easter gift the Church receives from the risen Christ and offers to humanity." The feast of Divine Mercy, as documented in the diary of Saint Faustina, is accompanied by a promise from Christ Jesus Himself that the soul that approaches Sacramental Confession and receives Holy Eucharist on that day shall attain the complete forgiveness of all sins and penalties. Furthermore, the Catholic Church grants a plenary indulgence (following the usual regulations) upon the recitation of certain simple prayers.

In response to the Church's call to Jesus' Divine Mercy, we observe in the readings at Mass today three of the most beautiful and profound sacred Scriptures that pertain to the mercy of God through some of the most essential and merciful sacraments of our faith: Baptism, Penance & Reconciliation, and the liturgy of the Mass. This is exemplified in today's First Reading from Acts 2:42-47, which states, "They devoted themselves to the teaching of the apostles and to the communal life, to the breaking of bread and to the prayers. Awe came upon everyone, and many wonders and signs were done through the apostles. All who believed were together and had all things in common." The liturgy of the Mass is an act of God's mercy towards us. While the primary purpose of the liturgy is to divinize us—to make us holy—the work accomplished within us is not conducted in isolation but within the community of believers who gather to worship and witness. This practice reminds us of our inherent human weakness, first observed by God in Adam, who said, "It is not good for the man to be alone. I will make a helper suited to him." Likewise, the human nature of the Bride of Christ is akin to Adam's; she was not created solely for herself but for a community of believers being sanctified.

Embracing the call to holiness is challenging enough; attempting to do so alone is likely impossible because we learn little about ourselves, our virtues, and our faults when our interactions are limited to self-reflection. Rather, it is through the community of believers, united in Christ, that the liturgy facilitates our understanding of God's mercy, as we hear testimonies and witness the transformative work in the lives of those whom He calls His children.

This journey toward communion with Christ and His People commences with our worthy reception of the Sacrament of Baptism, through which we become members of the Body of Christ by virtue of His sacrifice on the Cross and His resurrection. Today's Second Reading from 1 Peter 1:3-9 states: "Blessed be the God and Father of our Lord Jesus Christ, who in his great mercy gave us a new birth to a living hope through the resurrection of Jesus Christ from the dead, to an inheritance that is imperishable, undefiled, and unfading." Truly, God's greatest act of mercy toward us is the Sacrament of Baptism, through which we are not only cleansed of original sin, made members of the Body of Christ, and recipients of the Holy Spirit's indwelling, but most importantly, granted access to the Sacraments of Healing and Mission, through which we continue our journey of sanctification. The Sacrament of Baptism exemplifies God's abundant mercy, as it is the sole sacrament that bestows new birth upon us, thereby establishing us as citizens of the Kingdom of God.

Nevertheless, His boundless mercy did not cease there. Through the Sacrament of Baptism, our communion with God and His people was made possible, which had been an impossibility since our ancestors' exile from the Garden of Eden. Even more mercifully, God provided a means for us to never lose these relationships again through the Sacrament of Penance and Reconciliation, as recapitulated in today's Gospel reading in John 20:19-31. It states, "On the evening of that first day of the week, when the doors were locked, where the disciples were, for fear of the Jews, Jesus came and stood in their midst and said to them, 'Peace be with you.' When he had said this, he showed them his hands and his side. The disciples rejoiced when they saw the Lord. Jesus said to them again, "Peace be with you. As the Father has sent me, so I send you." And when he had said this, he breathed on them and said to them, "Receive the Holy Spirit. Whose sins you forgive are forgiven them, and whose sins you retain are retained." God understands our need for assistance because He dwelt among us, and leaving behind the Sacrament of Penance and Reconciliation is God's act of mercy towards us."

If we were to choose a single expression to reflect the depth of God's mercy, it might be something like agape-emet—a fusion of divine love (agape) and divine truth (emet). While no language offers a perfect word for this union, some cultures come remarkably close. In Hawaiian, aloha conveys not only love and compassion but also sincerity and truthfulness, embodying a way of life rooted in relational integrity. Similarly, the Maori word aroha encompasses love, empathy, and moral responsibility, reflecting a deep harmony between affection and truth. In every moment and every act of His mercy, God meets us face-to-face; He communes with us intimately so that we may grasp the truth, find true freedom, and live fully in His grace. To that end, He sent the Holy Spirit to dwell within us, guiding us into all truth. Our unwavering trust in Him flows from His unbreakable promise: He cannot lie nor lead us astray. His liturgy and Sacraments stand as radiant signs of this divine agape-emet—His steadfast love and truth, perfectly intertwined.

# Third Sunday of Easter

First Reading    Acts 2:14, 22-33
Responsorial Psalm    Psalm 16:1-2, 5, 7-8, 9-10, 11
Second Reading    1 Peter 1:17-21
Gospel Acclamation    Cf. Luke 24:32
Gospel Reading    Luke 24:13-35

# The Liturgy of the Catholic Mass is Unique, Exceptional, and Extraordinarily Transformative

For the Third Sunday of Easter, we have received a collection of readings that underscore one of the most profound truths of our faith: that Our Lord Jesus Christ's life with us was a singular, unique, exceptional, and extraordinarily transformative event. There was no one like Him, nor will there ever be, because everything that our Eternal Father needed to communicate through His Son had been spoken, and there would never be a need for another sacrifice for the redemption of our sins. Pertaining to this profound truth is also the profound reality that, since the liturgy communicates the fullness of Christ Jesus, the liturgy is therefore also a singular, exceptional, and extraordinarily transformative event.

At Pentecost, following the filling of the Apostles with the Holy Spirit and their subsequent commencement of speaking in various tongues, some among them experienced confusion concerning how individuals from different nations and speaking different languages could understand each other. According to Acts 2:10-13, it is recorded, "They were all astounded and bewildered, and said to one another, 'What does this mean?'" Yet, others, dismissing the phenomenon, responded skeptically, 'They have had too much new wine.' The current First Reading from Acts 2:14, 22-33 continues, stating, "Then Peter stood up with the Eleven, raised his voice, and proclaimed to them, 'You who are Jews, indeed all of you staying in Jerusalem. Let this be known to you, and listen to my words." Regrettably, the reading for today omits Peter's attempt at humor in the subsequent verse, where he asserts, "These people are not drunk, as you suppose, for it is only nine o'clock in the morning." In essence, it suggests that, notwithstanding criticisms that followers of Jesus may face, they refrain from becoming intoxicated early in the day. One can also imagine that there was someone in the crowd who responded to Peter's statement by remarking, 'It's 5 o'clock somewhere in the world.'

The First Reading resumes with Peter's Sermon at Pentecost in verse 22, where Peter continues to speak assertively, stating, "Jesus the Nazarene was a man acknowledged by God through mighty deeds, wonders, and signs, which God performed through him among you, as you yourselves are aware. This man, handed over according to God's predetermined plan and foreknowledge, you condemned and crucified using unlawful men. However, God raised him from the dead, freeing him from the power of death, for it was impossible for him to be restrained by it." Subsequently, Peter proceeds to highlight how the earthly kingship of David has been fulfilled in the eternal kingship of his descendant, Jesus of Nazareth.

The first thing to notice about Peter's Sermon at Pentecost is how he uses the prophecies of Joel and David to show his audience that the coming of Christ was special, one-of-a-kind, extraordinary, and deeply transformative. There might not have been a more powerful sermon in all of Christian history than this one.

The second thing to notice about it was how harsh Peter's tone was. Peter would be criticized on social media today for speaking like this. Not only was he speaking in a raised voice, but he was directly addressing people, saying, "You Jews, you Israelites – you are the ones who used lawless men to crucify Jesus." The text in verse 37 then says, "Now when they heard this, they were cut to the heart, and they asked Peter and the other apostles, "What are we to do, my brothers?" Here, Peter could have calmed down, softened his tone, and told them to simply be good people and treat others as they want to be treated, or he could have invited them to the Order of Christian Initiation (OCIA) program they held on Wednesdays in the upper room for more information. But no, he was inspired by the Holy Spirit to convict them of their sins, saying, "Repent and be baptized, every one of you, in the name of Jesus

Christ for the forgiveness of your sins; and you will receive the gift of the Holy Spirit. For the promise is made to you and to your children and to all those far off, whomever the Lord our God will call." The next verses tell us that Peter testified with many other arguments and exhorted them, "Save yourselves from this corrupt generation," and that those who accepted Peter's message were baptized, about three thousand people were added that day.

I find that this is the correct response whenever we fail to water down how singular, unique, exceptional, and extraordinarily transformative our faith is, because we received this faith directly from God's hand. It is hard to understand why we go to such lengths to diminish something so good as this. Today, we are more concerned about our tone than about the truth.

Today's Second Reading from First Peter 1:17-21 continues to emphasize the singular, unique, and transformative nature of Christ Jesus and our faith. The author, most likely the Apostle Peter, urges us to recognize that our conduct should be motivated by reverence, rooted in the awareness that Christ redeemed us from a futile existence—a life inherited from our ancestors. This redemption was not achieved through our own efforts or material possessions, such as silver or gold, but rather "with the precious blood of Christ as of a spotless unblemished lamb," who was "known before the foundation of the world but revealed in the final time for you."

Luke is the only Gospel that contains the narrative concerning Jesus encountering two of His disciples on the road to Emmaus, and this is the Gospel Reading for today, from 24:13-35. There are numerous topics we could discuss within this narrative; however, in keeping with the theme of this collection of readings, let us focus on the transformative moment. Recall, in the first reading, when, after hearing Peter's sermon, "they were cut to the heart." Now, while Jesus sat with them at the table, the text states, "he took bread, said the blessing, broke it, and gave it to them. At that moment, their eyes were opened, and they recognized him, but he vanished from their sight. Then, they said to each other, "Were not our hearts burning within us while he spoke to us on the way and opened the Scriptures to us?"

The hearers at Pentecost were cut to the heart after hearing Peter open the Scriptures, and now these two disciples' hearts were burning after Jesus opened the Scriptures. Those whose hearts were cut went on to be baptized, and these two disciples, whose hearts were burning, went to share their testimony with the disciples. Both of these accounts sound like extraordinarily transformative encounters. We should also note how the journey to Emmaus was very liturgical. There were scriptural readings, a homily by Jesus to the disciples, a prayer and blessings, a type of communion meal, and a dismissal.

Our faith, our religion, and our liturgy powerfully proclaim the truth of Jesus Christ, the eternal Word of God made flesh. He will come again in glory, and He is present among us daily in the sacred signs of bread and wine. There is nothing to be ashamed of or shy about in embracing the uniqueness and transformative power of our faith, for they reveal our Redeemer—Christ Jesus—who is both the same yesterday, today, and forever, yet wonderfully singular and unmatched. Let us emulate Saint Peter's courage, boldly sharing this divine truth through our words and the living witness of our lives, igniting hope and inspiring others to encounter the love of Christ.

# Fourth Sunday of Easter

| | |
|--:|:--|
| First Reading | Acts 2:14a, 36-41 |
| Responsorial Psalm | Psalm 23: 1-3a, 3b4, 5, 6 |
| Second Reading | 1 Peter 2:20b-25 |
| Gospel Acclamation | John 10:14 |
| Gospel Reading | John 10:1-10 |

# Through the Liturgy, Our Lord Shepherds Us

Today's First Reading for the 4th Sunday of Easter is a continuation of Peter's Sermon at Pentecost from Acts 2:14, 36-41. An interesting note here is that while the text informs us that thousands who heard Peter's Sermon at Pentecost were "cut to the heart," his appeal to them was not emotional at all. Rather, what the Holy Spirit had voiced through the Apostle Peter was simply the kerygma of the Church, which was based upon empirical evidence, the prophecies that Christ Jesus had fulfilled during His life on earth, and eyewitness accounts of Jesus' journey among us.

Moreover, the arguments that Peter was urging were specifically designed for a Jewish audience who had traveled to Jerusalem for the Feast of Pentecost (Shavuot) to celebrate the gift of the Torah to the Israelites at Mount Sinai. Therefore, Peter's message to this particular group of pilgrims was essentially to tell them that they no longer need to wait for the Messiah they had been promised long ago, because He has come to dwell among us, and you delivered Him to death. But if you "Repent and be baptized, every one of you, in the name of Jesus Christ for the forgiveness of your sins; and you will receive the gift of the holy Spirit," he said.

According to Luke, who is also the author of the Book of Acts, this marked the second occasion within fifty days that the city of Jerusalem hosted a congregation that experienced profound conviction regarding the execution of God. Luke 23:47-48 states, "Now when the centurion saw what had taken place, he praised God, and said, 'Certainly this man was innocent!'" And all the multitudes who assembled to witness the event, upon observing what had transpired, returned home, beating their breasts. Subsequently, fifty days later, many of those who had previously witnessed Christ's crucifixion accepted the teachings of the

Apostle Peter and were among the approximately three thousand individuals baptized that day. We acknowledge and celebrate the reality that, for many, conversion is a gradual process—and sometimes it occurs in as little as fifty days."

Today's Second Reading from 1 Peter 2:20-25 is believed by many to be derived from an early Christian hymn, which closely recapitulates or is based upon Isaiah's depiction of the Suffering Servant in Isaiah 53:4-12. Similar to Christ Jesus, the Suffering Servant was unjustly persecuted and executed; an evil permitted by God so that he might serve as a sacrificial lamb, offering himself for our sins. The Christian mystery lies in the transformation of this sacrificial lamb, who was resurrected to become the Shepherd of God's sheep that had gone astray. The author of 1 Peter expresses this joy, stating, "... but you have now returned to the shepherd and guardian of your souls."

Within the framework of a good shepherd being promised to us, as depicted in Psalm 23, "The Lord is my Shepherd," in Genesis 49:24, "...by the name of the Shepherd, the Rock of Israel," and in Ezekiel 34:11, "For thus says the Lord God: Behold, I myself will search for my sheep, and will seek them out," as well as through the archetype of good shepherds exemplified by the youthful Moses and David, we comprehend the Gospel's employment of the imagery of sheep, shepherd, and wolf. Furthermore, this tradition is continued in today's Gospel Reading from John 10:1-10, which, aside from Ezekiel, represents the longest continuous narrative concerning the imagery of sheep, shepherd, and wolf.

There is no esoteric aspect to the Gospel of John. It is arguably the most transparent of the four Gospels, as the author deliberately employs a comprehensive vocabulary to construct a self-explanatory text, implying that if one seeks to understand John's intent, one simply needs to observe and interpret, as John either explicitly states or sufficiently indicates his meaning. In this manner, John requires minimal prior knowledge of Old Testament prophecies from the reader, unlike the

Gospel of Matthew, which assumes a considerable familiarity with such prophecies. Specifically, the Good Shepherd narrative is exceptionally literal; it conveys exactly what it states. Furthermore, it is noteworthy that two 'I Am' statements are employed, wherein Jesus refers to Himself as both "the gate" and, in verse 11, as "the good shepherd." Subsequently, in chapter 21, Jesus instructs the Apostle Peter to engage in His pastoral mission by feeding and tending the Lord's sheep; a responsibility that has been inherited by successive successors within the line of Apostolic Succession.

That sacred act of shepherding is the divine work of our Catholic liturgy. Through it, we are not merely gathered as sheep; we are guided along the right paths to feast on the Body of Christ and be revitalized by His Precious Blood. In the Divine Symphony, we hear and recognize our Shepherd's voice through the sacred Scriptures read aloud and the Priest celebrated in Persona Christi—especially during the prayer of consecration—revealing His presence to us. The liturgy lovingly tends to us, ensuring that we lack nothing, and the Holy Spirit received in Baptism fills us with courage so unwavering that fear has no place. Even as the world presents us with trials, darkness, and the threat of wolves and false shepherds, the promise remains: the gates of Hell shall never prevail because Christ Himself is the Gate, the eternal protector of His flock. This liturgy is the inviter and the gatherer, calling us into the sacred mystery of His love and victory, forever inspiring hope and courage in our hearts.

# Fifth Sunday of Easter

First Reading    Acts 6:1-7
Responsorial Psalm    Psalm 33:1-2, 4-5, 18-19
Second Reading    1 Peter 2:4-9
Gospel Acclamation    John 14:6
Gospel Reading    John 14:1-12

# The Liturgy is not an Appeal to Diversity, but a Call to Oneness In Christ

Today's First Reading for the Fifth Sunday of Easter offers a compelling historical perspective. It is evident from the readings in the Book of Acts, particularly from the Third and Fourth Weeks of Easter, that the Christian community in Jerusalem is experiencing significant growth. Acts 2:41 reports that those who accepted Peter's sermon at Pentecost were baptized, totaling approximately three thousand individuals. Subsequently, chapters 3 through 5 of Acts largely document miraculous works performed by the Apostles, who were perceived as a threat by the Jewish religious authorities due to their expanding influence, leading to their subsequent treatment.

The current reading, Acts 6:1-7, introduces a specific issue: the rapid expansion of the early Christian community has strained its resources. It states, "As the number of disciples continued to grow, the Hellenists complained against the Hebrews because their widows were being neglected in the daily distribution." This reading indicates potential dissension or favoritism, whereby charity for widows appears to favor those of the Hebrew or Palestinian Jewish background over widows from the Hellenist or Greek diaspora Jewish community. The resolution devised by the Twelve Apostles to address this problem involved appointing seven Hellenist or Greek Jewish individuals to serve at tables, thereby allowing the Apostles to dedicate themselves to prayer and the ministry of the word.

The precise reasoning behind selecting solely disciples who were evidently Hellenist or Greek Jews, as indicated by their names, in balancing the distribution at the daily allocation remains unclear. Furthermore, Luke does not deem it necessary to account for any of these individuals performing that specific role; rather, he is primarily concerned with illustrating that their responsibilities expanded, as evidenced by Stephen and Philip preaching publicly in subsequent chapters of Acts.

Regardless, according to the current text, "the proposal was accepted by the entire community, so they chose Stephen, a man filled with faith and the Holy Spirit, as well as Philip, Prochorus, Nicanor, Timon, Parmenas, and Nicholas of Antioch, a convert to Judaism. They presented these men to the apostles, who prayed and laid hands on them." Once this administrative challenge within the Church was addressed through the ordination of these new servant ministers, Luke's momentous message concerning the early growth and expansion of the Church is resumed, stating, "The word of God continued to spread, and the number of disciples in Jerusalem increased significantly; even a considerable number of priests were becoming obedient to the faith." Here, Luke emphasizes not only the numerical increase of believers entering the Church but also the social and cultural diversity inherent within the community. This diversity included widows, ordinary Hebrews, Hellenists, converts to Judaism, such as Nicholas of Antioch, and even educated and well-trained Jewish priests adopting the faith in Jesus.

Nevertheless, diversity is an intrinsic aspect of how we initially come into our faith; however, it is not something we depart from. Rather, we arrive as many, yet depart as one into the many in the communion of saints. As Christ Jesus prayed in John 17:11, we are to be kept in the name given to Him, so that we may be united, just as He and the Father are. Similarly, the Apostle Paul instructs us in 1 Corinthians 10:17 that, "Because the loaf of bread is one, we, though many, are one body, for we all partake of the one loaf." Just as the Holy Trinity and the Body of Christ embody unity, so are we being shaped into a unified people for one God. What distinguishes us as a unique and set-apart community is not the manner in which we initially entered the faith, but who we are transformed into — who we were baptized into.

As the Second Reading from 1 Peter 2:4-9 affirms, "You are a chosen race, a royal priesthood, a holy nation, a people of His own, so that you may proclaim the praises of Him who called you out of darkness into His marvelous light." Our race does not consist of the labels that the world has assigned—black, brown, white, yellow, red—nor are these superficial skin pigments what the Holy Spirit teaches. Our actual race is defined by the fact that we were chosen; our calling is to belong to the royal priesthood, engaged in making spiritual sacrifices. Our birthplace or citizenship does not determine our nation; rather, it is called holy, signifying that our nationality is sacred. God calls us out of darkness into His marvelous light, and within this divine calling, our race, nation, and vocation are centered on proclaiming His praises.

The Gospel Reading from John 14:1-12 today exhibits elements reminiscent of a scene from a television sitcom. Our Lord takes considerable measures to reassure His disciples, stating, "Do not let your hearts be troubled. You have faith in God; have faith also in me. In my Father's house, there are many dwelling places. If it were not so, I would have told you that I am going to prepare a place for you. And if I go and prepare a place for you, I will come again and receive you unto myself, that where I am, there ye may be also. And whither I go, ye know, and the way ye know." As soon as Jesus concludes His exhortation to trust and assures them of His return, Thomas and Philip, displaying worry and a lack of faith, reveal that they have not been attentive to His teachings over the past three years. Thomas asks, "Master, we do not know where you are going; how can we know the way?" Philip requests, "Master, show us the Father,* and that will be enough for us."

The reason the One, Holy, Catholic, and Apostolic Church opposes certain forms of diversity is that it often promotes independence, isolation, and self-focus—shouting, 'look at me, I'm different!' Yet, God is completely unified; even the Son cannot point elsewhere but to the Father. When Jesus points to Himself, He is actually pointing to the Father. For example, when He responds to Thomas asking for the way, He says, "I am the way and the truth and the life. No one comes to the Father except through me," and when Philip asks to see the Father, Jesus replies, "How can you say, 'Show us the Father'? Don't you believe that I am in the Father and the Father is in me? The words I speak are not my own but come from the Father who dwells in me. Believe me when I say that I am in the Father and the Father is in me." Throughout His teachings, Jesus consistently underscores the unity and oneness of the Holy Trinity.

The central message of today's readings beautifully reminds us that our call to unity and oneness in Christ is a divine invitation to humble ourselves and serve others wholeheartedly, guiding them safely home to the Father's embrace. Every element of the liturgy—the words we speak, the actions we perform—powerfully echoes this truth: we are one family, united under one God. Though we come together as many, we leave transformed into one body in Christ. This divine unity calls the priest to speak only what the Church has entrusted to him and to perform only the sacred gestures it has ordained, so that all participants in the sacred sacrifice may be united in purpose and spirit.

Our responses, our sharing of one bread and one cup—all symbolize our communion, our union with Christ and with one another. True communion is found in unity; it cannot exist where sin has broken our bond with Him. Through the grace of confession and forgiveness, our sins are forgiven, and our union with Christ is restored and renewed. This sacred harmony, wrought through every sacrament, is a divine symphony—many voices, one melody. Just as Christ, the Bread of Life, is many grains made one loaf, so are we called to be many, yet united as one in Him. Let us embrace this profound mystery of unity, allowing it to inspire us to love more deeply and serve more selflessly, as we journey together toward our eternal home in Christ.

# Sixth Sunday of Easter

| | |
|--:|:--|
| First Reading | Acts 8:5-8, 14-17 |
| Responsorial Psalm | Psalm 66:1-3, 4-5, 6-7, 16, 20 |
| Second Reading | 1 Peter 3:15-18 |
| Gospel Acclamation | John 14:23 |
| Gospel Reading | John 14:15-21 |

# The Liturgy of the Catholic Church Prepares us for the Coming Persecution

Since our readings from the Fifth Sunday of Easter, several dramatic events have unfolded in Jerusalem. According to Acts chapters seven and eight, a harsh persecution—effectively a purge—was targeting the Hellenist Christians within the Jerusalem Church. Stephen, one of the seven chosen to serve the widows, was stoned to death for proclaiming the truth of Christ Jesus. Saul was on a rampage, "trying to destroy the church; entering house after house and dragging out men and women," whom he then imprisoned. It is possible that Hebrew Christians were protected from this persecution, which might explain why the Apostles stayed, while all other Christians fled Jerusalem to settle in the countryside of Judea and Samaria.

We lack knowledge regarding the reasons behind Philip's travel to Samaria. However, it is possible that he did so to continue his ordination work of ministering charity to the Hellenist Christian widows, or perhaps he was fleeing persecution. Today's First Reading from Acts 8:5-8, 14-17 informs us that while Philip was in the city of Samaria, he "proclaimed the Christ to them," marking the first occasion in the Acts of the Good News being preached to non-Jewish populations. Samaria was no stranger to miracles performed in the name of Jesus; Luke recounts that ten lepers were healed there not long ago. It is noteworthy that a people regarded by the Jews as heretics, and who are now experiencing an exodus of Jewish Christians fleeing into their city, were remarkably receptive to Philip's preaching, teaching, and healing ministries, which included exorcisms and the cure of paralytics and cripples.

Verses 14-17 further state, "Now when the apostles in Jerusalem heard that Samaria had accepted the word of God, they sent Peter and John to them, who went down and prayed for them, that they might receive the Holy Spirit, for it had not yet fallen upon any of them; they had only been baptized in the name of the Lord Jesus. Then they laid hands on them, and they received the Holy Spirit." This passage provides the earliest evidence of the Sacraments of Baptism and Confirmation being administered at different times—Baptism conducted by Philip, a deacon, and Confirmation conferred by the Apostles.

The Second Reading from 1 Peter 3:15-18, presented today, offers encouragement to the Church enduring persecution for their virtuous conduct. It builds on the previous verses, 13 and 14, with the words, "Now who is going to harm you if you are enthusiastic for what is good? But even if you should suffer because of righteousness, blessed are you. Do not be afraid or terrified with fear of them." In this context, Apostle Peter presents a new interpretation of Isaiah's 8:12-13, an ode to suffering, stating, "Do not call conspiracy what these people call conspiracy, nor fear what they fear, nor feel dread. But conspire with the LORD of hosts; he shall be your fear, he shall be your dread."

Furthermore, Peter draws from Jesus' Sermon on the Mount, addressing His message to those persecuted: "Blessed are they who are persecuted for the sake of righteousness, for theirs is the kingdom of heaven. Blessed are you when they insult you and persecute you and utter every kind of evil against you [falsely] because of me," which Peter rephrases as, "... those who defame your good conduct in Christ may themselves be put to shame. For it is better to suffer for doing good, if that be the will of God, than for doing evil."

Our Catholic Church has faced various persecutions throughout history, but the constant remains that we are a persecuted people because they persecuted our Lord first. However, the paradox of Christianity is that although we are persecuted, we do not see ourselves as victims – we do not have a Christ-grievance. The one who was guilty of our sins was sentenced to death in the flesh but rose again in the Spirit. Through Him, we also achieve victory over any persecution inflicted upon us by His enemies.

Considering today's Gospel Reading from John 14:15-21 alongside the First and Second Readings, it is clear that when Jesus says, "If you love me, you will keep my commandments," it suggests that following these commandments might lead to persecution. Loving Jesus likely means facing rejection from the world for loving Him. I believe this is true; the more fiercely we love God and openly testify to that love through words and actions, the more rejection we may face. However, the good news is that although loving God can result in persecution, He does not abandon us in our suffering.

Though He cannot be physically present among us as He was before the execution of His death sentence, the Third Person of the Holy Trinity, who has a mission, will stay with us. Our Lord promised this, saying, "And I will ask the Father, and he will give you another Advocate to be with you always, the Spirit of truth, whom the world cannot accept because it neither sees nor knows him. But you know him because he remains with you, and will be in you. I will not leave you orphans; I will come to you." In fact, He arrives at every Catholic Mass through the Holy Eucharist.

Once again, the words are beautiful, but in the context of today's readings, what does that sense of being adopted into the Holy Trinity look, smell, taste, sound, and feel like? It seems reminiscent of Stephen the martyr, who said, "You stiff-necked people, uncircumcised in heart and ears, you always oppose the holy Spirit; you are just like your ancestors." Given that this is what the Holy Spirit inspired Stephen to say, we need to reconsider how we interpret 1 Peter 3:16, which urges us to be prepared to explain our faith "but do it in gentleness and reverence," because Stephen's words were anything but gentle.

What does it taste like? Stones hitting your face and mouth. It feels like blood dripping from your skull. It looks and smells like the fear of people fleeing their homes to find safety in places we were told never to go, like Samaria. To be sure, there is a pedagogical side and works of charity in the Holy Spirit, where He uses us to edify and proclaim with our words in times and places of peace, but not only did the world kill Christ Jesus because it did not understand Him, but because we love Him, Christ has given us the gift of the Holy Spirit, whom He says the world cannot accept either. Therefore, our trajectory as Temples of the Holy Spirit is persecution. There is no way around it.

In this life, the only help we receive from God—who happens to come to us through every Divine Symphony—is certainly enough. It would be enough for us to share the same Spirit that dwells with Him, but just as human love naturally has its limits in showing love, so much more does the source of love extend into a divine and limitless capacity to share His fullness with us. This revelation is to remind us—always—that He has a deep and enduring interest and love for our lives.

More than that, the reception of the Holy Eucharist by the baptized—those in whom the Holy Spirit dwells—is both a profound sign and an unmerited grace. It calls and empowers us to participate wholeheartedly in our shared mission: to bring all of God's children into the fullness of knowledge and truth. As He assures us, "On that day you will realize that I am in my Father and you are in me and I in you." Every Catholic Mass becomes a sacred moment where this divine promise is fulfilled—renewing our hope, strengthening our unity, and igniting our collective purpose to transform the world through love and truth.

# Seventh Sunday of Easter

| | |
|--:|:--|
| First Reading | Acts 1:12-14 |
| Responsorial Psalm | Psalm 27:1, 4, 7-8 |
| Second Reading | 1 Peter 4:13-16 |
| Gospel Acclamation | John 14:18 |
| Gospel Reading | John 17:1-11a |

*The Liturgical Sense of the Readings at Mass (Year A)*

# The Lord is Risen, Now What?

After the anxious anticipation leading up to Resurrection Sunday and the rollicking joy that reverberates throughout Easter, many wonder as the season ends: 'Now what?' We have enjoyed the return of long-silent praises—the joyful 'Alleluia,' the triumphant 'Gloria in Excelsis Deo,' and ancient hymns like the 'Te Deum' echoing through our churches again. Our Lenten fast has transitioned into feasting and festivities, as the darkness of the tomb has given way to the brightness of new life. This question is not born from emptiness but from a desire to let that joy overflow into what comes next. Today's readings for the Seventh Sunday of Easter offer us three different responses to this core question of faith.

Peter's response to that, "Now what?" comes in today's Second Reading from 1 Peter 4:13-16. Writing around AD 62–64 from the Christian community in Rome—allegorically called "Babylon"—he addresses believers scattered across Asia Minor, many of them Gentile converts living as religious minorities under Nero's hostile regime. He does not urge them to lobby for religious freedom, keep a low profile, or escape their troubles. Instead, he invites them to reframe suffering as fellowship with Christ, writing, "Rejoice to the extent that you share in the sufferings of Christ, so that when his glory is revealed you may also rejoice exultantly."

The liturgical journey from Lent to Easter vividly symbolizes a transition from sorrow to joy, darkness to light, and preparation to fulfillment. However, after the final "Alleluia" is sung and the season ends, we are sent back into a world still entrenched in sin, brokenness, and the tragic effects of wounded nature. Our liturgical joy does not eliminate this reality; instead, it calls us to bring Christ's light into the darkness that resists it.

In today's First Reading from Acts 1:12-14, the Apostles and the Blessed Virgin Mary assemble in the Upper Room in Jerusalem following the Ascension. In typical urban dwellings of the first century, the ground floor was commonly utilized as a stable, shop, or storeroom, whereas the second floor contained the family's living quarters—spaces designated for meals, hospitality, prayer, and, ultimately, the earliest Eucharistic celebrations. This transition from a humble stable at the Nativity to a sacred upper chamber elegantly reflects the Church's own progression from humility to divine intimacy, moving from stable stalls to church pews. Here, prior to their departure into a world often antagonistic to Christ's name, they gathered in unity and anticipation for the promised outpouring of the Spirit, which would serve as their response to the question, "Now what?"

The most fitting response to "Now what?" comes from our Lord Himself in John 17:18, where He prays, "As you sent me into the world, so I sent them into the world." This means that Christ Jesus, the core of the liturgy of the Mass, was sent into the world to live in and through us. The liturgy then dismisses us into the world to share truth and life. Our faith's purpose is to be centered on Christ, guiding us to lead the world toward Him and to shape the world into a reflection of liturgy.

Today's Gospel from John 17:1–11a may not yet reveal the great sending commission, but it sets a profound foundation through Jesus' Bridegroom's Prayer. He begins with unwavering confidence, "Father, the hour has come; glorify your Son that the Son may glorify you," and fervently prays for eternal life—"that they may know you, the only true God, and Jesus Christ whom you have sent." He prays for the sanctification and unity of His followers in truth, demonstrating His deep love and desire for our collective destiny. In this intimate dialogue, Christ boldly claims His glory and actively shapes our purpose, equipping us through prayer for the mission ahead—one that He will empower and bless at Pentecost.

Our moment has arrived. Step forward with unwavering resolve. Embrace the calling, shine with the fullness of His glory, and ignite the mission with boldness and unwavering faith. Stand as beacons—His power lives within you, His purpose fuels your path, His love compels you to act. Transform your life. Transubstantiate the world. Refuse comfort. Refuse hesitation. Choose courage. Make the difference this moment demands.

# Other Holy Days of Obligation

# Solemnity of Mary, the Holy Mother of God

| | |
|---:|:---|
| First Reading | Numbers 6:22-27 |
| Responsorial Psalm | Psalm 67:2-3, 5, 6, 8 |
| Second Reading | Galatians 4:4-7 |
| Gospel Acclamation | Hebrews 1:1-2 |
| Gospel Reading | Luke 2:16-21 |

# Through the Catholic Mass, we are Born Again through the Womb of Mary, Mother of God, Mother of the Church, and Mother of the Liturgy

The Catholic Church's dogmatic teaching that the Blessed Mother Mary truly is the Mother of God, the Theotokos, necessitates a faithful assent to this Divine truth: that the Virgin Mary indeed is the mother—mother in every natural manner—to Christ Jesus, the Second Person of the Holy Trinity, the Word made flesh—flesh through her flesh. This fact signifies that through her womb and DNA, the Blessed Mother truly contributed to the formation of the human nature of Him who is the only begotten and beloved Son of God and is consubstantial with His Father. The Second Person of the Holy Trinity is truly related to the Blessed Mother by blood and lineage. Christ Jesus is, in every respect, the son of Mary and, simultaneously, the Son of the Eternal Father Almighty, without confusion or conflict.

This truth is affirmed in the sacred Tradition of the Church. In the Apostles' Creed, which states that the Son of God was "born of the Virgin Mary," the declaration made against Nestorius, the former Archbishop of Constantinople, at the Council of Ephesus in AD 431, says, "If anyone does not confess that the Emmanuel (Christ) in truth is God and that on this account the Holy Virgin is the Mother of God – since according to the flesh she brought forth the Word of God made flesh – let him be anathema." That is, anyone who teaches that Mary is not truly the Mother of God because from her, Jesus only took His human nature, but not His divine nature, is guilty of the heresy of Nestorius. For what Mary gave birth to was fully God and fully man; therefore, she is the Mother of God, the Theotokos. In other words, it is false to say that the Virgin gave birth to a human boy who later became God.

This reality is also confirmed in sacred Scripture: in Isaiah 7:14, which is echoed in Luke 1:31, "Behold a virgin shall conceive and bear a Son and His name shall be called Emmanuel;" in Luke 1:43 where Elizabeth refers to Mary as "the Mother of my Lord;" throughout the Gospel of Matthew where she is called "His Mother;" at the Incarnation in Luke 1:35 where the Angel Gabriel announces, "The holy Spirit will come upon you, and the power of the Most High will overshadow you. Therefore, the child to be born will be called Holy, the Son of God;" in John 2:1, where it states, ". . . the mother of Jesus was there," and in the Second Reading at Mass today from Galatians 4:4-7, which says, "When the fullness of time had come, God sent his Son, born of a woman, born under the law."

Therefore, as the Mother of God, the Blessed Mother persists in a dignity far above every other human, angel, and all other created things. For this, all generations will call her blessed, and no human has ever been closer to God than Mary, who carried the Second Person of the Holy Trinity in her womb and gave birth to Him, dressed Him, nursed Him, and raised him in the world. For this, she is the mother of adoration of the Blessed Sacrament and the glorious icon of worthy reception of the Body, Blood, Soul, and Divinity of Christ Jesus.

Given that Mary is regarded as the Mother of the body of Christ, it logically follows that she is also the Mother of all individuals who have been adopted into the Body of Christ. Accordingly, one of the privileges of the Blessed Mother is that she is the only woman born of flesh whose life is necessarily and intimately connected to the life of the Church; that is, the ecclesiology of the Catholic Church. Consequently, Saint Augustine stated that, since the Virgin Mary is truly the Mother of God and of the Redeemer, she is "clearly the mother of the members of Christ … since she has, by her charity, participated in the process of bringing about the birth of believers within the Church, who are united to its head."[38] Moreover, Pope Saint Paul VI bestowed upon our Mother the revered title of "Mary, Mother of Christ, Mother of the Church."

Let us consider further how the divine reality is incorporated into liturgical practice. If Mary is regarded as the Mother of the Church, then our discussion of the liturgy would be incomplete without acknowledging the extent to which it venerates her motherhood and her role in shaping us, similar to her role in the formation of Christ Jesus within her womb. I wish to elaborate further. Just as Christ was formed within Mary's womb—adopting her lineage, chromosomes, and many natural features—the liturgy also serves to shape us into tangible representatives of the Blessed Mother in the world. This mercy enables others to recognize our Mother and our Father through our actions and presence. For this reason, we also honor Mary under the title "Mary, Mother of the Liturgy."

I have often discussed in this series how the liturgical rhythm—standing, sitting, kneeling, praying, and confessing—shapes our formation. If we compare this process to what occurs in a woman's womb during birth, especially Mary's womb, we might say that this rhythm of formation is like being reborn into the world. The food our Mother provides is truly our daily bread; what she prepares for us is her Son. The procession to receive Him resembles an umbilical cord that only sin can sever. When we are dismissed from the liturgy—'*Ite, Missa est*'—it signifies us being pushed out of the womb and into the world, becoming who God has created and formed us to be.

The profound beauty of being sent forth from the liturgy—the sacred womb of Mary, Mother of the Church—invites us to embrace a mission far greater than ourselves. We are not merely dismissed; we are lovingly commissioned to return to her maternal embrace, where her gentle care renews us day by day as spiritual infants. Each time we receive her nurturing grace, we are offered the chance to be reborn in Christ, to be made new, and to be transformed at our core. This ongoing

---

[38] Cf. CCC 964, 502, LG 53; cf. St. Augustine, De virg. 6:PL 40,399.

renewal is not passive; it compels us to rise with courage, to answer God's call with steadfast commitment, and to become living vessels of His divine love in a world desperately yearning for hope. Let us not settle for comfort or complacency, but instead strive for true holiness by serving others with unwavering devotion, allowing the love that we have received to flow forth and transform every encounter. In the embrace of Mary, we find not only nourishment, but also the challenge to become Christ for others—bold, generous, and wholly alive in faith.

# The Feast of the Presentation of the Lord

## February 2

|  |  |
|---:|:---|
| First Reading | Malachi 3:1-4 |
| Responsorial Psalm | Psalm 24:7, 8, 9, 10 |
| Second Reading | Hebrews 2:14-18 |
| Gospel Acclamation | Luke 2:32 |
| Gospel Reading | Luke 2:22-40 or 2:22-32 |

# The Feast of the Presentation of the Lord

The Feast of the Presentation of the Lord dates back to the early 4th century, when the early Catholic Church in Jerusalem first commemorated it. Originally known as the 'Feast of the Encounter' (*Hypapante* in Greek, meaning 'meeting'), this celebration highlighted the meeting between Jesus and His people, represented by Simeon and Anna. By the 6th century, the feast had spread to Rome and was known as the 'Purification of the Blessed Virgin Mary', focusing on Mary's obedience to the law.

Over time, Western Catholic tradition placed increasing emphasis on Jesus as the Light, which led to the custom of blessing and carrying candles—a practice from which the name Candlemas is derived. In the 1960s, the liturgical reforms enacted following the Second Vatican Council officially designated the feast as the 'Presentation of the Lord,' underscoring its importance within both the life of Jesus and the liturgical calendar.

The Feast of the Presentation of the Lord celebrates the occasion when Joseph and Mary, in accordance with Jewish law, brought the infant Jesus to the Temple in Jerusalem forty days after His birth. According to the Law of Moses detailed in the Book of Leviticus (12:2-8), a woman who had recently given birth was considered ritually unclean and underwent a period of purification—forty days for a son, eighty for a daughter. At the conclusion of this period, the mother presented herself at the Temple, accompanied by offerings: a lamb for a burnt offering and a pigeon or turtledove for a sin offering. In cases where a lamb was unaffordable, two pigeons or turtledoves were permitted. Furthermore, Exodus 13:2 mandates the consecration of every firstborn male to God as a memorial of the Israelites' deliverance from Egypt. By presenting Jesus at the Temple, Joseph and Mary fulfilled this sacred obligation, thereby intertwining their personal story with the efficacy of salvation history.

While traditional beliefs and artistic representations often suggest that Joseph and Mary brought a pair of turtledoves in obedience to the law, today's Gospel Reading from Luke 2:22-40 does not specify which offering they brought, only that it was not a lamb.

Although the Feast of the Presentation is celebrated outside the traditional bounds of the Christmas season, it remains intrinsically united with the profound mystery of Christ's nativity. The feast powerfully affirms that the Light of the World—Christ Himself—transcends every barrier of status, distance, and time, and extends His transformative presence to all humanity through a seamless progression marked by three pivotal events.

First, the Nativity reveals how the divine light is bestowed initially upon those closest to its origin, most notably individuals marked by humility and simplicity. Mary, the Blessed Mother, gave birth to Jesus in humble surroundings—a cave repurposed as a stable—while the shepherds, emblematic of vigilant care and modest means, were chosen to witness this sacred moment. The angels, ever attendant upon God, filled the heavens with ceaseless praise, manifesting the first radiant outpouring of divine illumination.

Next, this radiant and divine light extends outward in the Feast of the Epiphany, reaching those at a greater remove in both geography and circumstance. The Magi, wise men journeying from the East, exemplify this expansion as they traverse considerable distances and face inherent dangers. Their unwavering devotion and courageous pursuit of the guiding star demonstrate the irresistible draw of Christ's light to all who seek truth beyond familiar borders.

Finally, the Feast of the Presentation stands as a testament to hope and perseverance fulfilled, embodied by figures who await the Messiah with steadfast faith. Simeon, led by the Holy Spirit, is honored for his righteousness and unwavering dedication, having received the divine promise that he would not die before beholding the Lord's Anointed. Anna, a prophetess and widow, devoted her life to prayer and fasting within the Temple. On this momentous occasion, she recognized the infant Jesus and proclaimed His arrival to all earnestly seeking redemption, thus emerging as one of the earliest heralds of the Gospel.

Together, these feasts form a continuous narrative, each interconnected and essential, demonstrating how Christ's light not only reaches those nearest in humility but is also extended to distant seekers and finally revealed to patient expectants. In contemplating this sacred progression, we are persuaded to recognize the universal and enduring power of Christ, whose presence transcends all limitations and calls each of us, regardless of our station or circumstance, to participate in the redemptive mystery unfolding throughout salvation history.

Neither Simeon nor Anna may have lived long enough to recognize Jesus as the one described in today's Second Reading from Hebrews 2:14-18, which states that He is the one who has come to "destroy the one who has the power of death." However, the reward for their patient waiting was monumentous: God permitted Simeon to behold the infant, destined to be the comforting light of Israel, and Anna to witness the child, born to redeem Jerusalem. Their stories become part of the divine narrative, illuminating the path of faith and hope, and teaching us to live with the same steadfast anticipation and unwavering trust in God's promises.

One more aspect shared by the Nativity, Epiphany, and the Presentation of the Lord is their observance in the present-day Liturgy of the Catholic Mass. This liturgy transcends all boundaries of status, distance, and time, renewing us in the illumination of Christ Jesus. Within our New Covenant Temple, Christ Jesus is presented to us as the Holy Eucharist—not merely as a human infant who came to resolve the political tensions troubling Simeon and Anna, but rather as the risen God-man who has come to heal the sins of the world, which are the source of bitterness, brokenness, despair, and vengeance.

Furthermore, the readings of today's Divine Symphony serve as a profound reminder that in every Mass, we are called to participate in this sacred encounter actively. As we gather within our Churches, we unite with Joseph and Mary in offering ourselves and our lives wholeheartedly to God. During the silent moments of the liturgy, we are beckoned to recognize Christ among us, just as Simeon and Anna did, and to bear unwavering witness to His redeeming presence in our lives and in the world. This sacred celebration challenges us all—near and far—to steadfastly remember that God's presence endures tirelessly with us, urging us to deepen our faith and commitment.

# The Solemnity of the Ascension of the Lord

## 40 days after Easter (or nearest Sunday after 40 Days)

| | |
|---:|:---|
| First Reading | Acts 1:1–11 |
| Responsorial Psalm | Psalm 47:2–3, 6–7, 8–9 |
| Second Reading | Ephesians 1:17–23 |
| Gospel Acclamation | Matthew 28:19a, 20b |
| Gospel Reading | Matthew 28:16–20 |

# The Relationship Between Ascension and Descension, *Anabainō* and *Katabainō*

The Ascension of Christ Jesus is regarded as the culmination of the theological concept known as the divine exchange, whereby God assumes human nature to enable humanity's participation in divinity. The event signifies the elevation of humankind through divine grace and establishes a path for union with God. Through this ascent, Catholic Christian doctrine holds that Christ provides an opportunity for deeper communion with God and access to His love and presence. The Ascension is commemorated as a moment representing transformation, hope, and the promise of eternal life, emphasizing humanity's potential for spiritual advancement.

Indeed, Catholic Christianity is a religion of ascent, an upward-moving faith, and we are a people being raised, lifted up, and ascending into Christ Jesus. For this reason, the liturgy itself is not only a participation in transforming our basic nature into a higher, divine nature, but in its very form, the liturgy physically lifts us upward, elevating our transformed natures into the Kingdom of God, our Father's house. If you doubt this essential mission of the Christian faith, consider the Gospels, where the imagery of ascent is almost always linked to some form of transformation, while the imagery of descent is consistently associated with our basic human nature, which is now ready to encounter Jesus Christ.

In the Gospels, the preferred Greek word for descending is katabainō, which contrasts with *kathēmai*, meaning simply to sit down. For example, in Matthew 14:29, "Jesus said, 'Come.' So, Peter got out (*katabainō*) of the boat and walked on the water toward Jesus." In Mark 15:30, they taunted Jesus to descend on their terms: "save yourself, and come katabainō from the cross!" Jesus would descend from the Cross to meet us, but it is always on God's terms. This idea of ascending from descending highlights that it is only by God's grace and mercy that we can come to the Father, ascending through Christ Jesus.

In the Gospels, the Temple in Jerusalem is seen as the pinnacle of ascent, and Jesus continually rises toward His passion. However, He first descends to preach, teach, and heal. From the very beginning, we see this pattern in Luke 2:51: "After the Finding in the Temple, He descended – katabainō – with them and came to Nazareth, and was obedient to them [Joseph and Mary]; and His mother kept all these things in her heart." It is true that the first encounter of our Lord was with His parents.

Before Jesus encounters the rest of us, He also undergoes His ministerial transformation, which John the Waymaker witnesses, saying, "I saw the Spirit descend as a dove from heaven, and it remained on Him."

Later, Jesus uses this same language in another sacrament, the Holy Eucharist, saying, "I am the living bread which *katabainō* from heaven; if anyone eats of this bread, he will live forever; and the bread which I shall give for the life of the world is my flesh."

Descending marks the beginning of the Christian encounter. It is the point where we realize how fallen and low we are in our natural state, yet in Christ Jesus, we find hope to rise above our miserable condition and into our Father's estate, which is our true inheritance. The Greek term best suited for this in this context is *anabainō*, meaning 'ascend,' contrasting with *katabainō*. It is not *egeirō*, which means 'to arouse,' as in, "God is able from these stones to raise up (that is, arouse) children to Abraham," not to ascend children to Abraham. Here, God is not promising any transformation of the rocks but simply that rocks will remain rocks, yet be aroused. Some uses of anabainō also refer to the Sacrament of Baptism. According to Matthew 3:16, "When Jesus was baptized, He *anabainō* – ascending immediately from the water, and behind, the heavens were opened and He saw the Spirit of God katabainō like a dove, and come on Him."

For Mark, the appointment of the twelve apostles was also a transformative ascent; he writes, "Jesus ascended the mountain, and called to Him those whom He desired; and they came to Him," meaning they too ascended to Christ to associate with Him, which is a type of Sacrament of Holy Orders, where the ordination, also called consecration (literally meaning, 'being associated with the divine'). Additionally, when describing the descent to meet His parents, Luke 2:42 states, "And when He was twelve years old, they ascended – anabainō according to custom."

There is always a relationship between ascension and descending, *anabainō* and *katabainō*. The same applies to the Sacrament of the Holy Eucharist in John, where Jesus says, "If this shocks you, then what if you were to see the Son of Man ascending to where He was before," which prophetically links the Eucharist's descent with His Ascension after the Resurrection.

This passage aligns with the account from the First Reading in Acts 1:1-11 for the Solemnity of the Ascension. Verses 6-9 state, "When they had gathered together, they asked Him, 'Lord, are You at this time going to restore the kingdom to Israel?" He answered them, "It is not for you to know the times or seasons that the Father has established by his own authority. But you will receive power when the Holy Spirit comes upon you, and you will be my witnesses in Jerusalem, throughout Judea and Samaria, and to the ends of the earth." When he had said this, as they were looking on, he was lifted up, and a cloud took him from their sight." The very thing that Jesus prophesied in John 6—"If this shocks you, then what if you were to see the Son of Man ascending to where He was before," happened."

Indeed, one thing we might overlook about the anabainō of our Lord is how shocking the actual ascension must have been. Jesus was right. The event of His ascension had to be much more shocking than His teaching that eating His flesh and blood would grant us eternal life. Consider this from the apostles' perspective: first, there was about a three-year ministry during which they followed Jesus everywhere; then an emotionally wrenching night that led to His crucifixion; then three days later, His shocking resurrection and return; and now, forty days later, He is lifted into the sky, and a cloud took Him from their sight.

That had to be shocking, maybe even a little overdramatic, even for God, who is the author of all drama. But instead of letting them stew in their shock, today's passage concludes, "While they were looking intently at the sky as he was going, suddenly two men dressed in white garments stood beside them. They said, "Men of Galilee, why are you standing there looking at the sky? This Jesus, who has been taken up from you into heaven, will return in the same way as you have seen him going into heaven.'"

If only our eyes could truly see what happens during the moment of consecration in the Mass, we would also be there, shocked, as the sky above the priest breaks open and Jesus descends again to meet us beneath the appearance of bread and wine.

It is true. The very reason we celebrate the Solemnity of the Ascension is because He first descended to us. This is the story of salvation history—God reaching out to us so that we can come to Him. In Christ Jesus, we now have the means to complete the journey. The Christian life begins with this pattern of descending and ascending in Baptism, where we are immersed and raised up—immersed and raised up—immersed and raised up a third time in the name of the Father, and of the Son, and of the Holy Spirit. Katabainō and Anabainō. Katabainō and Anabainō. Katabainō and Anabainō. In *nomine Patris et Filii et Spiritus Sancti*. It is a beautiful thing that we witness at every elevation of the Holy Eucharist during the Mass. The Body of Christ ascends before us and descends into our bodies. Katabainō and Anabainō.

The Second Reading at the Divine Symphony for the Solemnity of the Ascension, drawn from Ephesians 1:17-23; the optional Second Reading from Hebrews 9:24-28; 10:19-23, and the Gospel Reading from Luke 24:46-53, all pertain to the reasons why our Lord Jesus Christ ascended. These reasons include: for us, for our sake, for our salvation, for our intercession, and for our judgment. The justification for trusting Him in these matters is not solely because He is God and He is true, but because He dwelt among us and continues to reside within us to this very day.

The liturgy of the Mass captures all of this drama, from Baptism to the dismal moments and everything in between. From our ascending processions to the sanctuary, to communion. From standing, sitting, and kneeling, *Katabainō* and *Anabainō*. From the great descent of Christ Jesus, the Holy Eucharist into our bodies, so we might leave the Temple Mount of the New Jerusalem and go into the world to be a type of Him; that is, a eucharistic people in the world to encounter those far from Him, who is the true Temple, who has ascended for our sake. We cannot miss this key point of the Solemnity of the Ascension: it is not about Him alone, but about all of us being called to come to Him; to ascend to where He is through God's grace and the Sacraments of His Church.

# Pentecost Sunday
## First Sunday, 50 days after Easter

| | |
|---:|:---|
| First Reading | Acts 2:1-11 |
| Responsorial Psalm | Psalm 104:1, 24, 29-30, 31, 34 |
| Second Reading | 1 Corinthians 12:3b-7, 12-13 |
| Sequence | *Veni, Sancte Spiritus* |
| Gospel Reading | John 20:19-23 |

# The Liturgy of the Catholic Mass Fulfills the Human Desire for Unity

One of the most compelling pieces of evidence that we were created by a God who is truly one in being is the fact that, as human beings, we cannot help but to pursue and desire unity. We cannot help but to seek oneness because oneness created us. Not only does our physical DNA point to a common source and a universal relationship, along with the fruits of procreation—family—but in all our pursuits and interactions in the world, unity is our chief craving. Humans cannot help but believe that if everyone shared their beliefs, the world would be a better place. This pursuit is why we have designed rituals, religion, tribes, government, curriculum, brands, and countless other things: because we truly desire unity among each other.

We have a history of conquering other lands to unify them with us; a dark history of subjugating and killing those we deem unworthy of unification. All our self-driven efforts at unity always and inevitably fail. However, nearly two thousand years ago, the most perfect design for unity among humanity came to dwell among us, so that unity was no longer just an idea to grasp but a person named Jesus Christ, in whom we abide.

Today's First Reading from Acts 2:1-11 emphasizes the intrinsic human desire and profound yearning for unity, stating, "When the time for Pentecost was fulfilled, they were all in one place together." This revelation signifies their collective anticipation of the Lord. It is noted that there were no selfish desires among them; they were all united in purpose. The passage further describes, "And suddenly there came from the sky a noise like a strong driving wind, and it filled the entire house in which they were. Then there appeared to them tongues as of fire, which parted and came to rest on each of them. And they were all filled with the Holy Spirit and began to speak in different tongues, as the Spirit enabled them to proclaim." Thus, the unifying event of Pentecost serves as the fulfillment of Christ Jesus' Bridegroom prayer from John 17:20-23, which states, "I pray not only for them, but also for those who will believe in me through their word, so that they may all be one, as you, Father, are in me and I in you, that they also may be in us, that the world may believe that you sent me. And I have given them the glory you gave me, so that they may be one, as we are one, I in them and you in me, that they may be brought to perfection as one, that the world may know that you sent me, and that you loved them even as you loved me."

As Christ Jesus and the Holy Spirit share a joint mission—the Pentecost event, where Christ Jesus reveals His relationship with the Holy Spirit to us—we become co-partners in that mission. Our divine fellowship in Christ and the Holy Spirit makes us priests, prophets, and kings in Him through the indwelling and gifts of the Holy Spirit. Participating in this joint mission of the Holy Trinity not only unites us with each other but also sends us into the world as ambassadors and missionaries of unity through God's love and truth. This work of unity in Christ is carried out through the particular gifts of the Holy Spirit that each of us receives.

According to the Second Reading from 1 Corinthians 12:3b-7, 12-13, it is stated that "There are different kinds of spiritual gifts but the same Spirit; there are different forms of service but the same Lord; there are different workings but the same God who produces all of them in everyone. To each individual, the manifestation of the Spirit is given for some benefit." Once again, it is emphasized that the gifts of the Holy Spirit are not directed toward selfish desires or personal ambition, but are instead purely oriented towards fostering unity in Christ Jesus. They are aimed at enhancing and sanctifying the members of the Body of Christ. Further, in 1 Corinthians 12:28, the Apostle specifies some of these gifts, noting, "Some people God has designated in the church to be, first, apostles; second, prophets; third, teachers; then, mighty deeds; then, gifts of healing, assistance, administration, and varieties of tongues." At the initial Pentecost event, the Holy Spirit organized the work necessary to be accomplished among the diverse nations and languages present, resulting in all receiving the gift of tongues.

Given that the Sacraments, particularly the Sacrament of Baptism and the Sacrament of Confirmation, uniquely unify us with the Holy Spirit, they serve as means by which we remain connected to the Holy Trinity through reconciliation—specifically, through Sacramental absolution in the Sacrament of Penance for grave sins, and through non-Sacramental absolution during the liturgy of the Catholic Mass for venial sins. In this manner, the gifts bestowed upon the disciples at the Pentecost event, which support the joint mission of Christ and the Spirit, and the authority conferred upon them following the resurrection, are deeply interconnected and exhibit notable similarities. For instance, consider the Gospel reading from John 20:19-23, which begins: "On the evening of that first day of the week, when the doors were locked, where the disciples were, for fear of the Jews, Jesus came and stood in their midst and said to them, 'Peace be with you.'" Similarly, during Pentecost, the disciples were gathered together in unity, awaiting persecution. Just as at Pentecost, Christ's visitation resulted in the bestowal of power, authority, and a mission. Jesus again said to them, 'Peace be with you. As the Father has sent me, so I send you.' After these words, he breathed on them and said, "Receive the Holy Spirit. Whose sins you forgive are forgiven them, and whose sins you retain are retained."

In the Divine Symphony, God's hope and the joint mission of Christ Jesus and the Holy Spirit unite perfectly. Those who receive the gifts of the Holy Spirit come together to worship God, using those gifts. We are all gathered in one place in anticipation of our Lord. Our Catholic Masses, celebrated simultaneously at different times around the world, bring all of God's People into one assembly; communicating to us the word and love of our Creator; offering peace, healing us of venial sins so we may be worthy to receive Holy Communion; and then inviting us to partake in the one Bread and one Cup, so that we may become an image of who has entered us. In the world, when people see us, they should see Him. Our union with the one is only impeded by our sins, but even that has a remedy in the One in whom our heart finds their desire.

Thus, as we move from the celebration of Pentecost to the Solemnity of the Most Holy Trinity, we are reminded that this unity we experience in the liturgy is a reflection of the eternal unity within God Himself—Father, Son, and Holy Spirit. In each Mass, we are drawn deeper into the mystery of divine life, called not only to share in the communion of the Trinity but also to live out that unity in our daily lives. By receiving Christ in the Eucharist and continually seeking reconciliation, we are empowered to become true witnesses of God's love, embodying the peace, mercy, and holiness that flow from the heart of the Trinity into the world. The liturgy, therefore, is not merely a ritual but a participation in the life of God, shaping us into a people who—united in faith, hope, and charity—proclaim by word and deed the glory of the One who has made us one.

# Solemnity of the Most Holy Trinity

| | |
|---:|:---|
| First Reading | Exodus 34:4b-6, 8-9 |
| Responsorial Psalm | Daniel 3:52, 53, 54, 55, 56 |
| Second Reading | 2 Corinthians 13:11-13 |
| Gospel Acclamation | Cf. Revelation 1:8 |
| Gospel Reading | John 3:16-18 |

# The Solemnity of the Most Holy Trinity

The celebration of the Solemnity of the Most Holy Trinity, often simply called Trinity Sunday, has a rich historical development within the Church's liturgical calendar. Although Christians have always professed the belief in the Trinity—the Father, the Son, and the Holy Spirit—from the earliest days of the Church, a specific feast day dedicated to this central mystery did not exist in the universal calendar for many centuries.

Its origins can be traced to monastic communities in the early Middle Ages. By the 9th century, some monasteries in Europe began celebrating a special liturgical observance honoring the Holy Trinity. The feast gradually gained popularity, especially in northern Europe, but it was not yet universally observed.

The formal establishment of Trinity Sunday as a universal feast is attributed to Pope John XXII, who, in 1334, inserted it into the general calendar of the Roman Rite Church. He decreed that the Sunday following Pentecost would be set aside as a solemnity in honor of the Most Holy Trinity. This decision was influenced by the growing devotion to the mystery of the Trinity and the desire for a specific liturgical celebration that would invite the faithful to reflect more deeply on this foundational doctrine of the Christian faith.

Before its universal adoption, the Mass and Office for the Trinity had become widespread in various regions, and several popes and theologians supported its inclusion in the liturgical cycle. The timing—immediately after Pentecost—was intentional, as the descent of the Holy Spirit at Pentecost completes the revelation of the Trinity, following the Father's creation and the Son's redemption.

Since the 14th century, the Solemnity of the Most Holy Trinity has been celebrated throughout the Catholic Church, inviting believers to contemplate and honor the unity and mystery of the Triune God each year on the first Sunday after Pentecost.

It would be sufficient for us to believe in the Christian mystery that God is one God in three distinct persons, because our salvation is directly connected to that mystery. If the nature of God were not unified, and if there were not perfect communion between the Father, the Son, and the Holy Spirit, then we could never be certain that what Christ Jesus has promised us will be fulfilled by the Father, or that the Holy Spirit is genuinely working in us for our benefit. If the Godhead were not immutable, impassible, and truly unified in that aspect of their nature, then our hope would be in vain, as we would be believing in a God who may be at war with Himself. In this way, being a Christian would be no different than worshiping Zeus, Ra, or any ancient pagan gods. Therefore, for our faith to be rightly placed in the promises of Christ Jesus, there must be a Holy Trinity.

It is also true that our faith is not merely based on the sufficiency of what we profess. Rather, our faith is confirmed by the visible reality of our belief. That is, we do not just believe in the one nature of God because Scripture and Tradition tell us it is true, but we also know that Father, Son, and Holy Spirit are one because God has loved us perfectly, and there is no division in divine love. Additionally, we recognize that God's nature is love because love cannot hide itself from its object of love, whom it desires the best for, and God has never been able to hide His love for us.

The depiction of horses biting their mouthpieces before the commencement of a race—commonly referred to as 'biting at the bit'—may not serve as an ideal analogy to illustrate the Theophany event described in today's First Reading from Exodus 19:16-25. Nevertheless, it appears that God was eager to reveal Himself to His People, whom He had delivered from bondage in Egypt. This inference is drawn from the visual spectacle surrounding the event; God's initial appearance to the Israelites was far from modest—it was marked by "peals of thunder and lightning, a heavy cloud over the mountain, and a very loud blast of the shofar, so that all the people in the camp trembled."

This first Theophany was preceded by the establishment of a conditional covenant, as outlined in Exodus 19:5, where God states, "Now, if you obey me completely and keep my covenant, you will be my treasured possession among all peoples, though the entire earth is mine." The Hebrew term for 'covenant' is *barîṯ*, denoting an alliance and friendship. Following this initial Theophany, the Ten Commandments were issued. Subsequently, the First Reading from Exodus 34:4b-6, 8-9 describes another Theophany during the renewal of the Tablets on which the finger of God originally inscribed the Ten Commandments. These tablets were shattered by Moses shortly thereafter upon witnessing the Israelites' idolatry upon his return.

If your parents have ever given you a gift and somehow ended up feeling miserable for spoiling, ruining, or destroying what they gave you, you know how impossible it would have been to ask them for the same thing again. Most of us would never dare cross that line. Yet, if our parents, out of their knowledge, kindness, and mercy, knew how much we needed that gift, they might sound like God here; letting us know why they are doing it, "The LORD, the LORD, a merciful and gracious God, slow to anger and rich in kindness and fidelity, continuing his love for a thousand generations, and forgiving wickedness, rebellion, and sin; yet not declaring the guilty guiltless, but bringing punishment for their parents' wickedness on children and children's children to the third and fourth generation!" After being with them day and night for years in the desert, Moses knew the children of Israel very well. His knowledge of them was evident in his confession, "This is indeed a stiff-necked people; yet pardon our wickedness and sins, and claim us as your own." To which, in verse 10, God established a promissory or unconditional *barîṯ*; another alliance and friendship to perform marvels among them so that those who witness them will know that the Lord is with them.

This passage elucidates the Jewish understanding of God, emphasizing the belief that God is truly present among them. This presence is affirmed through the establishment of promissory and mutual covenants, as well as friendships. Correspondingly, similar language is evident in today's Second Reading from 2 Corinthians 13:11-13, where the Apostle Paul offers blessings: "The grace of the Lord Jesus Christ, and the love of God, and the fellowship of the Holy Spirit be with all of you." Such language reflects the concept of divine covenants and alliances, conveyed through the imagery of a Triune God. Additionally, this blessing bears a close resemblance to the well-known blessing from Numbers 6:24-26, which states: "The Lord bless you and keep you; the Lord make his face shine on you and be gracious to you; the Lord turn his face toward you and give you peace."

If we have not yet received the message that God genuinely loves us and that He continuously demonstrates His love through every moment of our lives, and that the enduring expression of His love is manifested through relationships, friendships, and alliances, then the Gospel Reading from John 3:16-18 serves as a reminder. It states, "God so loved the world that He gave His only Son, so that everyone who believes in Him may not perish but may have eternal life." Should one inquire about how this relationship is perceptible to the senses, it can be described as tangible through the New Covenant. For Christ Jesus entered the world through the Virgin Mary and was laid in a manger, a wooden or stone feeding trough—an animal feeding box—and that same Christ Jesus later assured us that by consuming His flesh and drinking His blood, we would attain eternal life. This mission of His was undertaken so that we might receive our daily bread and eternal life.

In this divine truth, the nature and mission of the liturgy are inseparably united with the very essence of the Holy Trinity — they are all love. Through the Mass, God reveals His profound desire for us: a love so vast and fierce that He longs to nourish us with eternal life through the Holy Eucharist. When we truly participate in the Holy Mass, Christ Himself comes to establish a relationship of friendship and alliance with us. Sending us forth as a Eucharistic people into the world, He empowers us to be His witnesses — to showcase His marvelous deeds through our acts as apostles of love. This is not just a day to honor The Most Holy Trinity; it is a call to live daily in the sacred order that renews our bond with the divine Source of life. Are we willing to accept this divine invitation — to transform the world by living out the love we receive, and to boldly declare His glory through our actions? We are called to be partners with God in His majestic plan of salvation. We must rise to this challenge, embodying His love with courage and conviction.

# Solemnity of the Body and Blood of Christ

|  |  |
|---:|:---|
| First Reading | Deuteronomy 8:2-3, 14b-16a |
| Responsorial Psalm | Psalm 147:12-13, 14-15, 19-20 |
| Second Reading | 1 Corinthians 10:16-17 |
| Gospel Acclamation | John 6:51 |
| Gospel Reading | John 6:51-58 |

# The Most Holy Body and Blood of the Lord

The Solemnity of Corpus Christi, also known as the Body of Christ, is traditionally celebrated worldwide on the Thursday following the Solemnity of the Most Holy Trinity. This occasion provides an annual opportunity to offer special reverence and commendation for the two manifestations of the Corpus Christi among us: firstly, the Holy Eucharist, and secondly, the Church.

The origin of this solemnity dates back to 1207, when a fifteen-year-old Belgian Augustinian nun named Giuliana di Cornillon had a vision of a full moon with a dark spot. The meaning of this vision, and another the following year, was that the Church—usually symbolized by the moon reflecting the sun's light—had a dark spot due to the lack of a feast dedicated to the Body of Christ. It was not until 1247, when Robert de Thourette became bishop of Liège, that Giuliana convinced him to create a diocesan feast for the Eucharist. In 1263, near Orvieto, Italy, in the town of Bolsena, a consecrated Host miraculously began to bleed onto the Corporal cloth beneath it.

The following year, Pope Urban IV, who had been the archdeacon of Liège and was living in Orvieto, believed in the Eucharistic miracle and issued the Papal Bull, *Transiturus*, to establish the solemnity of Corpus Christi. However, this bull was never put into practice because Urban IV died two months after issuing it. The celebration of Corpus Christi was only confirmed by his thirteenth successor, Pope Clement X (1305-1314), the first Avignon pope and the suppressor of the Knights Templar. Clement X's immediate successor, John XXII, officially established the traditional Corpus Christi procession in 1316.

During his pastoral visit to Orvieto on June 17, 1990, Saint John Paul II remarked: "Although the construction of this cathedral was not directly linked to the Solemnity of 'Corpus Christi,' established by Pope

Urban IV with the bull Transiturus in 1264, nor to the miracle that occurred in Bolsena the year before, it is undeniable that the Eucharistic miracle is powerfully represented here through the Bolsena corporal, which the chapel was built to honor and now protects with great reverence. Since that event, Orvieto has gained worldwide recognition as a place that symbolizes God's merciful love, which becomes the food and drink of salvation during life's earthly journey. Because of the veneration of this great mystery, your city continues to preserve and nurture the enduring flame."

There is a powerful mystery that Saint Pope John Paul II alludes to herein. This mystery pertains to the notion that the sole reason for the human condition requiring sustenance for continued existence is rooted in the fall of our first parents, Adam and Eve. Nonetheless, even within this lamentable state, God has maintained a connection with humanity throughout salvation history by providing food. The food, which was initially a matter of choice in the Garden—"... You are free to eat from any of the trees of the garden,"—has transformed into a necessity for survival. God has continually been present amidst daily needs, offering sustenance. In today's First Reading from Deuteronomy 8:2-3, 14b-16a, we are reminded of the manna bread in the desert that God fed us, "... a food unknown to you and your fathers, in order to show you that not by bread alone does one live, but by every word that comes forth from the mouth of the LORD." While this verse is not typically regarded as prophetic, it bears two significant prophetic implications: first, Christ Jesus is akin to the manna because He, too, was unknown to the ancestors, and He is also the word that proceeds from the mouth of the Lord. Additionally, in today's Gospel Reading from John 6:51-58, Jesus refers to Himself as the sustenance that fulfills the manna, saying, "I am the living bread that came down from heaven; whoever eats this bread will live forever; and the bread that I will give is my flesh for the life of the world." Unlike your ancestors who ate and still died, whoever eats this bread will live forever."

The concept of God being "edible" also finds resonance in Jewish tradition, particularly through the practice of wearing tefillin. Tefillin are small leather boxes worn on the head or arm by devout Jewish men, each containing verses of scripture written on parchment and wrapped in calf's tail hair. This ritual serves as a tangible reminder to the faithful that the word of God is meant to be internalized and, in a symbolic sense, "consumed." This theme of God as spiritual nourishment is further illustrated in the nativity story, where the infant Jesus was placed in a manger—a feeding trough for animals—underscoring the idea that God provides sustenance for His people. Moreover, this foundational belief is echoed in the prayer Jesus taught His disciples: "Give us this day our daily bread." This phrase points not only to the provision of material needs but also to the spiritual nourishment found in the Holy Eucharist.

Maybe it would be enough to understand that God is edible and that, as the bread of life, He came to sustain us both spiritually and physically. He is both a symbol and a reality, being our one essential person in this life. Perhaps knowing this would have been enough to help us persist on our earthly pilgrimage. However, for God, that was not sufficient. Instead, our Lord God needed us to be certain that partaking of His Body at the Divine Symphony of the Mass truly unites us as one body in Him.

This unity allows us to participate as one people in His and the Holy Spirit's ongoing work of salvation through the Church. In essence, receiving the Holy Eucharist truly aligns us with the Body of Christ and, by extension, with the mission of the Holy Trinity. Through this, our unity in Him not only signals to the world to find and follow Him but also reflects the reality of who we are becoming.

In this way, our reflection on the Holy Eucharist finds profound resonance in today's Second Reading from 1 Corinthians 10:16-17, which states: "The cup of blessing that we bless, is it not a sharing in the blood of Christ? The bread that we break, is it not a sharing in the body of

Christ? Because the loaf of bread is one, we, though many, are one body, for we all partake of the one loaf."

Thus, as we gather at the altar to receive His Body and Blood, we are not only nourished individually but are also drawn more deeply into the mystery of communion that defines our faith. The readings highlight how, through God's gift of spiritual nourishment—first in the manna of the Old Testament, then fulfilled in Christ, the living bread—we are united in a bond that transcends individuality.

This unity is precisely what the Apostle describes in 1 Corinthians: by partaking of the one bread, we become one body in Christ. Our sacred participation transforms us both as individuals and as a community, empowering us to embody Christ's presence in the world as living witnesses to His love and mercy. This transformation, rooted in our shared participation in the Eucharist, calls us to extend Christ's compassion to others and to build up His Church as one family in faith, just as the Apostle teaches that our unity in the one loaf makes us one body.

# Saint Joseph, Spouse of the Blessed Virgin Mary

## March 19

| | |
|---:|:---|
| First Reading | 2 Samuel 7:4-5a, 21-14a, 16 |
| Responsorial Psalm | Psalm 89:2-3, 4-5, 27 & 29 |
| Second Reading | Romans 4:13, 16-18 |
| Gospel Acclamation | Psalm 84:5 |
| Gospel Reading | Matthew 1:16, 18-20, 24a |

# The Liturgical Symphony of Saint Joseph's Obedient Faith

As the liturgical year proceeds through its sacred cycle, there comes a moment of contemplative stillness—a pause that regards with profound reverence the discreet figure of Joseph of Nazareth. He stands, not in the center, but at the crucial threshold: spouse to Mary, foster father to the Incarnate Word, and the silent "shadow of the Father." In the solemn architecture of the Church's worship, Joseph embodies the hinge between ancient prophecy and living fulfillment, between the longing of the First Reading and the radical obedience found in the Gospel. In this season, often marked by Lenten austerity, his feast emerges as a luminous shaft of light, inviting the faithful to revisit what it means to be "righteous" in the eyes of God.

From the opening chords of the First Reading, the promise of God to David in 2 Samuel resounds—a covenant that his house and kingdom will endure, a royal assurance that a descendant will establish the throne forever. This passage, regal and public in its proclamation, finds its quiet resonance in Nazareth's humble home. The grandeur of kingship meets the intimacy of familial life, and the enduring promise of Israel's throne is mysteriously realized in the straw-laden dwelling of a carpenter. The drama is thus transposed from the palace to the domestic, where cosmic significance is entrusted to the ordinary rhythms of family.

The Apostle, in today's Second Reading from Romans 4:13, 16-18, intensifies this mystery by re-situating the covenant not in legal observance or bloodline, but in the audacity of faith. He meditates upon Abraham, who trusted in God's promise even when hope defied reason, thereby fathering nations through faith. Joseph, in this sacred drama, emerges as a new Abraham: childless according to the flesh, yet paradoxically the very one through whom the Promise quietly enters and dwells. Into his home, through the risk of trust and the humility of surrender, is placed the One in whom all nations will be blessed. Joseph's righteousness, therefore, transcends moral propriety; it is a lived openness to the wild faithfulness of God—a willingness to risk honor and reputation for the sake of a plan he cannot fully comprehend.

The Gospel Reading from Matthew 1:16, 18-20, 24a brings this drama to its most intimate point in the narrative of the Annunciation to Joseph. Here, the mystery of the Incarnation is not merely announced to Mary, but also entrusted into the hands of Joseph, who, faced with a dilemma between law and mercy, contemplates a quiet dismissal of Mary. Yet it is the angel's word—"Do not be afraid"—that summons him to surpass the limits of conventional righteousness. Joseph utters no words in the Gospel; his obedience is articulated purely through action. He takes Mary into his home, embracing both her and the mysterious Child she bears. In this, Joseph's silent fiat becomes an anticipatory echo of Mary's own, preparing the path for the ultimate fiat that brings the Word into the world. The drama of Joseph's assent is not confined to a single moment, but is woven into the daily fabric of his life—through the anxieties, searches, and letting-go that mark the journey of fatherhood.

Thus, within the divine rhythms of the Mass, the readings converge in a symphony of faith and fulfillment. Joseph is present in the silent, steady gestures of the liturgy; he is the original layman, the sanctifier of ordinary life. The altar of the Holy Eucharist—where the Word becomes flesh anew for God's people—mirrors the kitchen table of Nazareth, where bread was shared, and the mysteries of God were pondered and lived. The act of Joseph's obedience is mystically repeated whenever the faithful utter their "Amen," consenting to receive the unpredictable Word into the hidden recesses of their own lives.

The Catechism of the Catholic Church speaks with clarity: "By his obedience, he [Jesus] replaces Adam's disobedience."[39] Yet it is the soil

---

[39] CCC 532.

of Joseph's obedience that nourishes this new beginning. The home, as the Catechism further attests, becomes "the first school of Christian life… where one learns endurance and the joy of work, fraternal love, generous—and even repeated—forgiveness, and above all divine worship in prayer and the offering of one's life."[40] Joseph models these lessons not by spectacle, but by steadfast presence; his dignity arises from choosing the good of another above his own standing—a logic governed by love's risk and the freedom it entails.

The Church's recognition of Joseph's greatness was a gradual unfolding—a devotion that blossomed in the obscurity of centuries before achieving universal prominence. The West's earliest references emerge around the year 800; only after the 15th century did his feast become universally observed. In 1621, it was made mandatory; in 1870, Pius IX proclaimed Joseph Patron of the Universal Church. Successive popes, from St. John XXIII to Francis, have deepened his place within the liturgical and devotional life of the Church, underscoring that "the logic of love is always the logic of freedom," as Joseph's story proclaims.

In drawing the gaze of the faithful to Joseph, the Church does more than prompt gratitude for his protection of the Holy Family. The feast presses a deeper question: Where in our own lives are we summoned to risk mercy over legalism, to choose justice above the preservation of reputation, to answer obedience's call beyond the limits of understanding? The vocation of Joseph—the "father in the shadows"—invites us to labor for others' good, to grant freedom in love, to relinquish control as God calls those we cherish beyond our embrace. It is within the quiet shadows of such everyday fidelity that true holiness is cultivated.

As we contemplate the mystery of the Annunciation, we are challenged to recognize that the Eucharist is not merely a sacrament to be received, but a school in the Josephian imagination. To partake of this mystery is to give our fiat anew, consenting to let the Word take flesh

---

[40] CCC 1657.

in the often unnoticed, hidden folds of our lives—a liturgical fulfillment that begins, as with Joseph, in the courage of silent, obedient faith.

"Blessed Joseph, to us too, show yourself a father and guide us in the path of life. Obtain for us grace, mercy, and courage, and defend us from every evil."

# The Annunciation of the Lord

## March 25

| | |
|---:|:---|
| First Reading | Isaiah 7:10-14, 8:10 |
| Responsorial Psalm | Psalm 40:7-8a, 8b-9, 10, 11 |
| Second Reading | Hebrews 10:4-10 |
| Gospel Acclamation | John 1:14ab |
| Gospel Reading | Luke 1:26-38 |

# A Feast of Incarnation, Obedience, and Liturgical Conversion

At the heart of liturgical theology lies not mere intellectual pursuit, but a summons to encounter—a sacred space where the memory of salvation is made vividly present and transformative. The Solemnity of the Annunciation of the Lord is both Marian and profoundly Christological; it is the pivotal moment in the Church's liturgical life—the axis point where the Word becomes flesh and, as the liturgy proclaims, "dwelt among us" (John 1:14). Mary's fiat, her courageous "let it be done," is not simply the beginning of Christ's incarnation, but the archetype of faith for all believers: attentive listening, surrender to the Spirit, and a willing participation in God's redemptive plan. In every Mass, this mystery is not only remembered but also re-presented, calling each Christian to risk their own "yes" amid the assembly.

The readings of the feast invite us into Isaiah's world, where the prophet's sign to King Ahaz—"the virgin shall be with child, and bear a son, and shall name him Emmanuel"—extends beyond its historical moment to reach the heart of the Church's worship. God's answer to human hesitation is not force, but humility; not triumph, but incarnation. Within the liturgy, Isaiah's prophecy is not a relic, but a living question: Will you trust the God who chooses the humble and the hidden? Will you allow your expectations to be reshaped by Emmanuel, God-with-us, in the unexpected? The Annunciation, then, is not history to be recalled but a present reality, a recurring invitation for God to break in anew.

The responsorial Psalm, "Here am I, Lord; I come to do your will," echoes Mary's response and situates her fiat as the heart of true worship. Her response is not mere obligation, but a joyful surrender: an interior openness that moves the assembly from ritual to reality. Every time these words are sung, the Church joins Mary's surrender, embodying her fiat in the present moment. The psalm becomes the anticipation of Christ, whose own obedience is the model for all faithfulness—transforming our participation in the liturgy into an act of profound trust.

Today's Second Reading from Hebrews 10:4-10, further deepens this reality, proclaiming that God desires not sacrifice or offering alone, but a body prepared for obedience: "Here I am...I have come to do your will." The Incarnation is presented as the supreme act of self-gift, a divine "yes" inaugurating a new covenant and a new liturgy. In the Eucharist, Mary's fiat and Christ's offering are united in a single movement of surrender, consecrating the faithful and drawing them into the mystery being enacted upon the altar. The Mass is not just remembrance, but participation—an invitation for each believer to echo Christ's obedience in the concreteness of daily life.

As the Acclaim from John 1:14ab proclaims, "The Word became flesh and made his dwelling among us," the assembly is drawn ever deeper into the mystery of God's abiding presence. The liturgy is the Annunciation made perpetual; the altar is where the Incarnation is encountered anew. The Church is no passive observer, but a living participant, summoned to receive the Word and be transformed by grace.

Luke's account of the Annunciation immerses the Church in the drama of faith: the angel's greeting, Mary's perplexity, her questioning, and ultimately her *agape-emet* act of participation. This narrative is ritually enacted in worship, offering a pattern for all discipleship—proclamation, openness, and consent to the Spirit's work. Mary's "let it be done" is not resignation, but the most active trust, a model for how every believer is called to become a vessel for God's redeeming action in the world.

The Catechism of the Catholic Church reminds us that the Annunciation is not merely an event but a summons to a way of life.[41] Mary's

---

[41] Cf. CCC 488-494; 967-969.

obedience unravels the knot of Eve's disobedience—her fiat becomes the paradigm for Christian existence: to hear the Word, trust beyond knowing, and yield to God's purposes. The Eucharist seeks to form in us this very readiness—that Christ might be conceived and brought to birth again through our surrendered lives.

For this reason, the feast of the Annunciation occupies a privileged place in the Church's calendar, affirmed by the Council of Ephesus in honoring Mary as *Theotokos*, God-bearer. Falling on March 25, nine months before Christmas, the celebration is both a marker of human gestation and a sign of hope fulfilled: the Word, conceived in faith, comes to term in the world's salvation. This solemnity, marked by joy even in the midst of Lent, is never lost to the calendar but always given its due, signifying its enduring place in the liturgical year.

Through the liturgical sense of the readings as Mass, we find that through these readings and prayers salvation history is rendered fully present—the prophecy of Isaiah fulfilled in Mary, the Psalmist's song embodied in Christ, the letter to the Hebrews offering the Incarnation as the highest form of worship, John proclaiming the Word's abiding presence, Luke providing the model for our response. The Mass is not a passive commemoration but a living participation in the drama of redemption. Here, Annunciation spirituality is not peripheral, but the very fabric of Christian identity: radical openness, trust, and cooperation with grace.

The pastoral and moral challenge of the Annunciation, celebrated in the liturgy, is relentlessly practical. It presses on every Christian and on the Church: Where must I yield to God's initiative beyond my understanding? Where is the message of the angel seeking a "yes" in my life? The liturgy demands an answer—not in abstraction, but in the willingness to risk obedience, to allow Christ to be conceived and brought forth anew, even in the hidden and ordinary stretches of our days.

To celebrate the Annunciation is to stake everything on the Word of God; to welcome the interruption of divine initiative; to bear, in our own flesh and history, the hope that saves the world. Every Eucharist is a fresh Annunciation, a living "fiat," a chance for the Word to seek flesh in us again. Nothing will be impossible for God. Faith is always this "yes"—the daily surrender that gives birth to Christ anew, in each soul, for the life of the world.

"Behold, I am the handmaid of the Lord. May it be done to me according to your word."[42]

We pray, Holy Mother Mary, full of grace – the first disciple, prophet, and mother, teach us to recognize God's arrival in the unexpected and the ordinary. Pray for us, that we may receive the Word with joy, embrace the cost of discipleship, and bear Jesus into a world longing for hope.

This Annunciation, let us move beyond mere commemoration to courageous participation. Where is God inviting a new "yes" in your life, beyond comfort or comprehension? Like Mary, may we trust that with God, nothing will be impossible.

---

[42] Luke 1:38.

# Nativity of Saint John the Baptist
## June 24

|  | **Vigil** | **During the Day** |
|---|---|---|
| First Reading | Jeremiah 1:4-10 | Isaiah 49:1-6 |
| Responsorial Psalm | Psalm 71:1-2,3-4a, 5-6ab, 15ab & 17 | Psalm 139:1-3b, 13-14ab, 14c-15 |
| Second Reading | 1 Peter 1:8-12 | Acts 13:22-26 |
| Gospel Acclamation | Cf. John 1:17; Luke 1:17 | Cf. Luke 1:76 |
| Gospel Reading | Luke 1:5-17 | Luke 1:57-66, 80 |

# The Turning of the Liturgical Year, the Herald of the Dawn

With the Nativity of Saint John the Baptist, the liturgical rhythm of the Church asserts a rare inversion, one that finds a meaningful reiteration in the feast of the Annunciation of the Lord. These two solemnities, distinct yet intimately entwined within the divine song of the Church's calendar, invite us into a deeper contemplation of the mystery by which God's salvific plan interrupts history. The Church, in her wisdom, celebrates the birth of John—alongside the births of Christ and Mary—marking these moments as thresholds of grace.

In the Mass for John's nativity, a proto-Eucharistic astonishment is voiced: the dawn kindles before the day, the forerunner is sent ahead of the Redeemer, the messenger is born to herald another's glory. Here, we are drawn to contemplate not only the ending of silence and barrenness but also the manner in which prophecy is enfleshed, anticipating the Word made flesh first announced at the Annunciation.

The interplay between John's Nativity and the Annunciation forms a liturgical and scriptural periodic phrasing. Isaiah's oracle, proclaimed on John's feast, narrates the emergence of a servant called "from the womb," destined to be "a light to the nations." While John stands as the immediate referent, the Church herself is drawn into this vocation: called from the womb, fashioned for a singular purpose, and bound to Israel's ancient hopes.

In this, we perceive the Annunciation as the moment when the Word's entry into the world is made possible—the fiat of Mary inaugurating the incarnation, while John's birth signifies the wilderness voice that precedes and prepares a people for that incarnate Word. John is not the Messiah; in announcing repentance and shining forth humility, he incarnates the paradox that the greatest among those born of women is precisely the one who steps aside, heralding the One whose coming was foretold at Gabriel's greeting.

The drama extends from prophecy to Apostolic witness, drawing the Church's memory through the Acts of the Apostles. Paul, preaching in Antioch, recalls, "John heralded [Jesus'] coming by proclaiming a baptism of repentance… 'What do you suppose that I am? I am not he. Behold, one is coming after me; I am not worthy to unfasten the sandals of his feet.'" The liturgy of the Catholic Mass thus becomes more than a Eucharistic meal; it is the ongoing proclamation of salvation history, an event still unfolding in the lives of the faithful.

Indeed, the liturgy does not simply recall John the Baptist's ministry—it renders his mission present, making the call to baptism, repentance, and humility a perennial summons for the faithful. This summons echoes the event of the Annunciation, where the Word of God pierces the silence of history, and the Virgin Mary's humility provides the womb for salvation itself.

The Gospel Readings, in its climactic narrative, draws these themes together. The miraculous birth of John, the muteness and restoration of Zechariah, the naming of the child—"John," meaning "God is gracious," chosen by divine initiative rather than human tradition—resonates with the newness announced at the Annunciation. "What, then, will this child be?" The question reverberates through the ages, pointing beyond itself to the One whom John will soon proclaim. Zechariah's blessing, the awe of the people, and the description of John as one who "grew and became strong in spirit, dwelling in the desert until the day of his manifestation," all serve as a prelude to the desert of preparation that the Mass itself enacts. Just as Mary's "yes" was spoken in the obscurity of Nazareth, so John's growth in solitude prepares the way for the public revelation of both the herald and the Lamb.

Each liturgical celebration, therefore, finds its meaning in this interplay: the preparatory humility of John the Waymaker is mirrored in the Liturgy of the Word, which readies the hearts of the faithful for the Liturgy of the Eucharist. Every Catholic Mass sings again the Waymaker's mission, and every Annunciation echoes the Blessed Mother's consent—"He must increase, I must decrease" in one, "Be it done unto me" in the other. Both feast days rehearse a humility that points away from self and toward Christ, the Lamb of God who continually comes in sacramental mystery. The Catechism of the Catholic Church reminds us, "To become 'a child of God,' one must be 'born from above' or 'born of God'... by receiving in faith the supreme gift of baptism."[43] John's birth prefigures the second birth of every Christian in Baptism, and just as the Annunciation opened the door for the incarnation, so John's nativity points forward to the new creation wrought in water and spirit.

In the desert's solitude, John discovers not isolation but mission. Each soul, likewise, must pass through silence and ascesis before fruitful proclamation. The Catechism affirms: "He [John the Baptist] inaugurates the Gospel, already from his mother's womb welcomes the coming of Christ and rejoices in being 'the friend of the bridegroom' whom he points out as 'the Lamb of God, who takes away the sin of the world.'"[44]

The Annunciation and Nativity of John thus converge: both feasts are celebrations of divine initiative, of vocations received in humility, and of roles accepted in faith. The Church stands at the junction of these mysteries, called to recognize that her deepest identity—her name, given in Baptism—is bestowed not by the world's traditions but by the creative word of God.

From the earliest centuries, the Nativity of John the Baptist was established as one of the first non-Christ, non-Marian feasts, set six months before the Nativity of Christ according to Luke's Gospel, and placed near the summer solstice, when the light begins to decrease—a cosmic echo of John's words, "He must increase, I must decrease." The Annunciation, celebrated in the vernal equinox's ascent, marks the dawn of incarnation as the world turns toward Christ's light. The

---

[43] CCC 678, 720.
[44] CCC 523.

Church, through these liturgical pairings, proclaims her perennial need for heralds and witnesses, for humility and hope rooted in surprising grace.

Thus, each feast places a mirror before the faithful: do we, in our living witness, truly prepare the way for the Lord by our humility and courage? Have we interiorized the humility that refuses self-reference and insists that salvation is a gift of God's mercy, not of our own making?

The liturgy, through the Nativity of John and the Annunciation of the Lord, warns against spiritual pride, insularity, and self-promotion, and instead calls us to decrease so that Christ may increase. Like John and Mary—each wonderfully made, each defined by grace—we are summoned to stand on the threshold, pointing to the Greater One, daring to receive a name, vocabulary, and vocation from Him who interrupts history with salvation and whose glory we are privileged to testify to.

# Feast of Saints Peter and Paul
## June 29

|  | Vigil | During the Day |
|---|---|---|
| First Reading | Acts 3:1-10 | Acts 12-1-11 |
| Responsorial Psalm | Psalm 19:2-3, 4-5 | Psalm 34:2-3, 4-5, 6-7, 8-9 |
| Second Reading | Galatians 1:11-20 | 2 Timothy 4:6-8, 17-18 |
| Gospel Acclamation | John 21:17 | Matthew 16:18 |
| Gospel Reading | John 21:15-19 | Matthew 16:13-19 |

# Liturgical Unity in Martyria, the Broken Rock, and the Outpoured Word

The Church gathers on June 29th in an extraordinary act of remembering: the joint feast of Saints Peter and Paul. These two apostles—so contrasting in background, personality, and apostolic scope—are united in the death that is the ultimate liturgical act: martyrdom. Their joint commemoration at the altar offers a catechesis not only on history but on the character of the very Church the liturgy constructs anew in every Mass.

Rooted in the earliest centuries of Christian tradition, the Feast of Saints Peter and Paul occupies a central and enduring place within Roman Christianity. Both apostles met their martyrdom in Rome—Peter by crucifixion, Paul by beheading—securing the city's status as a sacred locus of apostolic witness. Today's commemoration dates back to the Church's foundational memory, attested by early liturgical practice and patristic reflection. Saint Augustine notably emphasized the unity of their shared feast, despite their distinct deaths, as a symbolic convergence of the Church's dual apostolic mission: Peter representing pastoral leadership, and Paul embodying evangelical proclamation.

In today's First Reading from Acts 12:1-11, Peter is imprisoned by Herod and threatened with imminent execution. His rescue occurs not through human cunning but via the intervention of an angel. This liberation is nearly liturgical: surrounded by the power of death, the release signifies a paschal passage—delivering from bondage and darkness into the light of day, emerging from the fear of death into the mission of testimony. The Mass invites us to contemplate this same mystery—the Church, persecuted and frail, relying not on its own resourcefulness but on the liberating Word, the presence of God that breaks chains.

The Second Reading from 2 Timothy 4:6-8, 17-18 represents an almost divine liturgical elegy. The Apostle is described as "already being poured out as a libation." He has "fought the good fight, finished the race, kept the faith." Paul's impending death is not viewed as a defeat, but as an offering; his execution becomes Eucharistic, as his letters transform the Churches into the bread that sustains and fortifies them. The liturgy commemorates this memory as a present reality at every Mass, where the pouring out of Christ—and, by extension, the offering of all who are united with Him in death and witness—are made manifest.

Today's Gospel Reading from Matthew 16:13-19 addresses the profound mystery of the Church's authority and self-understanding. After a series of failures, Peter proclaims, "You are the Christ, the Son of the Living God." In response, Jesus does not merely affirm Peter's declaration; rather, He solemnly confers upon Peter a new identity and mission: "You are Peter [Cephas], and upon this rock [cephas] I will build my church... I will give you the keys to the kingdom of heaven."

By placing this narrative at the center of the feast, the liturgy encourages participants to reflect on a profound paradox: Peter, who once denied Christ, becomes the foundational rock, and Paul, a former persecutor, is transformed into an Apostle. This paradox underscores that the Church is not built upon flawless achievement but rather upon failures redeemed by divine grace and continual mercy. It signifies that the Church's nature parallels that of Christ—both human and divine—with humanity being elevated through participation in the divine.

This passage also introduces a significant theological paradox within the biblical narrative. Throughout sacred Scripture, it is God who is repeatedly described as the "rock" and "cornerstone"—the immovable foundation and source of security for His people, "He is the Rock, his works are perfect."[45] "The Lord is my rock, my fortress, and my deliverer,"[46] and "Behold, I lay in Zion a stone, a tested stone, a precious

---

[45] Deuteronomy 32:4.
[46] Psalm 18:2; Cf. 2 Samuel 22:2–3.

cornerstone, a sure foundation."[47] Yet here, in a moment of divine commissioning, God incarnate designates a human—Peter—as "the rock" upon which the Church will be built. This act, extraordinary in its humility and trust, demonstrates how divine authority chooses to work through human weakness, making the Church's very foundation a sign of both God's sovereignty and His willingness to transform and elevate the frail instruments He calls.

The Catechism of the Catholic Church clarifies that the foundation of the Church's unity lies not in organizational structures or administrative uniformity, but in a shared faith and liturgical life, with Peter's faith marking the rock upon which this unity is built and the Pope serving as the careful custodian of the keys entrusted to Peter.[48] Furthermore, it affirms that the Church is apostolic because it is established on the apostles themselves, remaining continually taught, sanctified, and guided by their successors in pastoral office until Christ returns.[49] Thus, our moral challenge is unity—not uniformity, but only through the grace of Jesus' promise we remain together as His Church, in root, branch, confession, mission, authority, and mercy.

In other words, the prayers and prefaces of this feast highlight that Peter, as the foremost confessor of faith, and Paul, as the outstanding preacher, together embody the dual vocation of the Church: steadfastness in maintaining the faith and courage in proclaiming it to the world. This unity, achieved not by erasing differences but by transforming them through shared confession and sacrifice, is at the heart of the Church's calling.

The unity symbolized and actualized in this feast is not the uniformity of perfect concord, but the harmony achieved when difference is reconciled around a common confession and sacrifice. The Mass, offering the one Christ through many hands and voices, challenges each

---

[47] Isaiah 28:16.
[48] CCC 552–553; 857.
[49] CCC 857.

community to persevere in unity—across ideological, linguistic, and cultural lines. Are we willing, like Peter and Paul, to be "poured out," to go where we would rather not go, to witness with our lives as well as our words?

# Feast of the Transfiguration of the Lord

### August 6

| | |
|---:|:---|
| First Reading | Daniel 7:9-10, 13-14 |
| Responsorial Psalm | Psalm 97:1-2, 5-6, 9 |
| Second Reading | 2 Peter 1:16-19 |
| Gospel Acclamation | Matthew 17:5c |
| Gospel Reading | Matthew 17:1-9 |

Feast of the Assumption of the Blessed Mother Mary

# Divine Majesty, Prophetic Fulfillment, and the Call to Transformation

The Feast of the Transfiguration shines in our calendar as a luminous moment in the Church's liturgical year. An invitation to all the faithful to contemplate the mystery of Christ's divine radiance. On this sacred day, the awe-inspiring Theophany of Jesus as the beloved Son beams from the mountaintop into our lives. This feast summons every disciple to gaze upon the majesty of God, to recognize the transformative call that reverberates throughout each reading.

In the deeply moving vision of Daniel in today's First Reading from Daniel 7:9-10, 13-14, the Ancient One sits enthroned amidst flames, surrounded by countless attendants. Envision Daniel, standing awestruck as the veil of heaven is drawn back in his prophetic vision. Before him blazes the throne of the Ancient One, set ablaze with fire, its brilliance scattering the shadows. A multitude beyond counting gathers in silent worship, their presence testifying to the grandeur that fills the celestial court. In this moving tableau, Daniel beholds not just the majesty of eternity, but the arrival of the Son of Man—Christ himself—radiant and vested with authority that will never fade. Here, the eternal kingdom is revealed, a dominion unshaken by time, summoning our hearts to bow in reverence, to kindle hope, and to stand in the holy awe that lies at the heart of our faith. This vision, echoing through the liturgy, draws us deeper into the mystery of divine sovereignty and invites us, too, to lift our eyes to the One whose reign is everlasting.

Just as Daniel's vision lifts our gaze to the majesty and sovereignty of God—inviting us into awe, hope, and reverence—the testimony found in today's Second Reading from 2 Peter 1:16-19 resounds with both fervor and challenge. Both passages draw us into the heart of divine revelation: Daniel witnesses the eternal reign of the Son of Man, while Peter recalls the encounter on the holy mountain, where Christ's majesty was revealed not by clever invention but through direct witness. In each case, the faithful are summoned to recognize and respond to God's glory—Daniel through prophetic vision, Peter through apostolic testimony. Peter's words affirm the truth and vitality of prophecy, urging us to attend "as to a lamp shining in a dark place," until the day breaks and Christ's light rises within. This apostolic witness calls believers to steadfast faith, readiness to hear God's voice, and courage to follow wherever it leads, echoing the awe and transformative call expressed in Daniel's vision.

The Gospel Reading from Matthew 17:1-9, which recounts the Transfiguration of Jesus before Peter, James, and John, serves as a living bridge between Daniel's prophetic vision and Peter's apostolic testimony. In Daniel's vision, the Ancient One's throne blazes with fire and majesty, and the Son of Man is vested with everlasting dominion—a scene saturated with awe and the promise of an eternal kingdom. This prophetic anticipation finds fulfillment on the mount of Transfiguration: Christ's face shines like the sun, his garments gleam, and Moses and Elijah stand beside him as living witnesses that he is the culmination of both Law and Prophets. The divine voice—"This is my beloved Son, with whom I am well pleased; listen to him"—echoes the eternal authority and sovereignty revealed to Daniel, now made manifest in the person of Jesus.

Similarly, Peter's later testimony recalls this very mountaintop encounter, insisting that the Apostolic proclamation is not "cleverly devised myth" but the fruit of direct witness to Christ's majesty. Peter urges the faithful to attend to this revelation "as to a lamp shining in a dark place," inviting us to let Christ's light transform our hearts and guide our journey, just as the disciples were summoned on the mountain to rise without fear and follow Jesus more deeply.

Within the Mass, these readings are not merely remembered but made present. The Divine Symphony draws us into the drama: Daniel's awe, Peter's testimony, and the Gospel's radiant vision converge in the celebration. The readings and Gospel proclamation invite us to recognize Christ as the fulfillment of all prophecy and the living Word to whom we must listen. The Father's command—"listen to him"—becomes the Church's call to attentive discipleship, echoed in the Alleluia, the homily, and above all, in the Eucharist. Here, Christ's glory is not just contemplated but received, that we may be transfigured and sent forth to bear his light to the world. Thus, the unity of these passages in the liturgy calls us to awe, attentive listening, and continual transformation by Christ's radiant presence.

In this way, the Transfiguration stands as more than a vision; it is a summons for hearts to allow Christ's radiance to transform every thought and motive. As the Catechism of the Catholic Church teaches, the event "reveals in the beloved Son the glory of the Godhead" and gives the Father's command to the Church: "This is my Son, the Beloved; listen to him."[50] The mountain revelation is thus both a foretaste of the Paschal mystery and an imperative to attentive discipleship.

The liturgy of the Catholic Mass makes that revelation present and operative. The Scripture readings and the Gospel proclamation present again the Father's voice; the Alleluia and Gospel acclamation call the assembly to attentive listening; the homily interprets the mountain vision as simultaneously a glimpse of the risen life and a summons to the way of the Cross. Above all, the Holy Eucharist effects the sacramental dynamic the Transfiguration signifies, forming the faithful so that, through communion, Christ's light may transfigure our minds and actions and we may bear that radiance into the world.[51]

To truly honor the Feast of the Transfiguration is to renew with unwavering resolve our commitment to the divine journey of faith: to pursue holiness relentlessly, to bear courageous witness to the truth, and to allow Christ's radiant brilliance to transform every action. The liturgical cycle calls us to be bold witnesses and attentive listeners amid the

---

[50] CCC 554.
[51] Cf. CCC 554.

chaos of the world; discipleship demands an ascent beyond complacency, an inward revolution, and steadfast trust in God's grace to transfigure even the most ordinary days. Anchored in God's unwavering promise, we are summoned to walk together into the luminous reality of His eternal glory—challenged to embody the light and courage necessary to transform ourselves and the world.

# The Assumption of the Blessed Mother of Mary
## August 15

|  | **Vigil** | **During the Day** |
|---|---|---|
| First Reading | 1 Chronicles 15:3-4, 15-16, 16:1-2 | Revelation 11:19A; 12:1-6A, 10AB |
| Responsorial Psalm | Psalm 132:6-7, 9-10, 13-14 | Psalm 45:10, 11, 12, 16 |
| Second Reading | 1 Corinthians 15:54b-57 | 1 Corinthians 15:20-27 |
| Gospel Acclamation | Luke 11:28 | Cf. Revelation 12:1, Psalm 45:10-16 |
| Gospel Reading | Luke 11:27-28 | Luke 1:39-56 |

# The Solemnity of the Assumption of the Blessed Mother of Mary

Today's First Reading for the Solemnity of the Assumption of the Blessed Virgin Mary opens with a striking vision from Revelation 11:19: "God's temple in heaven was opened, and the ark of his covenant could be seen in the temple." This verse is no mere poetic flourish—it is a liturgical unveiling of a theological reality long held in the heart of the Church. From the earliest centuries, the Mother of God, the *Theotokos*, has been venerated as the true Ark of the Covenant. Just as the Old Testament Ark contained the tablets of the Law, the manna from Heaven, and Aaron's priestly rod, so too did Mary carry within her womb the fulfillment of all these signs: Christ, the incarnate Lawgiver, the Bread of Life, and the eternal High Priest.

The Assumption was not defined in haste. Its veneration began in the East as early as the sixth century under the title Dormition of the Theotokos, and by the seventh century, the West also embraced its celebration. Over time, the feast spread throughout Christendom, nourished by the Church's deepening understanding of Mary's role in salvation history. The theological foundation remained steadfastly Christocentric: if Christ is the New Adam, then Mary is the New Eve—redeemed in advance and glorified in anticipation of the resurrection promised to all the faithful. This typological identification was articulated by Church Fathers such as Saint Gregory the Wonderworker and Saint Athanasius in the third and fourth centuries, respectively. Their witness affirms that Marian doctrine is not a theological embellishment but a necessary consequence of Christology rightly understood.

This gradual and prayerful development culminated in 1950, when Pope Pius XII, through the apostolic constitution *Munificentissimus Deus*, solemnly defined the dogma of the Assumption, writing:

This definition was not based on Scripture alone, but on the unanimous witness of tradition, the liturgical life of the Church, and the theological necessity of Mary's unique participation in her Son's redemptive mission. Her Assumption is not merely a reward—it is a sign of what awaits those who are conformed to Christ.

*Munificentissimus Deus* did not rest on Scripture alone, but drew upon the unanimous witness of tradition, the liturgical life of the Church, and the theological necessity of Mary's unique participation in her Son's redemptive mission. Thus, her Assumption is not merely a reward for her singular faithfulness; it is a sign and foretaste of the glory that awaits all who are conformed to Christ.

John's vision continues in Revelation 12:1 with the image that has inspired two millennia of Catholic iconography: "A great sign appeared in the sky, a woman clothed with the sun, with the moon under her feet, and on her head a crown of twelve stars." This celestial woman is not merely symbolic; she is both figure and fulfillment. She represents Israel—the Daughter of Zion perfected—and she is also the Virgin Mary, crowned in glory. Her appearance echoes Joseph's dream in Genesis 37:9, where the sun, moon, and stars bow down, prefiguring the eschatological exaltation of the one who bore the Messiah.

As John's vision deepens, he beholds a woman laboring in agony—an image that, for centuries, has been entwined with the ancient curse of Eve. Yet, in the luminous tradition of the Church, many theologians have gently contended that Mary, preserved from all stain through her Immaculate Conception, was shielded from the primal pains of childbirth. Instead, the suffering that unfolds in this celestial tableau is not Mary's alone; it is the collective anguish of Israel, humanity yearning and straining for the advent of her Redeemer. In this moment, the woman's travail becomes a sacred echo of every heart awaiting deliverance, every soul aching for the dawn of salvation.

Suddenly, the scene darkens as the red dragon coils into view—seven heads crowned with seven diadems, ten horns flashing with defiance—its very presence a chilling embodiment of hostility to divine life. With a thrash of its tail, it sweeps a third of the stars from the heavens, a gesture that many interpret as the harrowing fall of rebellious angels or the martyrdom of those faithful to God. The dragon's ravenous intent to consume the newborn child conjures the shadow of Herod's massacre of innocents, and resonates with the primordial enmity declared in Genesis 3:15: an ancient conflict between the woman and the serpent, a battle waged not in myth but in the very fabric of salvation history.

Yet, from this crucible of danger and suffering emerges the verse upon which the dogma finds its foundation: "Her child was caught up to God and his throne." This child is not merely a son, but the Sovereign, enthroned in glory. And the woman—having fulfilled the divine mission entrusted to her—finds herself led into the wilderness, a sanctuary prepared by the hand of God. This act of divine guardianship, this gentle ushering of the Mother of the Messiah into safety, stands as a radiant signpost pointing toward the mystery of the Assumption: the Church's steadfast belief that, at the completion of her earthly journey, Mary was received whole—body and soul—into the splendor of heavenly glory.

The readings for this Solemnity form a theological symphony. Revelation 12:10 resounds with the voice of heaven: "Now have salvation and power come, and the Kingdom of our God and the authority of His Anointed One." This vision is not just John's—it is the voice of the Church, echoing through the ages in the final doxology of the Lord's Prayer: "For the kingdom, the power, and the glory are yours, now and forever." The proclamation of the Kingdom and the authority of Christ in Revelation finds its fulfillment in the Church's liturgical and doctrinal life, as seen in the solemn definition of the Assumption. This connection underscores that the mysteries celebrated are not isolated events but are woven into the divine melody of salvation history, continually proclaimed and made present in the Church's worship and belief.

The Second Reading, from 1 Corinthians 15:20–27, proclaims the sovereignty of Christ, who will subject all things to the Father. Mary's Assumption is a foretaste of this cosmic restoration. She is the firstfruits of redeemed humanity, the living proof that death does not have the final word. In this way, the readings are intimately linked: the triumphant declaration of Christ's victory in Revelation finds concrete expression in Mary's Assumption, as described by Paul. Her glorification anticipates the ultimate fulfillment of Christ's reign, when all creation will be brought under His dominion. Thus, the Solemnity's scriptural texts harmonize to reveal Mary not only as a participant in Christ's victory, but as a sign of hope for all the faithful, pointing toward the destiny promised to those who are united with her Son.

The Gospel from Luke 1:39–56, then, recounts Mary's visitation to Elizabeth and her Magnificat. But it also draws deeply from Old Testament typology. Mary's journey to the hill country mirrors David's journey to retrieve the Ark.[52] Elizabeth's exclamation—"How does this happen to me, that the mother of my Lord should come to me?"—parallels David's awe: "How can the Ark of the Lord come to me?"[53] The infant's leap in Elizabeth's womb recalls David's dance before the Ark. Mary's hymn of praise mirrors David's psalm of thanksgiving. Even her three-month stay echoes the Ark's temporary dwelling in the house of Obededom.[54]

The Assumption is not merely commemorated—it is participated in. When we approach the priest and hear the words "Corpus Christi," our "Amen" is not a passive assent. It is a Marian fiat. We echo her response at the Annunciation: "Let it be to me according to your word." The elevation of the consecrated host is a visual echo of Gabriel's promise: "The Holy Spirit will come upon you, and the power of the Most High will overshadow you."[55] Every knee bows, not out of ritual habit, but in

---

[52] 2 Samuel 6:2.
[53] 2 Samuel 6:9.
[54] 2 Samuel 6:11.
[55] Luke 1:35.

recognition of the Presence that once dwelled in Mary and now dwells in us.

Just as God filled Elizabeth's barren womb with miraculous life, so too does He transform the humble elements of bread and wine into the very essence of Christ—living, eternal, and divine. The miracle of the Holy Eucharist is the Incarnation itself, extended across the chords of time, bridging heaven and earth. Through this sacred sacrament, we become living tabernacles—the Ark of the Covenant—carrying the presence of Christ into the very heart of the world.

Mary, our luminous prototype, stands as a radiant torch guiding us. Her Assumption is not merely a privilege bestowed upon her but a promise—a divine song singing what it truly means to be fully conformed to Christ. The liturgy of the Catholic Mass does more than honor her; it calls us to imitate her, to become Eucharistic people—radiant vessels of grace. It challenges us to allow divine love to transform us, to be shaped by grace, and to live with unwavering hope that we, too, might be loved into the fullness of Heaven.

So, I ask you: Will you answer this divine call? Will you open your heart to the mystery of the Assumption and let it sculpt your life, your worship, your witness? The journey to Heaven is a sacred adventure—active, vibrant, demanding our wholehearted `fiat`—our heartfelt `Amen`.

# Feast of the Exaltation of the Cross

*September 14*

| | |
|---:|:---|
| First Reading | Numbers 21:4b-9 |
| Responsorial Psalm | Psalm 78:1-2, 34-35, 36-37, 38 |
| Second Reading | Philippians 2:6-11 |
| Gospel Reading | John 3:13-17 |

# The Exaltation of the Cross: Liturgical Paradox and Promise at the Heart of the Catholic Christian Faith

Each year on September 14, the Church invites her faithful to contemplate the deepest paradox of the Christian mystery: the Cross, once a tool of execution and humiliation, stands at the very center of our worship as the wellspring of life and hope. We do not venerate the Cross as a mere historical artifact or symbol of defeat, but as the place where divine blessing is poured out upon humanity. Here, the liturgy compels us to gaze upon that which the world would avert its eyes from—a Roman instrument of capital punishment, reserved for non-citizens and the disgraced—now transformed into a sign of exaltation and eternal life. The scandal and glory intertwine: through the shame of crucifixion, the Church proclaims, comes salvation.

To appreciate the magnitude of this paradox, we must recall that in Jesus' era, crucifixion was the empire's ultimate deterrent—a public, excruciating death meted out to slaves, revolutionaries, and foreigners. No Roman citizen could be subjected to such ignominy, except by choice or under extraordinary circumstances.

According to tradition, the Apostle Paul, though a Roman citizen, was given the death penalty; yet out of respect for his citizenship, he was beheaded—a more "honorable" death—rather than crucified, which was reserved for the most disgraced. In contrast, Peter was not a Roman citizen and, therefore, was condemned to die by crucifixion. Church tradition further holds that, out of humility, Peter asked to be crucified upside down, deeming himself unworthy to die in the same manner as his Lord. This distinction between the fates of Peter and Paul underscores the shame and horror associated with crucifixion in the ancient world.

The death penalty executed on the Cross was not only a sentence of physical annihilation but a spectacle of disgrace, intended to erase memory and dignity. Yet it is precisely this gallows, this sign of utter defeat, that has become for Christians the throne of the world's Redeemer and the object of our highest adoration.

The lectionary readings for this feast immerse us in the profound scriptural roots of this mystery. In the first reading from Book Numbers 21:4b-9, Israel's rebellion in the wilderness elicits a plague of fiery serpents—agents of death. In response, God commands Moses to lift a bronze serpent upon a pole; all who turn their gaze upon it in repentance are healed: "Moses accordingly made a bronze serpent and mounted it on a pole, and whenever anyone who had been bitten by a serpent looked at the bronze serpent, he lived." This account is not an insignificant account but a typological foreshadowing: salvation is found in the very place of suffering, healing in the vision of what wounds.

The Second Reading from Philippians 2:6-11, the Apostle deepens this vision. Christ, "though he was in the form of God, did not regard equality with God as something to be grasped, but emptied himself...becoming obedient to death, even death on a cross." Here, the Church's song is not detached dogma but a summons to enter into the drama of descent and exaltation—kenosis into glory, self-offering into resurrection. In this way, the liturgy does not simply re-present salvation history; it enacts this movement of love poured out and raised up.

Finally, the Gospel Reading from John 3:13-17 articulates the decisive fulfillment: "Just as Moses lifted up the serpent in the desert, so must the Son of Man be lifted up, that whoever believes in him may have eternal life." The Cross, then, is simultaneously the nadir of human violence and the zenith of divine love. The Mass, in every generation, is the Church's great "lifting up," commanding us not to look away from suffering but to behold, in the Crucified, the medicine of immortality.

The Catechism of the Catholic Church frames this paradox with clarity and authority: "The Cross is the unique sacrifice of Christ, the 'one mediator between God and men.'" [56] The faithful are not called to a religion of comfort and self-assurance, but one that dares to embrace the wounds of God. "The Christian must deny himself and take up his cross... There is no holiness without renunciation and spiritual battle." [57] The Cross is not an obstacle to be avoided, but the very path to sanctity and victory.

Historically, the feast of the Exaltation of the Holy Cross traces its origins to the fourth-century discovery of the True Cross by Saint Helena and the dedication of the Basilica of the Holy Sepulcher in Jerusalem. Over the centuries, this double commemoration—both historical and mystical—has enshrined the Cross as a universal sign of hope, not despair. Every "lifting up," in the Christian life, is marked by this tension: suffering and exaltation, weakness and triumph, death and resurrection, forever joined in the mystery of Christ.

The challenge of this feast is both searching and urgent: Where, in our lives and communities, have we misunderstood or fled from the Cross? Do we dare to gaze upon it—prayerfully, trustingly—or do we seek escape in distraction and comfort? The liturgy insists: suffering is not the final word, nor is death the end of our song. The call to us Catholics is clear and uncompromising—to transform every cross-bearing into participation in the world's redemption, to seek the "exaltation" hidden in sacrificial love, and to lift up, day by day, all labor, pain, and hope as offering to the God who conquered death through the wood of shame. This is the paradox we celebrate: the instrument of execution becomes the gateway to eternal life, and in every crucifixion, the seed of resurrection is sown.

---

[56] CCC 618.
[57] CCC 2015.

# Dedication of the Lateran Basilica
## November 9

|  |  |
|--:|:--|
| First Reading | Ezekiel 47:1-2, 8-9, 12 |
| Responsorial Psalm | 45:2-3, 5-6, 8-9 |
| Second Reading | 1 Corinthians 3:9c-11, 16-17 |
| Gospel Acclamation | 2 Chronicles 7:16 |
| Gospel Reading | John 2:13-22 |

# The House Not Made by Hands

On November 9, the universal Church contemplates the mystery of sacred space through the celebration of the Dedication of the Lateran Basilica, the cathedral of Rome and, in tradition, the "mother and head of all churches of the city and the world." In this liturgical moment, the faithful are summoned to consider not only the physical structure of the basilica, but the deeper reality it signifies—a spiritual indwelling, the temple of the people of God.

The scriptures proclaimed in this feast offer rich images, drawing from Ezekiel's vision in the First Reading (47:1-2, 8-9, 12) of an eschatological temple: water flows from its threshold, bearing life and healing, transforming wastelands into gardens, salt water into fresh, fruit trees abundant along the banks, their leaves and fruit for nourishment and medicine. This prophetic vision mirrors, in sacramental sign, the Church's vocation to become a living source of grace and renewal for the world, reminding all that worship is never an isolated pursuit but a spring that purifies and heals beyond its boundaries.

Saint Paul, writing to the Corinthians in our Second Reading (3:9c-11, 16-17), deepens the liturgical mystery, declaring, "You are God's building... Do you not know that you are the temple of God, and that the Spirit of God dwells in you?" Here, the sacredness of the basilica is transposed from marble and gold to the hearts of the faithful, transformed by encounter with the divine in worship, and sanctified by baptism and the Spirit. The celebration thus directs reverence toward the assembly itself, the living stones of which Saint Peter speaks, whose holiness renders the structure truly sacred.

Today's Gospel Reading from John 2:13-22 finds Jesus purifying the Jerusalem temple, further amplifying this theme. His words—"Destroy this temple, and in three days I will raise it up"—draw a thread from the physical building to the new Temple of Christ's Body, a mystery both personal and ecclesial. The Lateran Basilica stands as a witness to history and unity, ever reminding the Church of her vocation to ongoing reform: each Christian community, like the temple of old, remains in need of cleansing and renewal, always "under construction" in Christ.

In contemplating these mysteries, the feast points inevitably to the Annunciation of the Lord, where the eternal Word becomes flesh and dwells among us. Here, the Incarnation reveals the most profound sanctification of space and time: the very body of the Virgin Mary becomes the new Ark of God's presence, the dwelling place of the Most High. In this light, the dedication of a church is not merely a commemoration of brick and stone, but a proclamation that God continues to pitch His tent among humanity, drawing every place and every home into participation with His saving presence.

The Catechism of the Catholic Church affirms that the Church herself is the temple of the living God, the house where the Father's children are welcomed and nourished, described as a place of prayer and the dwelling of God's presence.[58] This teaching is extended to the Christian home, which serves as the foundation of faith and the first place where the Gospel is proclaimed and received.[59] Thus, the unity between the physical spaces of worship and the spiritual realities they signify is established: both church and home are called to embody God's presence, fostering prayer, faith, and communion in daily life.

The liturgy, therefore, challenges all who celebrate these feasts to recognize that sacred space matters only insofar as it leads to the transformation of lives, to lives lived as "living stones," temples indwelt by the Holy One.

The annual remembrance of the Lateran Basilica's dedication, much like the Annunciation, is not ultimately about the building itself, but about the universal call to holiness, unity, and mission. Every gathering at the table of the Holy Eucharistic sings again the Lateran's summons,

---

[58] Cf. CCC 756, 1181.
[59] Cf. CCC 1666.

inviting the Church to continual self-examination: Are our hearts true temples? Are our communities sources of mercy, healing, and life-giving water? True dedication is ongoing, demanding the conversion of every facet of personal and communal existence into a dwelling place for God, just as Mary's fiat inaugurated the divine habitation in the world. In this way, the feasts draw the faithful into deeper contemplation and more fervent commitment, that all may become living signs of God's transforming presence in creation.

# The Solemnity of All Saints
## November 1

| | |
|---:|:---|
| First Reading | Revelation 7:2-4, 9-14 |
| Responsorial Psalm | Psalm 24:1bc-2, 3-4ab, 5-6 |
| Second Reading | 1 John 3:1-3 |
| Gospel Acclamation | Matthew 11:28 |
| Gospel Reading | Matthew 5:1-12a |

# The Solemnity of All Saints

The Solemnity of All Saints, celebrated on November 1$^{st}$ in the Western Church, is a feast that honors all the saints—both those who are canonized and those whose holiness is known only to God. Its origins are deeply rooted in the early Christian tradition of venerating martyrs. As the number of Christian martyrs grew during the persecutions of the first centuries, it became impossible to assign a separate day to each. By the 4$^{th}$ century, the Church in the East began to commemorate all martyrs collectively, initially celebrating this feast in May.

The Western Church adopted the practice in the 7$^{th}$ century, when Pope Boniface IV consecrated the Pantheon in Rome to the Blessed Virgin Mary and all martyrs on May 13$^{th}$. However, it was in the 8$^{th}$ century that Pope Gregory III moved the celebration to November 1$^{st}$, coinciding with the dedication of an oratory in St. Peter's Basilica to all saints. This date was later extended to the entire Church by Pope Gregory IV in the 9th century, establishing November 1$^{st}$ as the universal date for the Solemnity of All Saints in the Western tradition.

The feast's placement at the end of the liturgical year is significant, as it invites the faithful to reflect on the "last things"—death, judgment, heaven, and hell—and to fix their gaze on the ultimate goal of Christian life: union with God in the company of all the saints. The celebration is also closely linked with All Souls' Day on November 2$^{nd}$, forming a triduum of remembrance and prayer for both the saints in heaven and the souls in purgatory.

In this way, the Solemnity of All Saints, with its roots in the early veneration of martyrs and its establishment as a universal feast by the Church, invites us each year to join in communion with the countless holy men and women—both known and unknown—who have gone before us. This tradition not only honors their memory but also reminds us that we are surrounded by a great "cloud of witnesses," ever ready to intercede for us and accompany us on our own journey toward holiness.

In today's First Reading from Revelation 7:2-4, 9-14, the servant John received a vision of the Holy Mass across the span of centuries, wherein he observed "a great multitude, which no one could count, from every nation, race, people, and tongue. They stood before the throne and before the Lamb, wearing white robes and holding palm branches in their hands." It is evident from this vision that John was presented with a Palm Sunday Mass, with the faithful holding palm branches during the procession. The text further states that they cried out in a loud voice: "Salvation comes from our God, who is seated on the throne, and from the Lamb." In the subsequent part of his vision, it appears that the servant John heard the Gloria in Excelsis Deo, which would not typically be sung during Lent but would be sung aloud on Easter Sunday.

At the conclusion of this segment of John's vision, one of the elders addressed him and inquired, "Who are these individuals clothed in white robes, and from where have they come?" John responded, "My lord, you are the one who knows." The elder then informed him, "These are the ones who have endured the great distress; they have washed their robes and made them white in the Blood of the Lamb." This vision of the holy and pure saints in Heaven, as observed by the servant John, fulfills the prophecy in today's Second Reading from First John 3:1-3: "We know that when it is revealed, we shall be like him, for we shall see him as he is. Everyone who has this hope based on him makes himself pure, as he is pure."

I believe that the words of Tertullian in his Apology (197 A.D.) powerfully illustrate the unbreakable spirit of our saints during times of intense suffering. He writes: "Crucify us, torture us, condemn us, destroy us! Your wickedness exposes our innocence. It is precisely because of our purity that God permits us to endure such trials. When you recently condemned a Christian maiden to a panderer rather than to a panther, you openly acknowledged that a stain on our purity is regarded as more dreadful than any punishment or even death. Your cruelty, no matter how severe, only fuels our faith. The more you persecute us, the more our numbers grow. The blood of martyrs is truly the seed of Christians." These words challenge us to recognize that suffering and persecution have historically strengthened, rather than weakened, our faith and resolve.

The path to sainthood illuminated by the Synoptic Gospels is beautifully demonstrated in today's Gospel reading from Matthew 5:1-12. The nine Beatitudes are more than mere words; they are divine opportunities—gifts of grace—that invite us to unite our mind, body, and soul with the sacred heart of Christ. When we embrace and practice these nine blessings consistently, they transform into our supernatural behaviors, guiding us like a shining light along that narrow path to Mount Calvary. There, in dying in Christ, being buried in Him, and rising anew, we find our true salvation and purpose. Let us open our hearts to these divine opportunities and walk confidently on the path toward eternal life.

In this way, the liturgy of the Holy Mass, herself a divine opportunity, not only provides us with a perfect way to journey to Calvary, but with the hosts of angels and the communion saints gathered around our sacred space as we adore Him and consume Him, the Mass also foreshadows what Heaven will be like when we see Christ in His full glory, raised high on His throne. By gathering all of God's people from every nation, race, people, and language to worship Him from sunrise to sunset, the Catholic Church shows us what Heaven will look like.

The saints of our faith began their journey to the throne of God from the very same place where we are now, yet their commitment was unwavering. They actively participated in the liturgy of the Mass: sitting in our pews, kneeling on our floors, listening intently to the readings, praying earnestly, confessing their sins in union with the universal Church, and receiving the Holy Eucharist. Today, on this Solemnity, we celebrate their steadfastness in faith and their triumphant finish. But let us ask ourselves: are we truly following their example? Are we exercising the same devotion and perseverance? We must heed their righteous quest—pray for us that we might have the grace and courage to finish our race with the same unwavering resolve.

# The Commemoration of all the Faithfully Departed (All Souls' Day)
## November 2

| | |
|---:|:---|
| First Reading | Isaiah 35:6, 7-9 |
| Responsorial Psalm | Psalm 23:1-3a, 3b-4, 5-6 |
| Second Reading | Romans 6:3-9 |
| Gospel Acclamation | Cf. John 6:40 |
| Gospel Reading | John 6:37-40 |

# The Liturgy of Remembrance, Intercession, and the Hope Beyond Death

November 2 stands as a singular testimony to a Catholic instinct: love that persists in prayer for those "who have gone before us marked with the sign of faith." All Souls' Day, paradoxically one of the most hopeful of feasts, confronts the reality of death not with resignation but with the triumphant proclamation of Easter.

Here, the Church affirms that Christ's victory is neither abstract nor distant, but reaches into the depths of human mortality, extending mercy and binding the living and the dead within a single bond of love. In the readings for this day, the voice of Wisdom resounds, assuring the faithful that "the souls of the righteous are in the hand of God, and no torment will ever touch them... their hope is full of immortality."[60] Against the tide of forgetfulness that so easily overtakes the world, the assembly of believers participates in an act of holy memory, refusing to surrender to the finality of death.

Today's First Reading from Isaiah 35:6, 7-9 offers a vision of restoration and hope that echoes powerfully through the readings of All Souls' Day and the liturgy of the Catholic Mass. In this prophetic passage, the promise that "the lame shall leap like a deer, and the tongue of the speechless sing for joy" speaks to the transformative mercy of God, who brings healing and new life where there was once sorrow and death. The assurance that "no lion shall be there, nor any ravenous beast come up on it" reflects the Church's proclamation that, in Christ, death and danger are overcome and the faithful are led safely to the joy of communion with God. This resonates with the liturgical remembrance of the departed, affirming that the journey beyond death is not one of isolation or peril, but of hope and restoration, as celebrated in the Eucharist and the prayers of intercession for all souls.

---

[60] Wisdom 3:1–4.

The Apostle's words to the Romans in our Second Reading (6:3-9) deepen this unfolding vision of hope and mercy, echoing the Church's unwavering confidence in Christ's triumph over death. Paul proclaims that through baptism, we are united with Christ not only in His death but also in His resurrection—a mystery that extends its promise beyond the confines of individual comfort to embrace the whole human family.

Christ's reconciling death, offered "while we were still enemies," is not simply a personal solace; it is the very ground of a hope that refuses to be limited by time or circumstance. The Eucharistic sacrifice, then, is not a memorial for the present assembly alone, but a perpetual act of intercession and love for all who seek mercy, for all souls on the pilgrimage toward the fullness of communion with God. In this, the Church lives out its vocation as a people who remember, who intercede, and who trust that God's mercy knows no boundaries.

Today's Gospel Reading from John 6:37-40 further amplifies this assurance, as Jesus stands not only before the tomb of Lazarus, but before every place of sorrow and loss in human experience. His declaration, "I am the resurrection and the life; whoever believes in me, even if he dies, will live," resounds as the heart of Christian hope. The tears of Jesus are not signs of resignation, but the compassionate gaze of God who enters into the reality of death in order to transform it from within. His weeping becomes the overture to the divine command that breaks the silence of the grave, calling forth new life and revealing that death's dominion is not final.

In the liturgy of remembrance and intercession, the Church clings to this promise, confident that every prayer for the departed is heard by the One who holds the keys of death and life, and who gathers all the faithful, living and dead, into the inexhaustible communion of His love. Indeed, every Eucharistic bread that is broken is, in essence, a "shout into the tomb"—an unwavering prayer that the Lord would summon the departed into the company of saints, affirming that the communion of the Church is never interrupted by death.

This dynamic of remembrance and intercession finds deep resonance in the Church's doctrine. From the earliest days, Christians have honored the memory of the dead and have prayed for their purification, trusting that such love and supplication draw the souls of the departed into the light of God's presence. The Church's teaching, as expressed in the Catechism, declares that these prayers are not mere sentiment, but a participation in the unity of the Body of Christ, a unity rendered visible in the Eucharist and sustained by the prayers of intercession.

To unite one's own death with that of Christ is to understand dying not as an ending, but as a passage—a birth into everlasting life with Him. Thus, in commemorating All Souls, Catholics are challenged to consider not only the fate of their own souls, but the enduring bonds of mercy and love that unite the living and the dead, calling all to the slow and shared work of divine mercy.

Yet the liturgical calendar does not isolate the commemoration of the dead from the mysteries of redemption and incarnation; rather, it weaves these commemorations into a seamless tapestry. Just as All Souls' Day confronts mortality by invoking the hope of resurrection, the feast of the Annunciation proclaims the very moment when eternity entered time, when the Word was made flesh in the womb of Mary.

The Annunciation, far from being merely a celebration of divine initiative, is inseparably linked to the destiny of every soul: it marks the inauguration of the saving work that will culminate in Christ's victory over death, the very victory celebrated at Easter and pleaded for at every Mass for the departed. In Mary's fiat—her "yes" uttered on behalf of all humanity—the Church glimpses the beginning of the path by which death is overcome and immortality is made possible. The hope that animates All Souls thus has its roots in the mystery of the Incarnation, whose promise is not undone by the grave but rather fulfilled in resurrection glory.

Thus, within the rhythm of the liturgical year, the faithful are continually invited to contemplate the profound unity between these feasts: the Annunciation and All Souls' Day. Both proclaim that God's love abides, that the Eucharist is the pledge and presence of Christ's victory, and that the bonds of intercession and communion transcend the boundaries of time and mortality.

The Church, ever ancient and ever new, persists in hope—remembering, offering, and trusting that, in Christ, "death does not end the song," but gathers the choir anew. This is not only comfort, but a call: to pray for the dead, to accompany them with love, and to allow the mysteries of faith to shape our vision of life, death, and the promise of eternal communion.

# The Solemnity of the Immaculate Conception of the Blessed Virgin Mary
## December 8

| | |
|---:|:---|
| First Reading | Genesis 3:9-15, 20 |
| Responsorial Psalm | Psalm 98:1, 2-3ab, 3cd-4 |
| Second Reading | Ephesians 1:3-6, 11-12 |
| Gospel Acclamation | Cf. Luke 1:28 |
| Gospel Reading | Luke 1:26-38 |

# Far Above All Angles and Saints

For many, one of the most challenging of all the distinctively Catholic doctrines to accept is the dogma of the Immaculate Conception of the Blessed Virgin Mary. That the Mother of our Lord was preserved, from the first moment of her existence, from the stain of original sin is not a theological novelty, but a truth long cherished in the *sensus fidelium*—the deep intuition of the People of God—centuries before it was solemnly defined. It was not until 1854, in his encyclical *Ineffabilis Deus*, that Blessed Pope Pius IX formally declared this belief as dogma:

> Therefore, far above all the angels and all the saints so wondrously did God endow her with the abundance of all heavenly gifts poured from the treasury of his divinity that this mother, ever absolutely free of all stain of sin, all fair and perfect, would possess that fullness of holy innocence and sanctity than which, under God, one cannot even imagine anything greater, and which, outside of God, no mind can succeed in comprehending fully.

In this declaration, Pius IX does not introduce a new doctrine but rather articulates with precision what had always been latent in the Church's liturgical life, patristic witness, and theological reflection. He demonstrates, with both pastoral sensitivity and doctrinal rigor, that the Immaculate Conception is not an innovation but a divine truth safeguarded, defended, and gradually clarified through the centuries.

And yet, paradoxically, for some it remains easier to believe that bread and wine become the living Body and Blood of a divine Person; or that a crucified Man rose bodily from the dead; or that the invocation of the Triune Name over water effects a real ontological transformation in the soul—than to believe that the Eternal Father would will His Son to be conceived in the womb of a woman "resplendent with the glory of most sublime holiness and so completely free from all taint of original sin."

But if one accepts the central ontological claim of Christianity—that the personal sin of Adam and Eve wounded human nature itself, such that the effects of original sin are transmitted to all by propagation (as taught by the Council of Trent, Session V, and rooted in Genesis 3)—then one is faced with a theological necessity. Scripture affirms that Christ "appeared to take away sins, and in Him there is no sin."[61] Therefore, either Mary was preserved from original sin so as not to transmit it to her Son, or Christ Himself would have had to be conceived immaculately.

But the latter option is untenable. It is not sufficient to argue that Christ's divinity simply "overcame" a sinful humanity, as if His divine nature neutralized a corrupted human nature. Such a view would fracture the hypostatic union. On the contrary, given that Jesus Christ is truly God and truly man, united in one divine Person without confusion or division, there can be no internal contradiction between His humanity and His divinity. He must be fully human, like us in all things but sin, and yet without any trace of inherited corruption. Thus, either He was conceived holy and remained sinless, or He was born with original sin and overcame it. The latter position is not only theologically incoherent—it would unravel the very foundations of Christian soteriology, ecclesiology, and eschatology.

In affirming the former, the Church's dogma of the Immaculate Conception ultimately says more about Christ than it does about Mary. It is not that Mary's dignity required her to be sinless, but that Christ's mission demanded it. If Jesus had been conceived immaculately by His own divine prerogative, apart from the natural order, He would not have assumed a human nature like ours in every way. He would have been an exception to the very condition He came to redeem. But if He is to be the New Adam, recapitulating humanity in Himself, then He

---

[61] 1 John 3:5; cf. Hebrews 4:15; 2 Corinthians 5:21; 1 Peter 2:22.

must be born of a woman who is fully human yet uniquely prepared—redeemed in advance by the merits of the Cross.

This is the *admirabile commercium*—the wondrous exchange—celebrated in the Church's liturgy and crystallized in the Catechism of the Catholic Church:

> The Word became flesh to make us 'partakers of the divine nature' (2 Peter 1:4). 'For this is why the Word became man, and the Son of God became the Son of man: so that man, by entering into communion with the Word and thus receiving divine sonship, might become a son of God' (St. Irenaeus). 'For the Son of God became man so that we might become God' (St. Athanasius). 'The only-begotten Son of God, wanting to make us sharers in his divinity, assumed our nature, so that he, made man, might make men gods' (St. Thomas Aquinas).[62]

The theological heart of the Immaculate Conception is revealed most clearly in the liturgy of the Eucharistic sacrifice. Christ had to be born naturally without stain or blemish to be offered as a spotless victim for sin.[63] As the Agnus Dei proclaims at every Mass, He is the Lamb of God who takes away the sins of the world. And just as the Passover lamb had to be "without blemish,"[64] so too must the true Paschal Lamb be perfect in His humanity.

Mary, then, was chosen by the Eternal Father to bear this Lamb—not because of her own merit, but because the sacrifice required it. We had nothing to offer God that could redeem us, for all we possess is already His. Only God could offer God. And so He prepared a woman, full of grace, to be the living tabernacle of His Incarnate Son. Through her, the Lamb was born. Through Him, the sacrifice was made. And through the Eucharist, that same spotless Lamb is offered to us again and again, that we might become one with Him.

As one ancient Eastern Christian hymn proclaims:

---

[62] CCC 460.
[63] cf. 2 Corinthians 5:21.
[64] Exodus 12:5.

> "You alone and your Mother
> are more beautiful than any others;
> For there is no blemish in you,
> nor any stain upon your Mother.
> Who among my children
> can compare to these?"

Ultimately, the doctrine of the Immaculate Conception stands not as an embellishment of Marian devotion, but as an indispensable affirmation of Christological truth. Far from being a sentimental addition or an excessive veneration of Mary, it functions as a doctrinal safeguard, preserving the integrity of the Gospel itself. Without the Immaculate Conception, the foundation of Christ's sinless humanity would be compromised, and the very logic of redemption would be undermined. The Gospel's narrative demands that the Lamb offered for the sins of the world be truly spotless, and that the vessel chosen to bear Him be wholly pure. Thus, the Immaculate Conception is not merely an ancillary belief—it is the necessary prelude to the Incarnation, ensuring that the redemptive mission of Christ unfolds without contradiction or blemish.

# Feast of the Holy Family

*First Sunday after Christmas (or December 30 if Christmas is Sunday)*

| | |
|---:|:---|
| First Reading | Sirach 3:2-6, 12-14 |
| Responsorial Psalm | Psalm 128:1-2, 3, 4-5 |
| Second Reading | Colossians 3:12-21 |
| Gospel Acclamation | Colossians 3:15a, 16a |
| Gospel Reading | Matthew 2:13-15, 19-23 |

# The Liturgy of the Domestic Church: Holiness in the Ordinary

In the heart of the Church's liturgical calendar, the Feast of the Holy Family stands as a radiant beacon, illuminating the path to holiness not through grand gestures but through the quiet sanctity of the ordinary. This treasured feast invites every Catholic family to recognize that their home is a sacred place—a domestic church—where God's love is made manifest daily. In celebrating the Holy Family, we are called to see the extraordinary grace woven into the everyday moments of family life, and to answer the call to sanctity within our own homes.

The Feast of the Holy Family, honoring Jesus, Mary, and Joseph, has its roots in the Church's deep reverence for family life. While devotion to the Holy Family existed in earlier centuries, it was not until the late nineteenth century that the feast found formal recognition. Pope Leo XIII specifically promoted devotion to the Holy Family in several of his encyclicals. Notably, he wrote the encyclical *Neminem Fugit* (issued on December 14, 1892), which is dedicated entirely to the devotion of the Holy Family. In this document, Pope Leo XIII encouraged all Christian families to look to the Holy Family of Nazareth as a model of virtue, unity, and faithfulness. Additionally, his teachings on the Christian family and the importance of the domestic church are found in other encyclicals such as *Arcanum Divinae Sapientiae* (on Christian marriage, 1880), though *Neminem Fugit* is the primary encyclical focused on devotion to the Holy Family.

Pope Benedict XV officially established the Feast of the Holy Family for the universal Church in 1921 through the decree *Bonum Sane*. This document set the feast on the Sunday within the Octave of Christmas, or on December 30 when Christmas falls on a Sunday. This formal recognition was both a response to societal upheaval and a reaffirmation of the family as the bedrock of Christian life. Earlier forms of the feast had appeared in local calendars and religious communities, reflecting the Church's perennial appreciation for the holiness found in family bonds.

The concept of the "domestic church" springs from the earliest traditions of Christianity, where the home was regarded as the first and most intimate place of worship. The Second Vatican Council articulated the concept of the family as a "domestic church" in its Dogmatic Constitution on the Church, *Lumen Gentium*. Specifically, section 11 states: "The family is, so to speak, the domestic church. In it, parents should, by their word and example, be the first preachers of the faith to their children."[65] Within this sacred space, parents and children become living witnesses to Christ, and daily routines transform into liturgies of love, forgiveness, and service. The domestic church is not merely an ideal; it is a reality accessible to all who welcome God into the ordinary rhythm of their family life.

The readings appointed for the Feast of the Holy Family provide profound insight into the sanctity of family life and the call to holiness in the ordinary. The First Reading, Sirach 3:2-6, 12-14, exhorts children to honor and care for their parents, reminding us that reverence within the family is a path to divine blessing. Sirach's wisdom speaks directly to the heart of the domestic church, where respect, kindness, and compassion are the building blocks of holiness.

In the Second Reading, Colossians 3:12-21, Saint Paul offers a blueprint for Christian living within the home. He calls the faithful to clothe themselves with compassion, kindness, humility, and patience, urging forgiveness and love as the bonds that unite families. Paul's words are both practical and profound: they reveal that holiness is not reserved for the extraordinary, but is found in the daily acts of love and mercy that shape family life. His exhortation to let the peace of Christ rule in our hearts and to let the word of Christ dwell richly among us is a direct invitation to transform our homes into places of prayer and grace.

---

[65] *Lumen Gentium*, 11.

The Gospel Reading, Matthew 2:13-15, 19-23, recounts the flight into Egypt and the return to Nazareth, highlighting the trials and faithfulness of the Holy Family. In their obedience, trust, and perseverance through uncertainty, Jesus, Mary, and Joseph exemplify the courage required to embrace God's will in daily life. Their journey teaches us that holiness often emerges in the midst of difficulty, and that the ordinary challenges faced by families can become occasions for extraordinary grace.

The Feast of the Holy Family is not merely a commemoration—it is a call to action. Every family is invited to embody the virtues of the Holy Family, transforming the routine of daily life into a living liturgy of faith. Simple acts of kindness, moments of forgiveness, prayers shared at the dinner table, and the patient bearing of one another's burdens are the seeds of holiness. In these ordinary moments, God's presence becomes tangible, and the family home becomes a sanctuary of love and peace.

This feast reminds us that holiness is not out of reach. It is found in the laughter of children, the gentle guidance of parents, the quiet sacrifices made for one another, and the steadfast commitment to walk together in faith. By embracing the liturgy of the domestic church, every family can participate in the mystery of God's love and become a sign of hope and renewal for the world.

As we celebrate the Feast of the Holy Family, let us renew our commitment to make our homes places of prayer, love, and service. Let us recognize that the path to holiness is paved with ordinary acts, transformed by grace. The liturgy of the domestic church is not confined to special occasions—it is lived each day, in every family that seeks to follow the example of Jesus, Mary, and Joseph. May we, inspired by their witness, welcome holiness into the ordinary and become, in our own homes, living temples of God's presence.

# If You Enjoyed This Book, Check Out These Others at Saint Dominic's Media
## http://www.saintdominicsmedia.com

Since its publication in 2018, *The Divine Symphony: An Exordium to the Theology of the Catholic Mass*, by David L. Gray, has been consistently called the best book ever written about the liturgy of the Church.

This book consists of four very accessible and easy-to-read movements that narrate, explore, and explain the meaning, mystery, theology, history, symbolism, and continuity of the Catholic Mass.

*The Liturgy of Gregory the Theologian: Critical Text with Translation and Commentary*, by Dr. Nichols Newman, offers a new edition, translation, and commentary of the Greek Liturgy of St. Gregory the Theologian. In this discussion of the Greek text, which exists alongside a Coptic version, the origins of the liturgy and its programmatic use in the turbulent theological world of the fourth century are discovered. This book offers a new translation of several of Remigius dei Girolami's political works, the *De Bono Communi, De Bono Pacis, Sermones de Pace,* and the *De Iustitia*.